Uncle John's CERTIFIED Organic BATHROOM READER®

By the
Bathroom Readers'
Institute

D0043411

Bathroom Readers' Press
Ashland, Oregon

Dedicated to the memory of Jean Srnecz

UNCLE JOHN'S CERTIFIED ORGANIC BATHROOM READER®

For information, write:
The Bathroom Readers' Institute, P.O. Box 1117, Ashland, OR 97520
www.bathroomreader.com • 888-488-4642

Cover design by Michael Brunsfeld, San Rafael, CA (*Brunsfeldo@comcast.net*)

Printed on Rolland Enviro100 Book, which contains 100% post-consumer fiber, is Environmental Choice, Processed Chlorine Free, and manufactured in Québec by Cascades using biogas energy.

By using 25,680 lb. of Rolland Enviro100 Book instead of virgin-fiber paper in the printing of this book, we saved: 218 trees, 130,917 gallons of water, 13,871 lb. of solid waste, 31,741 cubic feet of natural gas, and 30,459 lb. of air emissions.

ISBN-13: 978-1-59223-981-8 / ISBN-10: 1-59223-981-1

Library of Congress Cataloging-in-Publication Data
Uncle John's certified organic bathroom reader.
   p. cm.
Prepared by the Bathroom Readers' Institute.
ISBN 978-1-59223-981-8 (pbk.)
1. Organic living—Miscellanea. 2. Sustainable living—Miscellanea. 3. Environmental protection—Citizen participation—Miscellanea. 4. American wit and humor. 5. Handbooks, vade-mecums, etc. I. Portable Press (Ashland, Or.) II. Bathroom Readers' Institute (Ashland, Or.) III. Title.
GF77.U53 2009
640—dc22

                                               2008051404

Printed in Canada
First Printing
1 2 3 4 5 6 7 8 9 13 12 11 10 09

Hiya, Sam! Hiya, Gideon!

THANK YOU!

*The Bathroom Readers' Institute would like to thank the people
whose advice and assistance made this book possible.*

Gordon Javna

Jay Newman

Amy Miller

Thom Little

Brian Boone

John Dollison

Angela Kern

Claudia Bauer

Julia Papps

Michael Brunsfeld

Judy Plapinger

Kait Fairchild

Jef Fretwell

Kyle Coroneos

Jude Wait

Jeremy Bloom

Matt Smith

Kelly Smith

Michele Tune

Loaf Newman

Sara Elliott

Katherine Butler

Susan Milam

Tamara Orr

Paige Usyk

Jennifer Graue

Alison Kroulek

Robin Langford

Theodore Scott

Miranda Marquit

Chris Clark

Emma Lloyd

Jennifer Heigl

Angela West

Luke McKinney

Barb Koch

Paul Seaburn

Rose Kivi

Megan Boone

Christine DeGueron

Sydney Stanley

JoAnn Padgett

Melinda Allman

Ginger Winters

Monica, Amy, and Lisa

Elise Gochberg

Julie Bégin

Steven Style Group

Publishers Group West

Raincoast Books

(Mr.) Mustard Press

Thomas Crapper

Hiya Porter, Zephyr, Gilli, Proudfoot, Fangorn, Montana, Kitsy, Iniki, Caesar, Deja, and Zappa!

CONTENTS

Because the BRI understands your reading needs, we've
divided the contents by length as well as subject.
Short—a quick read
Medium—2 to 3 pages
Long—for those extended visits, when something
a little more involved is required
* Extended—for those leg-numbing experiences

*   *   *

**OFFICIAL U.S. FOREST SERVICE GUIDELINES
FOR DESTROYING "WOODSY OWL" COSTUMES**
*The Forest Service updated their mascot's look in 2008 and
posted these instructions for the disposal of old costumes.*

1. Incinerate the complete costume with the oversight of an
official USDA Forest Service law enforcement officer.

2. The entire Woodsy Owl costume, including each of the separate
pieces, is to be destroyed beyond recognition.

INTRODUCTION

GREETINGS, EARTHLINGS!
Here at the Bathroom Readers' Institute, we've written dozens of books since 1988, but none that have challenged us more than this one. We wanted to unscramble one of the most talked-about issues of our time—the environment. But at the same time, we wanted to bring you the kinds of things you've come to expect from us: pop culture, unknown origins, fast facts, and simple explanations of complicated subjects—all sprinkled with a healthy dose of humor (and a little weirdness).

With that in mind, you'll read about:

• **Pioneers:** The mother of the green movement, the father of soil conservation, the man who found the hole in the sky, and Leonardo da Vinci's theories on climate change.

• **Nature:** Worms that eat toxic waste, frogs that tell our future, owls that heal, and trees that talk to each other.

• **Alternative power:** Provided by wind, the sun, nuclear energy, microbes, tornadoes, Japanese commuters, beer, poop...

• **Great debates:** Paper vs. plastic, Flinstones vs. Jetsons, drilling in Alaska, and organic food—is it really all it's cracked up to be?

• **Tips:** New uses for old TP rolls, reducing your energy bills, surviving society's collapse, and going green in the afterlife.

Before you get started, remember that a lot of what you'll read about here is still unfolding. Even in the last few months of writing this book, we saw a lot change (for example, the U.S. overtook Germany as the world's number-one user of wind power). Think of these pages as a time capsule—where the environmental movement stands one decade into the 21st century.

So get ready for a fun, eye-opening ride through our ever-changing world.

And as always:

Go with the Flow!

—Uncle John, the BRI Staff,
and Porter the Wonder Dog

GREEN SUPERHEROES

Batman saved Gotham City, and Superman saved Metropolis. Big deal—these superheroes save trees, plants, rivers, and animals.

CAPTAIN PLANET. The 1990 cartoon series *Captain Planet and the Planeteers* was created by media mogul Ted Turner. Captain Planet battled barons of industry such as Looten Plunder, Sly Sludge, and Captain Pollution—villains who were hell-bent on destroying the environment. With his blue skin and green hair (to resemble Earth), Captain Planet fought them with strength, speed, and the ability to control weather and matter.

CHLOROPHYLL KID. This was a minor DC Comics character in the 1960s. As a child on the planet Mardru, the green-skinned hero fell into a vat of plant-growth serum that gave him special abilities: He could magically produce plants out of thin air, accelerate their growth, and communicate with them.

THE BLACK PANTHER. As king of Wakanda, a fictional African nation, the Black Panther fought evildoers in a series of comics in the 1970s. His arch-enemies, the White Gorilla Cult, obtained their superpowers by killing the rare white gorillas who live in Wakanda.

ANIMAL MAN. In 2008 this obscure character was honored by People for the Ethical Treatment of Animals (PETA). Why? He's a vegan and animal-rights advocate, and his special powers are the abilities to mimic animals and understand their thoughts and feelings.

THE TOXIC AVENGER. In the 1984 movie *The Toxic Avenger*, Melvin Ferd is a scrawny janitor who falls out of a window and lands in a jug of toxic waste that instantly transforms him into a superstrong, but disgustingly mutated, ooze-dripping monster. While he doesn't fight environmental crime (he goes after petty thieves), the Toxic Avenger is a good example of why you shouldn't leave nuclear waste laying around.

A recycling operation creates 6 times as many jobs as a landfill.

ECO-TOWNS

*A few of the most environmentally
friendly cities in the world.*

CHATTANOOGA, TENNESSEE. There's a sign near the
Tennessee River Gorge in Chattanooga that says, "You can
see seven states from here." That wasn't true in 1969, when
there was too much air pollution to see 100 yards, earning Chattanooga the reputation as the most polluted city in the United
States. But in the 1970s, citizens launched a revitalization plan
focused on affordable housing, crime prevention, economic development, and the environment. They cleaned up the city's waterways, cut emissions from industrial plants, and switched to a fleet
of electric buses—made right there in Chattanooga.

KAMIKATSU, JAPAN. In 2003 this town of about 2,000
people banded together around the goal of reducing their waste
output...to nothing. Now families sort their trash into 34 separate
categories of recyclables, from plastic to cardboard to bottle caps
to batteries. As of 2008, Kamikatsu recycles 80% of all the trash
generated in the town, and by 2020 they plan to be a Zero Waste
town.

GREENSBURG, KANSAS. In May 2007, a ferocious tornado
ravaged this town of 1,500. Twelve people were killed—and more
than 90% of the buildings in the town were destroyed. When the
weary residents met in the days after to draft a rebuilding plan,
they agreed that every structure in the city would meet the highest standards of the U.S. Green Building Council—a first in the
country. To meet that goal, residents are given tax rebates to
build energy-efficient homes (all new homes will use rainwater
collected in cisterns to flush their toilets, for example), and a
wind farm will take the place of the local electric plant. So
extraordinary are the town's plans that they've received a lot of
attention...including from Hollywood heavyweight Leonardo
DiCaprio, who produced the documentary *Eco-town*, which
chronicles Greensburg's efforts.

Highest point in Hamilton County, Ohio: the pile of trash at the Rumpke Sanitary Landfill.

ENVIRONY

Who knew trying to save the planet could be so ironic?

PLAYFUL IRONY

In 1974 the Consumer Product Safety Commission issued 80,000 buttons that read, "For Kids, Think Toy Safety." Shortly after, the buttons were recalled because they had "sharp edges, parts that a child could swallow, and toxic lead paint."

FENG-SHUIRONY

Rising above a village in Southern China was a barren, brown mountainside that had been quarried...until county officials decided in 2007 that it was hurting the area's feng shui. So they had it painted green. The villagers were perplexed—not only did the mountainside now look like Astroturf, but the estimated $60,000 spent on the job could have been used to plant trees and shrubs throughout the entire village, making the area naturally green.

BEASTLY IRONIES

• In 2000 a save-the-whales advocate was forced to call off his ocean voyage after his boat was damaged by two passing whales.

• How did the city council of Woodstock, Ontario, try to curb the noise pollution caused by thousands of invading crows in 2002? They scared the crows away with repeated blasts of loud fireworks.

FOUL IRONY

The Dave Matthews Band has long championed environmental awareness, but apparently one of their tour-bus drivers didn't get the message. In 2004 the band's bus was traveling across Chicago's Kinzie Street Bridge when the driver decided that the bridge's open metal grating made it a great place to empty the bus's septic tank. So he illegally dumped about 100 gallons of human waste into the Chicago River below...and it landed on a group of elderly people taking a boat tour. The state of Illinois sued, and the band ended up paying $200,000 and donating another $100,000 to the Friends of the Chicago River and the Chicago Park District.

THE IRONY OF FORCE

- In 2005, while studying the effects of global warming on a fragile underwater coral reef, Greenpeace's *Rainbow Warrior II* accidentally ran aground, causing significant damage to the reef.

- Two activists were preparing to throw a bottle of acid at a whaling ship in the Antarctic when their own boat became lost in the fog. They sent out a call for help, and who came to their rescue? The whaling ship. After the activists were steered into clearer waters, one of them said, "I guess we're back on schedule," and threw the bottle of acid at the whaling ship before racing away.

IRONIC WEATHER

Stories of global-warming conferences being canceled due to snow are numerous. Here's the opposite: In August 2008, a conservative advocacy group called Americans for Prosperity scheduled two meetings in Florida to discuss the "global-warming hoax." But the meetings had to be cancelled because Tropical Storm Fay was approaching—a storm that eventually flooded the state. (Climatologists claim a sign of climate change is more intense tropical storms.)

BACKYARD IRONY

In Sunnyvale, California, two neighbors got into a dispute after the redwood trees in one yard grew so tall that they blocked the sun from hitting the solar panels on the other house's roof. The matter was taken up in 2005 by county officials, who cited California's Solar Shade Control Act. The ruling: The redwoods would have to be trimmed or removed, as they were an "environmental hazard."

* * *

A KILLER RECYCLING PROGRAM

The tiger keelback (*Rhabdophis tigrinus*) is a snake native to Asia with an amazing adaptation: The toads upon which it feeds have a gland that dispenses toxic venom to ward off predators. After eating the toad, the snake actually extracts the toxin, stores it in its own special gland...and then releases it to kill other prey (including more toads).

Endangered breed: In the 1830s, the Bulldog nearly went extinct.

WASTEFUL FACTS

Throwing the occasional can away doesn't seem like much, does it?

• Each month, Americans throw away enough aluminum to rebuild every commercial airplane in the country.

• Not every state has a deposit system for soda cans. In 2007 about 36 billion aluminum cans were sent to landfills. Lost scrap value: about $600 million.

• Toilets made after 1992 are water-efficient, using as little as 1.3 gallons per flush. Pre-1992 toilets use between 3.5 and 7 gallons per flush.

• Leaving the water running while brushing your teeth wastes up to 1,500 gallons of water per year.

• The average coal-powered electrical plant can convert only 35% of coal's energy into electricity—the rest is lost as waste heat.

• A leaky faucet that drips once per second wastes 3,000 gallons of water in a year.

• A bath requires about 70 gallons of water. A five-minute shower: 15 gallons.

• A home loses up to 25% of its heat if the windows aren't properly sealed and caulked.

• A refrigerator built 20 years ago uses 70% more energy than one built today.

• Each year, the average American uses wood and paper products equivalent to a 100-foot-tall Douglas fir.

• Over 70% of all metal is used only once, then discarded.

• Most Americans drive to work alone, collectively leaving enough unused space in their cars to carry everyone in western Europe—about 140 million people.

• Each month, Americans discard enough glass jars and bottles to fill the Sears Tower…eight times over.

• The average baby generates a ton of garbage in its first year—mostly diapers.

• Each year, more than 21 million shopping bags' worth of food is discarded in landfills.

• Over a lifetime, the average American will create 90,000 pounds of garbage.

"Willful waste makes woeful want." —Thomas Fuller

YOU CAN RECYCLE THAT

*At last—what to do with that clunky old monitor
taking up space in your basement.*

APPLIANCES. Even if they don't work anymore, you can
send them to the Steel Recycling Institute (recycle-steel.org),
who will salvage the metal parts and resell them.

BATTERIES. Batteries, both rechargeable and disposable, are full
of metal and caustic chemicals that are hard to get rid of safely.
For about $24, Battery Solutions (batteryrecycling.com) sends you
a thick plastic tub that you can fill with up to 12 pounds of batteries. You send it back, they take care of it.

ELECTRONICS. For $50, GreenDisk sends you a cardboard box.
You then fill it with up to 70 pounds of what the company calls
"technotrash"—VHS tapes, CDs, monitors, video game cartridges,
digital cameras, wall chargers, cords, keyboards, computer mice,
and iPods. Send it back, and GreenDisk recycles it all.

STYROFOAM. Some pack-and-ship stores (Mailboxes Etc., the
UPS Store) accept donations of styrofoam peanuts for reuse, or
you can mail them to the Alliance of Foam Packaging Recyclers
(epspackaging.org/info.html).

EYEGLASSES. The Lions Club collects eyeglasses, either to send
them to needy people or to grind up the glass to make new lenses.

CELL PHONES. The charity Call to Protect (donateaphone.com)
collects old phones and reprograms them so they only dial 911.
They are then given to domestic-violence victims.

ATHLETIC SHOES. Athletic shoes can cost more than $100,
which puts them out of reach for many athletes in developing
nations. One World Running (oneworldrunning.com) collects
shoes that are still in good shape and sends them to athletes in
Africa, Haiti, and Latin America.

ANCIENT ENVIROS

*Proof that people were standing up for the land
and the animals long before it was in style.*

H IPPOCRATES (460–377 B.C.E)
Claim to Fame: The first true physician
Environmental Impact: Back then, everyone agreed that
sickness was caused by divine influence. Hippocrates introduced
the radical notion that diseases could be caught from the environment. His *Treatise on Air, Water, and Places* looked at the effect of
the environment on people throughout Europe and Asia, and
noted that people needed to pay more attention to what was in
their food and water. With proper attention to diet and environment, he wrote, many diseases could be prevented. Thanks to
these seemingly simple concepts, both personal health and environmental awareness took a giant leap forward.
Famous Quote: "Everything in excess is opposed to nature."

ARISTOTLE (384–322 B.C.E)

Claim to Fame: Greek philosopher

Environmental Impact: It's only been in the last century that
Aristotle's contribution to biology has been fully appreciated. His
extensive zoological writings make up the first thorough record of
animal life, and the classification system he created was the first of
its kind—it separated animals first into live-bearing and egg-lay-
ing, and then into several subcategories. In total, Aristotle cata-
loged nearly 500 species and introduced modern methods of
biological research.

Famous Quote: "In all things of nature there is something of the
marvelous."

PLINY THE ELDER (23–79 C.E.)

Claim to Fame: Roman historian and military officer

Environmental Impact: Born Gaius Plinius Secundas, Pliny com-
piled *Naturalis Historia*, the world's oldest surviving encyclopedia.
In 37 volumes, it exhaustively catalogues the plants, animals,
geography, astronomy, known history, and medicine of the time.

Though it's peppered with superstition, the work is considered one of the first scholarly texts to argue that seemingly disparate aspects of life are connected.

Famous Quote: "It is this Earth that, like a kind mother, receives us at our birth and sustains us when born; it is this alone, of all the elements around us, that is never found an enemy of man."

ST. FRANCIS OF ASSISI (1182–1226)

Claim to Fame: Patron saint of animals

Environmental Impact: Born Giovanni Bernardone, the Italian friar was somewhat unique in the Middle Ages because of his belief that animals should be treated humanely—and that the land, water, and sky should be as well. Legends of St. Francis tell of his preaching to his "sisters the birds" while they perched attentively, and calming a savage wolf that was terrorizing a town. In recent years, several eco-organizations have adopted St. Francis as the patron saint of the environment.

Famous Quote: "If you have men who will exclude any of God's creatures from the shelter of compassion and pity, you will have men who deal likewise with their fellow men."

LEONARDO DA VINCI (1452–1519)

Claim to Fame: Artist, inventor, Renaissance man

Environmental Impact: Endlessly fascinated by the world around him, da Vinci formulated many theories that were way ahead of their time. For example, he believed that global sea levels had changed over the millennia. His evidence: marine fossils found on mountaintops. By studying the layers of sediment, da Vinci theorized that there had been a gradual shift in water levels rather than a massive flood, as the Church taught.

Also an accomplished naturalist, da Vinci's drawings of plant life were the most accurate of his time. Biologists today still refer to them to note how various species have changed over the centuries. (Da Vinci didn't get everything correct—we now know that the center of Earth is not full of water.)

Famous Quote: "Human subtlety will never devise an invention more beautiful, more simple, or more direct than does nature…in her inventions nothing is lacking, and nothing is superfluous."

Indian winter? A freak snowstorm dumped 20 inches of snow in Vermont in 1816…in June.

NATURE'S CUSTODIANS

Whenever a plate of food gets dropped at the BRI, we just let Porter the Wonder Dog clean it up. Here are some other creatures that assist us in tidying up the planet.

SUPER WORMS

In 2008 researchers at the University of Reading in England discovered a new type of heavy-metal fan: a previously unknown species of earthworms. Found in abandoned, contaminated mine sites all over Great Britain, these worms actually eat toxic waste, including lead, zinc, arsenic, and copper residue from mining. Best of all, after the worms metabolize them and poop them out, the metals are much less toxic. The hope is that these "super worms" may someday be used to clean up contaminated sites. "They could become 21st-century eco-warriors by helping to tackle soil pollution much more efficiently than man has been able to," said researcher Mark Hodson.

CARRION MY WAYWARD SON

Imagine how disgusting life would become if the world's sanitation workers suddenly went on strike. It would be even worse if the vultures did. Without these scavenging birds of prey, we'd be up to our eyeballs in festering carcasses. The vulture's unique digestive tract, which can safely consume bacteria like the one that causes botulism, makes it an ideal garbage collector—especially suited to swooping in after natural disasters and cleaning up the inevitable scattering of dead animals. How important are vultures? In India, the government has mounted a nationwide campaign to revive their dwindling numbers, fearing that their disappearance could cause a spike in diseases such as anthrax and brucellosis. And if you kill one in the U.S., you could be fined $15,000 and thrown in jail for six months. So the next time you see a flock of vultures slowly circling overhead, thank them. (And get to a doctor!)

ELECTRIFYING NEWS

Researchers at the Medical University of South Carolina reported in 2005 that some bacteria commonly found in freshwater ponds can consume harmful pollutants, including PCBs and chemical solvents. Even better, while consuming the pollutants, the bacteria generate electricity at levels that could be used to operate small electronic devices. According to researcher Charles Milliken, "As long as the bacteria are fed fuel, they're able to produce electricity 24 hours a day." Milliken looks forward to a day when his microscopic multitaskers will detoxify contaminated places while harvesting usable amounts of energy.

I'LL HAVE THE PORT

In busy harbors and ports around the world, frequent small spills of fuel, oil, sewage, and chemicals wreak havoc on their estuarine ecosystems. For decades, the only countermeasure has been dredging—digging up the contaminated areas of the seafloor and depositing the sediment somewhere else, where it can (hopefully) be decontaminated. In 2001 U.S. Navy scientists discovered that dredging may be detrimental: It stops a natural cleanup process called *intrinsic bioremediation*. After decades of exposure, microbes in the sediment "learn" to metabolize the pollutants. So removing them causes even *more* damage. Research into the phenomenon—currently underway at several large harbors around the world—could one day lead to safer and cheaper cleanup procedures.

HERE COMES PETER COTTONWOOD

In 2007 scientists at the University of Washington spliced a rabbit gene onto the DNA of a poplar tree—creating a "super poplar tree" that can suck up toxins from contaminated soil. Any tree can safely absorb a few toxins, but the mutant trees can absorb hundreds, including cancer-causing pollutants such as benzene, vinyl chloride, and chloroform. And they do it up to 50 times faster. Opponents claim that these "mad scientists" are entering dangerous territory. Sharon Doty, one of the mad scientists, assures the skeptics that a lot more research remains before these mutant trees will get out of the lab. "It's a beautiful thing that a rabbit gene is perfectly readable by a plant," she says. "I don't think it's something to fear." (That is, until the giant poplars start hopping around.)

MOONSTRUCK

*Building sustainable housing on the Moon may
sound like science fiction, but some are
taking the idea very seriously.*

NICE ATMOSPHERE
In 2007 a team of 30 astronomers, engineers, and students
from around the world unveiled their plan for a project
called Luna Gaia, or "Moon Earth." Though the materials will initially come from down here, the scientists believe the site could
one day be 95% self-sufficient, needing very little help from Earth
to survive. Some details:

• The complex will consist of inflatable "pods" the size of small
apartments made of a durable Kevlar-like material and linked by
inflatable tunnels. The first installation will be built in a mile-
wide crater near the Moon's north pole. This will keep the inhabi-
tants in the shade of the crater's rim, protecting them from solar
radiation.

• A dozen 100-foot-wide mirrors on the rim will direct sunlight to
a power station, where it will be used to heat water to produce
steam to drive turbines, as in a typical power plant.

• Some of the pods will be greenhouses for growing food. Plants
will also provide some (and eventually all) of the oxygen necessary to survive. Other pods will house aquariums where fast-grow-
ing fish can be raised to provide a sustainable food source.

• Water from washing—as well as urine—will be filtered and
treated to convert it back into drinking water.

• There will be zero waste. All refuse, including human waste,
will be broken down via microbes into fertilizer.

• NASA has already announced plans to build a lunar post
sometime around 2020. Will they use the Luna Gaia model?
Stay tuned.

Each year, 70,000 Americans die as a result of air pollution.

TERMS OF ENPOOPMENT

*In the world of wastewater treatment, that nasty stuff has a
lot more names than Number One and Number Two.*

Wastewater: All the liquid waste—including the solid waste within it—produced by a community (homes, factories, etc.).

Sewage: The part of wastewater that contains significant amounts of poop. (The term is also often used to describe all wastewater.)

Influent: The wastewater that flows into a treatment facility.

Raw sewage: Another name for wastewater that has not been treated (as well as the name of a death-metal band from Mt. Blanchard, Ohio).

Slurry: A mixture of mostly urine and feces from cattle or pig farms.

Graywater (or sullage): Wastewater from nonindustrial sources—primarily homes—from showers, bathtubs, sinks, washing machines, and other sources that aren't used for the disposal of food, urine, feces, or toxic materials.

Blackwater: Wastewater that *does* contain urine, feces, or toxic material.

Scum: The foamy stuff that floats on top of wastewater, consisting mostly of fats and grease. (Yum!)

Sludge: The first step in wastewater treatment is the separation of the solids from the liquid—the gooey, solid, and sort-of-solid stuff left over is called sludge.

Biosolid: After the sludge is further treated by physical filtering, it is biologically processed, or "eaten," by microbes and converted into nutrient-rich organic material.

Clean water: Wastewater that that hasn't come into contact with humans (from ice machine drains, air conditioners, and basement drains).

Effluent: This is the end result of the treatment process—the "cleaned" liquid from wastewater that flows out of a treatment plant.

THE ♻ SYMBOL

How cool would it be to have this tidbit on your resume?
"1970: designed a symbol that millions of people
around the world see every day."

THINKING OUTSIDE THE BOX

The first Earth Day, celebrated by 20 million people in April 1970, not only led to the formation of the EPA (see page 255), it also launched an unusual contest. A Chicago-based cardboard-box company called Container Corporation of America (CCA), a pioneer in manufacturing recycled products, was looking for a simple design to print on all of their recycled boxes. Inspired by the success of Earth Day, Bill Lloyd, the graphic designer at CCA, decided to advertise the contest nationally at America's high schools and colleges. "As inheritors of the Earth, they should have their say," he said.

In Lloyd's grand vision, the winning design would be more than a symbol printed on CCA's boxes; it would serve as a symbol to promote the nationwide recycling movement. First prize: a $2,500 scholarship to the winner's choice of colleges. More than 500 entries came in from students all over the nation.

TWISTED

The winner: Gary Anderson, a 23-year-old graduate student at USC. He drew his inspiration from 19th-century mathematician August Ferdinand Möbius, who noted that a strip of paper twisted once and joined at the tips formed a continuous one-sided surface. Commonly referred to as a "Möbius strip," the geometric shape has since shown up in engineering (conveyor belts that last twice as long) and in popular art, such as M. C. Escher's fantasy-based woodcuts "Möbius Strip I" and "Möbius Strip II (Red Ants)."

It was that combination of practicality and art—along with the recycling-friendly notion that everything eventually returns to itself—that put Anderson's design at the top of the contest finalists. "I wanted to suggest both the dynamic—things are changing—and the static equilibrium, a permanent kind of thing," he later recalled. (After the design was chosen as the

---

There are 120 "green"-themed charter schools nationwide.

winner, Bill Lloyd altered it slightly; he darkened the edges and rotated the arrows 60 degrees so the interior of the symbol resembled a pine tree. In Anderson's version, one of the pointy ends faced down.)

CCA attempted to trademark the recycling symbol, but after they allowed other manufacturers to use it for a small fee, the trademark application was held for further review. Rather than press the matter, Lloyd and the CCA decided that a petty legal battle over such a positive message was a bad idea. So they dropped the case and allowed Anderson's creation to fall into the public domain. The three arrows have since come to represent the three components of conservation: Reuse, Reduce, Recycle.

SYMBOLOGY

Although anyone is free to use the recycling symbol as part of an advertising campaign (or as a graphic on a page…like in a *Bathroom Reader*), its use to advertise a commercial product's recycling properties is strictly regulated by the Federal Trade Commission's "Guides for the Use of Environmental Marketing Claims." There are several variations, but here are the symbol's two main classifications:

• **Recycled:** If the arrows are surrounded by a solid black circle, then the product is made from previously recycled material. A percentage displayed in the center of the symbol denotes how much of the product was made from recycled material. (If no percentage is denoted, it is 100% recycled.)

• **Recyclable:** If the arrows are not surrounded by a circle, then the product is recyclable, but only if the "regulations and/or ordinances of your local community provide for its collection."

STILL AT IT

Nearly four decades later, Gary Anderson remains active in the green movement. After earning his Ph.D. in geography and environmental engineering from Johns Hopkins University in 1985, the architect-by-trade has spent the bulk of his career as an urban planner with a focus on controlled growth. When asked how it feels to have created one of the most popular symbols in the world, Anderson tries to downplay his accomplishment, but admits that it's "pretty neat."

BAD MOVIE SCIENCE

The moral: When movie characters use scientific-sounding words, remember that some Hollywood screenwriter probably made that stuff up.

THE DAY AFTER TOMORROW (2004)

Premise: The Gulf Stream, an Atlantic ocean current that helps regulate Earth's temperature, has become so affected by global warming that it essentially stops. The ocean suddenly rises and massive icy tidal waves flood New York City. Within days, North America is a frozen wasteland.

Bad Science: Global warming can have a detrimental effect on the oceans, but it can't stop the Gulf Stream that fast. Even if it could, in order for New York City to flood like it did in the movie, the entire continent of Antarctica would have to melt. For *that* to happen, all of the sunlight that hits Earth would have to be collectively beamed at the South Pole...for three years.

THE MATRIX (1999)

Premise: After the machines take over the world, the human resistance "scorches the sky" to block out the machines' power supply—sunlight. So the machines use the humans for power, keeping them alive in a vegetative state while subjecting their brains to a life simulation. The machines "liquefy the dead so they can be fed intravenously to the living."

Bad Science: Neither the machines nor the humans know much about sustainable energy production. Blocking out the sun would just destroy Earth's biosphere; the machines could easily build solar panels in space to get all the power they need. Second, human energy is inefficient—only about 35% of the energy from food converts to mechanical energy. And feeding humans to humans can lead to a disease called kuru, which causes insanity—and would screw up the simulation.

THE CORE (2003)

Premise: This big-budget actioner stars Aaron Eckhart and Hilary Swank. After Earth's inner core suddenly stops rotating, the planet's magnetic field collapses. This allows the sun's microwaves to

---

On average, food travels 1,400 miles before it ends up on your plate.

penetrate the atmosphere and cause havoc on the surface. Humanity's only hope is a ragtag group of scientists who must travel down to the center of the planet in an experimental vehicle. Their plan: detonate several nuclear bombs in the hopes of "jump-starting Earth's engine."

Bad Science: If Earth's core—which spins at 550 mph (although the movie says 1,000 mph)—suddenly stopped rotating, all of its rotational energy would be released up into the mantle, and then to the surface, causing a massive earthquake that would last for years. Also, microwaves couldn't fry the surface; they're too weak, and they aren't even affected by magnetic fields. And as far as building a ship that can withstand the immense pressure inside Earth to detonate nuclear bombs that will jump-start the core...we don't have nearly enough room to go into how impossible that is.

WATERWORLD (1995)

Premise: The surface of Earth has been completely covered in water. In one scene, the Mariner (Kevin Costner) swims around an abandoned underwater city that's revealed to be none other than Denver, Colorado, once known as the "mile-high" city.

Bad Science: If the temperature of Earth increased 8°F, sea levels would rise by three feet due to melting polar ice caps, which would be ecologically catastrophic. But sea levels could never rise to the point where Denver was completely submerged—the city's elevation is 5,280 feet. If all the world's ice melted, the ocean would rise 250 feet, submerging many coastal cities, but not Denver.

THE HAPPENING (2008)

Premise: (*If you haven't seen this and don't want to have the "twist ending" spoiled, stop reading!*) Throughout the movie, some unknown force is causing people all over the northeastern United States to spontaneously kill themselves. The cause is revealed to be trees—angry, angry trees. Retaliating en masse against humans for polluting the planet, the trees emit neurotoxins called *pyrethrins*, which scramble the brain and lead to suicide.

Bad Science: Pyrethrins come in very small quantities (in liquid form) in chrysanthemums native to Australia. And the liquid can be toxic, which is why it's used in pesticides. But trees could never emit suicide-causing neurotoxins.

YOU'VE GOT JUNK MAIL

"You're approved!" "Save big $$ on your next oil change!" "Time to refinance!"
"You may already be a winner!" "Take the cable TV challenge!"
"We'll clean your carpets!" "Sale ends Monday!"

THE STATS

Each year, the average mailbox receives approximately 848 pieces of junk mail—and that number is significantly higher in election years.

• The U.S. Postal Service reports that in 1980, 35 billion pieces of unsolicited mail were sent to U.S. homes. Since then, the number has grown to 100 billion per year.

• According to the U.S. Department of Energy, every year direct mail campaigns use the paper equivalent of 100 million trees. The bulk of these trees come from rain forests.

• In 2005 alone, nearly six million tons of junk mail ended up in municipal waste systems.

• According to the Environmental Protection Agency, less than 36% of the junk mail sent in 2005 was recycled. And nearly half of it never even gets read.

So what can you do to help curb this massive waste?

THE SOLUTIONS

A direct-mail campaign is considered a success if 1% to 3% of the recipients actually become customers. So 97% or more of all that paper is going to waste. Still, there are steps you can take to significantly reduce the amount of junk mail you receive. Here are a few from the consumer advocate organization Privacy Rights Clearinghouse.

Direct mailing lists. The best avenue is to go online to the Direct Marketing Association's Mail Preference Service Web site. There you'll find instructions on how to take your name off of national mailing lists. That alone will significantly reduce your junk mail.

Local ads. If you want to stop getting those envelopes full of coupons for restaurants, car repair, etc., that are addressed to "Resident" or "Occupant," contact the distribution company

Team name of SUNY College of Environmental Science and Forestry: the Stumpies.

directly (such as Valpak or Pennysaver). Their address or phone number can usually be found somewhere on the envelope. Your best bet is to send them the address label along with a letter requesting them to remove you from their list. The company may even have a Web site that will allow you to remove your name online. Privacy Rights Clearinghouse warns that "you may have to notify the distribution company more than once to make sure your address has been removed."

Catalog mailings. Most of them are managed by a company called Abacus, which sells your name and address to these publications. Contact Abacus directly and request that you be removed from all of their lists. (Other catalogs may need to be contacted directly.)

Preapproved credit card solicitations. They're usually handled by the four major credit bureaus: Equifax, Experian, TransUnion, and Innovis. According to the Fair Credit Reporting Act, they are required by federal law to remove you from their list if you request it, but you must contact each one separately.

MORE WAYS TO STOP JUNK MAIL

• Whenever possible, keep your address to yourself. It gets added to a computer database (along with your buying habits) every time you apply for a credit card, buy a car, fill out a survey, donate to a charity, enter a contest, subscribe to a magazine, etc. Keep an eye out for a box to indicate that you do not want to receive any advertising in the mail. If there isn't one, then write in big block letters: "Do not give or sell my info to any mailing lists."

• Most phone-book white pages—where many of these lists get your information—will allow you to have only your name and number printed without your address, but you must specifically request it.

• For individual pieces of junk mail, use a big magic marker to write "Junk Mail: Return to Sender" on the envelope. The satisfying part is that you make the company pay for postage twice *not* to get your business; on the flip side, it means that the package will most likely be thrown in the trash and end up in a landfill. Also, it doesn't guarantee that your name will be removed from any list.

As you can see, getting your name off of these lists requires a lot of effort. And in the end it probably won't eliminate junk mail altogether, but it will significantly reduce it. The good news is that with each passing year, more and more state and national initiatives are being proposed with the ultimate goal of creating one national "Do Not Send" list (there are several petitions available online). But the fact of the matter is that direct mailing is among the least expensive ways for a company to advertise itself—so the practice won't be going away anytime soon.

GET CREATIVE

So what can you do with all that junk mail that floods your mailbox? Recycling it is the obvious choice. Just throw it in the bin (but first make sure to shred anything, such as credit card applications, that have your personal information). Beyond that, here some fun ways to take the "junk" out of junk mail.

Get free envelopes. Many applications come with a perfectly good envelope, and sometimes it even has an unused stamp. Save them for your future mailing needs, or store records or receipts in them.

Shred them. Now you have packing material to keep your boxed goods safe the next time you move.

Save for a scrapbook. Cut out the funny pictures and tacky advertising slogans, and you'll have a free, fun collection of accents for your next scrapbook.

Make a basket. Junk mail and catalog pages can be used to weave surprisingly beautiful baskets. Several Web sites can show you how.

Make art. It's a growing fad among modern artists: Sculptures, tapestries, and even "trees" made from junk mail have been featured at galleries all over the world. According to Aurora Robson, a Canadian artist, "The activity of opening up the mail and finding a depressing mass of garbage and credit card applications is now a pleasant experience wherein I find a new batch of art supplies. The language, costly graphic devices, and fancy printing used in junk mail give it a persuasive, positive, and personal flavor, making it great fodder."

*   *   *

"What is a weed? A plant whose virtues have not yet been discovered."

—**Ralph Waldo Emerson**

ENDANGERED ELEPHANT HEART PLUMS

Everyone wants to save the whales, or the forests, or the ozone layer.
But what about food? Won't somebody please think of the food?

SLOOOOOOW DOWWWWWN

In 1986 an Italian wine journalist named Carlo Petrini founded the "Slow Food Movement." His goal: to convince people to stop scarfing down Big Macs as fast as they can. Slow Foodists (there are 85,000 of them worldwide) buy only locally grown organic food, prepare it with care, and, most importantly, take plenty of time to savor the "sensual pleasure" and "slow, long-lasting enjoyment" of their meals. "I'm not trying to over-throw the system," says Petrini, "but I'm hoping we can offer an alternative to the fast life. We won't throw bombs at McDon-ald's—maybe handfuls of tagliarini."

A major goal of the movement is preservation of certain foods. In 1996 Slow Food International founded the Ark of Taste, a sort of endangered species list. In the last 100 years, they claim, 75% of European and 93% of North American food diversity has been lost. Here are a few of the U.S.'s most endangered dishes. (We have no idea what most of these are.)

- Cherokee Trail of Tears Dry Beans
- Black-Seeded Tennis Ball Lettuce
- Bull Nose Large Bell Pepper
- Sheepnose Pimiento
- Anishinaabeg Manoomin Rice
- Amish Deer Tongue Lettuce
- Bronx Grape
- Black Republican Cherry
- Petaluma Gold Rush Bean

- Black Sphinx Date
- Elephant Heart Plum
- Gilfeather Turnip
- Aunt Molly's Husk Tomato
- Yellow Indian Woman Bean
- Early Blood Turnip-Rooted Beet
- Inchelium Red Garlic
- Grandpa Admire's Lettuce
- Traditional American Root Beer

How about you? One in six Americans lives within a mile of a toxic waste site.

ACCORDING TO THE LATEST RESEARCH

Every new day brings some bold new study. Some are interesting, and some are weird. For example, did you know that science says...

DIVORCE IS BAD FOR THE ENVIRONMENT

With funding from the National Science Foundation and National Institutes of Health, a team of researchers from Michigan State University studied household energy use and divorce rates in 12 countries. Findings: Rising divorce rates around the world lead to fewer people living in more houses—for all 12 countries studied, divorces resulted in 7.4 million extra households and 38 million extra rooms. "The increases in consumption of water and energy and using more space are being seen everywhere," said head researcher Jack Liu. According to the study, if the U.S. couples who were divorced in 2005 had stayed together, it would have saved 73 billion kilowatt-hours of electricity and 627 billion gallons of water. And it isn't just divorce: Fewer multigenerational households—combined with single people living alone for longer—also result in more strain on energy resources.

CLIMATE CHANGE KILLED AN EMPIRE

In 1993 geologist John Valley led a team from the University of Wisconsin, along with another from Hebrew University in Israel, to study stalactites found in a Jerusalem cave. Valley used a tool called an *ion microprobe*, which utilizes tightly focused light to find calcite deposits, the amounts of which vary with levels of rainfall. By carbon dating the deposits, the team was able to reconstruct climate patterns from 200 B.C.E., which marked the beginning of the Roman Empire, all the way to its fall in the 5th century C.E. Over that time, there was a gradual and consistent reduction of rain...which coincided with a steady decline in agriculture and trade. After the 15-year study was concluded, the scientists announced that the drier climate may have led to the decline of the Roman Empire.

Surprise: It takes less water to use a dishwashing machine than to wash dishes by hand.

CHEMICALS ARE TURNING MALES INTO FEMALES

In 2008 the British chemical watchdog organization CHEMTrust published the combined results of more than 250 worldwide studies. It revealed that over the past century, humans, animals, and fish have been exposed to roughly 100,000 toxic chemicals. Many of those chemicals have since been discovered to be *endocrine disrupters*, or "gender-benders"; prolonged exposure to them interferes with sex hormones. Some of these chemicals include *phthalates* (found in cosmetics), flame retardants used in furniture, and, most notably, pesticides. Among the damage:

• Half the male fish in English rivers now develop eggs in their testicles.

• Male alligators in Florida have lower testosterone levels, increased estrogen levels, and smaller penises than their ancestors did.

• Polar bears with both sets of sex organs have been discovered in the Arctic Circle.

• The damage has affected humans, too. Sperm counts in 20 industrialized nations have declined by nearly 60% in the last 50 years. And baby boys born to American women who endured prolonged exposure to chemicals have smaller penises.

THE TREES ARE SPEAKING TO EACH OTHER

Scientists from the National Center for Atmospheric Research measured chemical emissions from trees in a walnut grove in Davis, California. The area was in the midst of a drought, and the nights were very cold. How did the scientists know this? The trees told them by producing a chemical called *methyl salicylate*. It works just like aspirin relieves fever and pain in humans, except this chemical raises biochemical defense mechanisms in trees. And not only did the trees use the aspirin to makes *themselves* feel better, they emitted it into the air so other nearby trees could be warned about the danger and begin producing their own methyl salicylate. In other words, the researchers believe that the trees can actually "talk" to each other to warn of environmental threats.

* * *

"We trees do what we can. We keep off strangers and the foolhardy; and we train and we teach, we walk and we weed."
—**Treebeard the Ent,** *The Lord of the Rings*

THE GOLF WAR

Golf is a great game—it requires strength, precision, strategy, and luck. And it's one of the world's most popular leisure activities, inspiring people young and old to take long walks in green fields. But that "green" comes at a price.

A COURSE OF A DIFFERENT COLOR

When golf was born in Scotland in the 16th century, there were no specialized courses used solely for the sport. Golf was played in pastures, where grazing flocks of sheep kept the fairways both trimmed and fertilized (and provided their own special kinds of hazards). The terrain was uneven and the grass mostly brown. It was truly "man vs. nature."

The designers of 20th-century golf courses, however, tried to control much of this natural uncertainty before the player ever teed up. They decided the grass in each section—fairway, green, or rough—must always be cut at a specific height and have its own definitive shade of green. Maintaining this requires a small army of full-time employees practicing "turfgrass science," the technical term for golf course maintenance. It's such a lucrative and sought-after position that many top universities offer a four-year degree in it.

SEA OF GREEN

In the past 100 years, the popularity of golf has exploded. Roughly 26 million U.S. golfers can now choose from 15,000 courses, which collectively cover an area the size of Delaware. That's a lot of grass to keep watered. A well-manicured course requires about 3,400 gallons per golfer per round of 18 holes. To use the same amount of water, that golfer would have to flush a toilet 87,000 times. The world over, golf courses use 2.5 billion gallons of clean water every single day.

And it takes more than water to keep a golf course green, which is why turfgrass scientists must become experts in chemical pesticides and fertilizers. Courses are covered with whatever chemicals will do the job. If one isn't working, they try another.

Setting the standard for this manicured look is the Augusta National Golf Club in Georgia, the site of one of golf's most prestigious events, the Masters tournament. Augusta is famous for its almost surreal, Technicolor landscape with immaculate fairways surrounded by thousands of ornamental flowers...all thriving thanks to copious amounts of water and chemicals. So important is this appearance that when the Masters was first televised in color in 1967, the groundskeepers were ordered to dye the creeks, ponds, and water hazards so they'd look more blue on camera. That kind of dedication to "beauty" spread throughout the sport.

GAG ORDER

But as the environmental movement grew more mainstream in the final three decades of the century, golf courses turned into a big green target. Several organizations sprang up, culminating with the Global Anti-Golf Movement (GAGM) in 1996, with chapters in Europe, Asia, Australia, Latin America, and the U.S. To these groups, the problems with the sport go deeper than high water usage and pesticide contamination—courses also destroy wildlife habitats. And proving just how much they despise the sport, GAGM's manifesto says, "Golf course and golf tourism development violate human rights in every sense of the word....It promotes an elitist and exclusive resort lifestyle and notion of leisure."

For their part, the United States Golf Association (USGA) and the Professional Golfers Association (PGA) have acknowledged that the high water and pesticide use is out of control (though they steer clear of the human-rights argument). Around the same time the GAGM formed, the two golfing associations joined with Audubon International to announce their "Golf & the Environment Initiative" (GEI), which is working to "enhance golf course environmental responsibility and performance through cooperation in environmental stewardship and public education." GAGM claims that this is essentially a public-relations campaign mounted by the golf industry, but whether that's true or not, the general approach to maintaining golf courses has started down a new path.

GOING TO REHAB

In the first decade of the 21st century, the field of turfgrass science began moving away from heavy pesticide use in favor of a broad approach referred to as Integrated Pest Management, or IPM. For the most part, this means using fewer synthetic pesticides and more organic gardening techniques to maintain healthy turf. To be fair, this change isn't necessarily because golf course owners *want* to be more responsible. They're forced to: 30 states have drafted pesticide restrictions for playgrounds and athletic fields…including golf courses.

Regardless of the catalyst, the "Greening the Green" movement is under way. And so far, the first few years have been difficult. Cornell University professor of turfgrass science Frank Rossi explains why: "A lot of golf courses are like drug addicts—they are chemically dependent. The first several years of adhering to an IPM, they're going to be strung out. They aren't going to look so great because they're going through chemical withdrawal." After the courses are weaned off of heavy pesticide dependency, Rossi says, they can actually become "far healthier and cheaper to maintain than before."

THE FAIR WAY

Is it possible to maintain a completely pesticide-free golf course? In the ideal climate (cool, relatively dry, and without too much snow in winter), it's possible…but expensive. The most famous example of an "organic" course is the Vineyard Golf Club in Martha's Vineyard, Massachusetts, which doesn't use pesticides at all. But they can afford it, being a private course that charges $350,000 to join and $1,000 per month in membership fees.

For most courses, a much more realistic goal is to reduce pesticide use to a minimum. The good news is that a lot of information exists on how to do this, including this tip from the GEI: "When designing a golf course, it is important to identify existing ecosystems. Emphasizing the existing characteristics can help retain natural resources, allow for efficient maintenance of the course, and will likely reduce site development costs."

So as the "Augusta look" falls out of favor, the old "Scottish style" is enjoying a resurgence in popularity. The new retro courses feature a much wilder, more windswept look. The putting greens themselves are still manicured, but the fairways are more natural and much of the rough is left to grow wild, giving today's golfer a direct link to the links of the past. The result: less water, less pesticide use, less habitat destruction, and less guilt among golfers who only wish to pursue their "notions of leisure" in peace.

TOILET TECH

·The typical toilet is a real water waster. Here are
two that save water via modern technology.

DUAL FLUSH

In the vast expanses of the Australian outback, water is such a limited resource that flushing a toilet several times per day is considered wasteful. So in 1980, the Australian government allocated $130,000 to a company called Caroma Industries to design a more efficient toilet. The task went to engineer Bruce Thompson, who created the two-buttoned Dual Flush toilet. The #1 flush, for liquid waste, uses only 0.8 gallons of water, while the #2 flush, for solid waste, uses 1.6 gallons (most toilets use about 2 gallons). Result: 67% less water is used, saving up to 9,000 gallons per toilet per year. In addition to the lower water and sewer costs, the Dual Flush has a stronger flow than conventional toilets, which means almost no clogging. It also utilizes a "wash down flush system," which, unlike typical siphonic systems, cleans the bowl as it flushes and doesn't cause the occasional "splash back" problems of standard toilets. (Bonus: The toilet seat can be snapped off for easy cleaning.)

WATERLESS

Used in restaurant restrooms since the mid-1990s, waterless no-flush urinals emit fewer odors than flush urinals because they're less susceptible to the backflow of sewer gases. According to the Waterless Co., each urinal saves up to 45,000 gallons of water per year. How does it work? "The conventional water-filled urinal's trap drain is replaced by a disposable EcoTrap filled with BlueSeal liquid. The trap seal blocks out sewer gases, and the BlueSeal liquid blocks out urine odors from the room. A 3-oz. dose of BlueSeal lasts over 1,500 uses." But the waterless urinal hasn't quite been perfected. The problem is with the chemical filters—if they're not changed often enough, they do develop odor. And some find the "chemical" smell of a fresh filter offensive. But these urinals do have another thing going for them (other than saving all that water): You don't have to touch them.

THE TOXIC TRAVEL GUIDE

Bored with Disneyland? Had enough of the Bahamas? Have a real vacation at one of these exotic—and toxic—locales!

HOT SPOT: Mailuu-Suu, Kyrgyzstan
HIGHLIGHTS: Located in one of the most fertile regions of Central Asia, Mailuu-Suu is just minutes from majestic mountains, alpine lakes, and scenic rivers.

TRAVEL TIPS: Bring a Geiger counter. Once part of the Soviet Union, from 1946 to '67 Mailuu-Suu processed uranium for the U.S.S.R.'s nuclear power and weapons programs. Today, nuclear waste—millions of pounds of it—is buried in pits in the hills surrounding the town. Bonus: It's an earthquake- and flood-prone region. Since many of the storage containers are already damaged, the area is overdue for a disaster of unprecedented proportions.

LODGING: There's little employment in the town of 24,000, so many people have just up and left. You can probably rent an empty (radioactive) house for next to nothing.

HOT SPOT: Linfen, China
HIGHLIGHTS: This out-of-the-way city of four million is located in Shanxi Province. Widely considered the ancient birthplace of Chinese culture, Linfen is home to the Yao Miao temple, the Yao Tomb, and the Iron Buddha Monastery.

TRAVEL TIPS: If you're not fond of inhaling coal dust, wear a mask. Linfen lies in the heart of China's coal country, and everything in the city is covered in black soot. How bad is it? In 2008 *Time* magazine named Linfen "The Most Polluted City in the World." Tourism officials will even give you a mask emblazoned with the words "I Can Breathe!"

LODGING: Consider the four-star Tang Yao Hotel, which features a "pavilion in the yard which makes you linger on with no thought of leaving when you enter just as in fairyland!"

According to the EPA, the 2nd-most-frequent cause of lung cancer after smoking is radon gas.

HOT SPOT: La Oroya, Peru

HIGHLIGHTS: This mountain paradise offers stunning views of the Andes from its perch at 12,000 feet above sea level.

TRAVEL TIPS: Bring all the water, food—and air—that you'll need. La Oroya processes copper, zinc, and lead, and the massive smokestack in the center of town has been spewing out black smoke and dust for 80 years. The once-lush hills have gone gray from decades of acid rain, which has contaminated the area with toxic levels of lead, arsenic, and sulfur dioxide.

LODGING: Rent an airtight Winnebago…and a haz-mat suit, should you feel the need to take a walk.

HOT SPOT: Ranipet, India

HIGHLIGHTS: Nestled in the southeastern state of Tamil Nadu, Ranipet sits on the banks of the majestic Palar River, and the city teems with Indian history and folklore.

TRAVEL TIPS: It also teems with *hexavalent chromium*—a carcinogen (made famous by the movie *Erin Brockovich*) that's a waste product of the leather tanning business, which the town is famous for. More than half the leather in all of Asia moves through Ranipet's factories—and it pollutes the groundwater at the highest levels on Earth. Local farmers say the water they use for irrigation actually "stings like insect bites" if it gets on their skin.

LODGING: There are many fine hotels in Ranipet; just think twice before drinking the water.

HOT SPOT: The Irish Sea, located between England and Ireland

HIGHLIGHTS: Boating, scuba diving, whale watching—the foggy Irish Sea has it all for the cold-water-loving adventurer!

TRAVEL TIPS: Don't go in the water. Since the 1950s, the Sellafield nuclear power plant on the coast of Cumbria, England, has discharged untold amounts of radioactive waste into the Irish Sea. It's still at it, too—dumping an estimated two million gallons *per day*, giving the Irish Sea a dubious honor: "the most radioactive sea in the world." So don't go fishing, either, as the fish contain dangerously high levels of plutonium-239 and cesium-137.

LODGING: Since you're going to be exposed to radiation anyway, why not go all the way and book a nuclear submarine?

GOING SOLAR

The sun is so big that it makes up more than 99% of all of the matter in our solar system—more than a million Earths could fit inside it. Its energy makes life possible. Yet only now are we truly beginning to harness the power of this massive tank of gas.

DAY BREAK
Humans have known for thousands of years how to capture the sun's energy. In many ancient cultures, homes were built facing south to take advantage of its warmth. The Romans first used glass windows to enhance and hold the sun's heat during winter. But for the next two millennia, that was about the extent of solar power.

Then, about 150 years ago, a Frenchman named Auguste Mouchout invented a solar-powered steam engine. Never heard of Auguste Mouchout? That's because his contraption was so expensive to build, and coal (which fueled most engines at the time) was so cheap, that no one saw the point in going solar. No one, that is, except American scientist Charles Fritts. In the 1880s, he figured out that a substance called selenium, when coated with an extremely thin layer of gold and exposed to sunlight, could create electricity. It was the world's first solar cell. But by then, the Industrial Revolution was in full swing, and cheap, abundant fossil fuels were the power source of choice.

APPROACHING CLOUDS

In the 20th century, many scientists contributed to the development of solar power, including Albert Einstein, who discovered the *photoelectric effect*—how matter absorbs photons (light particles) and emits their energy as electrons. But solar power wasn't looked at seriously until 1953, when Bell Laboratories developed the first silicon solar cell—the kind that would become the industry standard. Still, most people at the time viewed solar technology, technically called *photovoltaic energy*, as a novelty.

And then came the 1970s and the Arab oil embargo, which threatened to cut off the main supply of the world's oil. Governments scrambled to jump-start research into alternative energies.

But the solar revolution fizzled out when the embargo ended and gas prices again dropped. It wasn't until this century that the growth of the solar-energy market in Europe and Asia, coupled with the record-high oil prices of 2008, reinvigorated interest in producing solar power on a larger scale...kind of.

It still hasn't caught on in many countries, most notably the United States and Great Britain. Other nations—Italy, Brazil, Paraguay, Germany, Japan, and India—use solar to a greater degree. More than 25,000 Japanese homes have solar panels on their rooftops. And in some cities in Germany, the sun provides up to 40% of the power. Still, only 0.039% of the world's electricity comes directly from the sun.

OVERCAST

There are four major obstacles to making solar power viable.

Cost. Only about 23% of the light that strikes a silicon solar cell is converted to electricity. As a result, silicon solar panels have to be very large, making them expensive to manufacture.

Shade. At night, on cloudy days, and during the shorter days of winter, solar cells produce little or no power. Inventors and engineers haven't yet found a way to bypass this "darkness" problem.

Storage. Once the electricity is harnessed, it's difficult to store it in the large quantities needed to distribute it from sunny solar farms to remote locations that need the power.

Environmental Impact. One solution to the storage problem— storing the electricity in batteries—has its own set of problems. Batteries are costly to manufacture, and the processes used to both make and dispose of them can release toxins into the environment. And then there's the fact that, using current technology, a solar farm large enough to power a large city would need to be the size of a small city—requiring a construction project that would take a huge environmental toll on the land it's built on.

Just as it was in the late 1800s, it's still cheaper in the short term to just keep on using fossil fuels, which is what 99.961% of the world is doing.

THE SILVER LINING

But it's too early to give up on solar. Scientists, engineers, economists, and politicians are taking some serious looks at ways to improve it. Here are a few of the ideas being considered.

Sharing the Cost. One short-term solution is for utility companies to rent the rooftops of large buildings, where they can install solar panels. Warehouses are ideal, but some utility companies are also offering to install panels on people's homes at no charge. In most cases, the homeowner gets their power at no cost; the excess energy is then collected for the utility's power grid. These urban and suburban solar installations mean less disruption of natural habitats.

Hydrogen. Because one of the obstacles to cost-efficient solar power is storage, scientists at the Massachusetts Institute of Technology have figured out how to turn sunlight into hydrogen, which is easier to store than electricity. The idea is to use solar power to split water into hydrogen and oxygen atoms. The hydrogen could then be stored for later use in fuel cells. Water has been split (through a process known as *hydrolysis*) for years, but it takes a great deal of energy and high temperatures. This latest breakthrough could, theoretically, create a cost-efficient method of hydrolysis at room temperature.

Space Panels. In space, the sun never stops shining and it's not filtered through our thick atmosphere. So why not put huge solar panels up there? Answer: Because no one has figured out a cost-effective way to get that energy down to the planet's surface. One idea is to "beam" it down in a process utilizing microwaves. If the theory works, solar panels in space may become a new power source.

Fold Them Up. Most of the cells that make up solar panels and arrays are flat, and they reflect a great deal of sunlight back into the sky. Folded V-shaped solar cells, however, would reflect some of that light back into the collector, increasing efficiency. This low-cost interim measure may decrease the overall cost of solar energy.

Make Them Smaller. One type of solar cell is made from a thin film composed of copper, indium, gallium, and selenide (known as CIGS). It works roughly the same way a silicon solar cell does: Electrons become excited when light strikes them. Thin films are less efficient than silicon at converting sunlight into electricity, but they're less expensive and can be produced in greater amounts more easily.

Make Them *Way* Smaller. Nanotechnology may be the wave of the future, and tiny titanium oxide particles have proven to be much more efficient than large silicon crystals. Other products being tested include plastic solar cells that can work on cloudy days, and even spray-on solar composites, similar to paint, that may lead to sweatshirts that power cell phones and hydrogen cars that get their "juice" from their paint job. This technology is still very new and very expensive (but very cool).

HERE COMES THE SUN

Ideas are one thing; practical solutions are another. Many scientists and policy makers are urgently trying to put solar energy to work in the face of a fragile world economy and our finite oil reserves—not to mention climate change linked to greenhouse gas emissions. If all goes well, harnessing the sun's ample energy could be the solution to all of these problems. "If adequate policy measures are put in place today, solar electricity has the potential to supply energy to more than four billion people by 2030," claims Ernesto Macias, president of the European Photovoltaic Industry Association. And some studies estimate that a concentrated push toward solar energy could create 10 million new jobs and supply two-thirds of the world's energy needs.

By then, microscopic solar cells may power cars, homes, and even robots. And future generations will (hopefully) look back at today's gargantuan, unsightly, inefficient silicon solar panels...and laugh.

*   *   *

REDUCE, REUSE, DOWNLOAD

Tapes replaced records, compact discs replaced tapes, and in 2003, digital storage began to replace CDs. That's when Apple's iTunes Music Store debuted. Since then, the service has sold more than five billion electronic song files, the equivalent of about 415 million compact discs. Environmentally speaking, this amounts to 415 million compact discs that were not pressed, 415 million plastic CD cases that were not manufactured, and 415 million paper liner-note booklets that were not printed.

FLINTSTONE V. JETSON

Who's the bigger environmental (Hanna) barbarian?

AN ANIMATED DEBATE

One is from the Stone Age, and one is from the distant future, but Fred Flintstone (of *The Flintstones*, 1960–66) and George Jetson (of *The Jetsons*, 1962–63) are a lot alike: Both are middle-class family men just trying to get by. Here's where these two fictional characters from 40-year-old cartoon shows truly and most importantly differ: Who had the larger carbon footprint?

FRED FLINTSTONE: GOOD

• He lives in the Stone Age. All building materials, tools, cars, and consumer products are made out of natural, mostly unadulterated—and extremely eco-friendly—stone. Flintstone lives off of the Earth, literally.

• Flintstone doesn't use fossil fuels. He lives alongside plants and animals that will one day putrefy and *become* petroleum. Without a drop of oil, Flintstone powers his car by rapidly pedaling his feet, perhaps the greenest alternative energy source in history. Further, since electricity hasn't been harnessed yet, all of the appliances in his home are powered via the mechanical labor of various birds and animals. Carbon emissions from the Flintstone home: zero.

• One could argue that this is animal cruelty, as the birds and mammoths are forced to work as indentured servants. However, instead of running away, the animals seem perfectly content to insult Fred with their clever wisecracks.

• Finally, Flintstone doesn't wear shoes or pants, so he doesn't contribute to the pesticide-dependent cotton industry. Conclusion: Fred Flintstone is quite "green."

GEORGE JETSON: BAD

The Jetsons was a product of the early 1960s idea that "the future" would be all about technology and labor-saving devices. What didn't seem to occur to anyone was all the energy it would take to power a world full of robots, flying cars, and self-cleaning kitchens.

• Jetson eats food prepared by a Food-a-Rac-a-Cycle, a microwave-

Designer Nguyen La Chanh created Moss Carpet, a bath mat made out of living moss.

size machine that prepares any meal at the push of a button. Because it's a tiny device that can't store bulky items, it can't produce just *any* food. According to an article by David Freedman in *Discover*, it would only produce "blobs of tasteless but nutritious paste" with flavoring chemicals added. So the Jetsons subsist on highly processed chemicals, decidedly not locally grown or organic.

• The food machine is just one of many sophisticated gizmos that preclude any work for Jetson and his family (his boy Elroy, daughter Judy, and Jane, his wife). The Jetsons enjoy talking watches, machines that control their dreams, holographic 3-D television, video phones, a machine that gets them out of bed and dresses them, and Rosie, the robot maid. Every single one of these gadgets requires a tremendous amount of electricity.

• Jetson drives a flying car. It looks like a cross between a Volkswagen Beetle and a flying saucer, but the closest thing we have to compare it to is a Sikorsky S-76C, a common commercial helicopter that gets terrible gas mileage—less than two miles per gallon. Today's gas-guzzling Hummer H2 gets about 10 mpg, meaning that Jetson's "futuristic" car is only 20% as efficient as a Hummer.

• Even if Jetson wanted to drive an energy-efficient car on the ground, he couldn't. All of the buildings in his hometown of Orbit City are elevated hundreds of feet off the ground—he can't even *walk* anywhere. Flying is the only option. And when Jetson steps out of the car at his destination, the sidewalks move. (It's truly amazing, then, that Fred Flintstone is fatter than George Jetson.)

• And why exactly are all those buildings sky-high? It's not touched upon in the show (creators say they based the buildings on the futuristic Space Needle in Seattle), but maybe Al Gore was right: By the time *The Jetsons* takes place, in the year 2062, all the electricity used to power *our* labor-saving devices has produced so many carbon emissions that the polar ice caps have melted, covering the surface of the Earth in water, leaving humanity no choice but to build upward. (Sorry, George. Our bad.)

*　　*　　*

Fred: How can you be so stupid?
Barney: Hey, that's not very nice! Say you're sorry.
Fred: I'm sorry you're stupid.
—*The Flintstones*

DUMPSTER DIVING

One man's trash is another man's treasure.

CROSS TO BEAR

After an Austrian hotel owner died in 2004, his family threw most of his "junk" away. A woman happened upon the pile of refuse and found an old wooden cross. She took it home, but later decided she didn't want it and almost threw it away herself. But a friend stopped her and said they should take it to the local museum. There, curator Hermann Mayrhofer immediately knew that this was much more than just an old cross. He did some research and discovered that it was more than 800 years old and had been missing since World War II—the Nazis had stolen it as part of an art collection of a Polish aristocrat, then stashed it in an Austrian castle. Estimated worth: $600,000.

IT'S GREEK TO US

The *Codex Sinaiticus* contains most of the Old Testament and all of the New Testament. One of the most important sources for modern Bible translators, it was handwritten in Greek on several scrolls in the fourth century. Today it's in the British Museum, thanks to a German book historian named Constantin von Tischendorf. In 1859, while visiting a monastery near Mt. Sinai, he came across a basket of old parchments to be used as fuel for a fireplace. Curious, von Tischendorf started leafing through them and knew right away that he had found something irreplaceable.

MANHATTAN TRANSFER

In 2003, while heading to work, Elizabeth Gibson saw a painting in the garbage near 72nd Street in Manhattan. She liked it, took it home, and got it appraised...and learned it was *Tres Personajes*, a 1970 abstract of three people by Mexican artist Rufino Tamayo. It had disappeared after it was stolen in the mid-1980s. Gibson returned the painting in nearly perfect condition to its owners, who gave her a $15,000 reward. In 2008 *Tres Personajes* sold at auction for $1 million. "I know nothing of modern art," she said, "but it didn't seem right for any piece of art to be discarded like that."

A well-rounded meal: A company in Taiwan makes edible dinner plates out of wheat.

KEEP EARTH CLEAN: IT'S NOT URANUS!

And other bumper stickers that will either amuse or offend...or both.

Compost! A Rind Is A
Terrible Thing To Waste

Save the Earth. It's the only
planet with chocolate.

*Red Meat Isn't Bad For You,
Green Fuzzy Meat Is*

**Honk if you like
noise pollution!**

I don't just hug trees—
I talk dirty to them, too

SAVE WATER, TAKE A
BATH WITH YOUR
NEIGHBOR'S WIFE

*THIS IS A GREEN CAR
(they were all out of red ones)*

*Yuppies: The Other
White Meat!*

*Serious about reducing CO$_2$?
Stop breathing so much.*

People are more opposed to
fur than leather because it's
easier to harass rich women
than motorcycle gangs

Bald people for
global warming!

I'M A TREE HUGGER—
I PINE FOR YEW

**Preserve wildlife:
Pickle a toad**

Compost happens!

*Don't like logging? Try
wiping with a pinecone.*

*Suburbia: Where they cut down
all the trees and name the
streets after them*

***Drive a hybrid—my SUV
needs the gas you save***

*If you're living like there's
no global warming,
you'd better be right.*

THE EARTH DOES NOT BELONG
TO US—IT BELONGS TO THE
ZORGONS OF PLANET KRON.
(SO DON'T TICK THEM OFF!)

**Ignore the environment
and it will go away**

ROOSEVELT

*The 26th president of the United States was number
one when it came to protecting the land.*

SEALING HIS FATE

Long before he dreamed of being a military leader or president, a sickly seven-year-old named Theodore Roosevelt wanted to be a zoologist. In the summer of 1865, the boy got hold of a severed seal's head from a local New York City market, then found some other animal skeletons and opened up the "Roosevelt Museum of Natural History." Capturing animals for study became his hobby. When Theodore grew into a teenager, his father gave him boxing lessons to fight back against the bullies at school, which helped him grow into the man who would later lead his men to victory at the battle of San Juan Hill in the Spanish-American War before being elected governor of New York. Later, after serving as vice president for only six months, Roosevelt took the top office when William McKinley was assassinated in 1901. Combining progressive domestic programs with a strong national defense policy, Roosevelt's eight-year presidency is regarded by historians as one of the most successful ever. And environmentalists remember him well, too—they call him "The Great Conservationist." Here's why.

The National Wildlife Refuge System. By executive order, on March 14, 1903, Roosevelt declared Florida's Pelican Island a permanent wildlife refuge. Exotic migratory birds such as snowy egrets, herons, and pelicans, who flocked to the island, had been hunted nearly to extinction because their elegant plumes were used in fashionable women's hats (in 1903 an ounce of bird feathers was worth more than $32—twice the price of gold). Roosevelt went on to establish 53 National Wildlife Refuges, 51 of them bird sanctuaries. Today there are 538 wildlife refuges—at least one in every state, and one within an hour's drive of every major city.

The Newlands Reclamation Act. Under this act, passed by Congress in 1902 and named after its chief sponsor, Sen. Francis G. Newlands of Nevada, Roosevelt authorized the sale of public lands in 16 western states and used the money to develop federal irriga-

The first pair of Doc Marten boots had soles made from old rubber tires.

tion projects, transforming the western United States. Proving that not every plan is perfect, the act led to the building of massive dams to irrigate arid areas for settlers and agriculture...which blocked river flows in other areas, causing severe water shortages and other damage that's still being dealt with today.

The National Antiquities Act. Finally passed into law in 1906 after decades of efforts on the part of lawmakers, naturalists, and archaeologists, this law gave the president the power to create national monuments that would protect "historic landmarks, historic and prehistoric structures, and other objects of historic or scientific interest." In all, Roosevelt authorized the creation of 18 national monuments, most in the West and Southwest, including the first—Devils Tower, Wyoming—plus Gila Cliff Dwelling, New Mexico; Petrified Forest National Monument, Arizona; and Muir Woods, California, which he had once visited with his good friend, naturalist John Muir. In 1907 Roosevelt set aside more than 1,000 acres for the Grand Canyon National Monument (made a national park in 1919), thereby protecting it from development by railroads and mining companies.

The U.S. Forest Service. In 1905 Roosevelt consolidated three federal agencies to form the Forest Service, which set aside 150 million acres for national forests. Members of Congress, particularly in the West, objected to the federal government having so much power in their states, and in 1907, they passed a law prohibiting the government from creating or enlarging any national forests in Oregon, Washington, Idaho, Montana, Colorado, or Wyoming. Roosevelt thwarted Congress one last time when he issued an executive order making 16 million acres of prime timberland—now known as the Midnight Forests—part of the national forest system the night before he signed the bill. "Optimism is a good characteristic," Roosevelt told Congress, "but if carried to an excess, it becomes foolishness. We are prone to speak of the resources of this country as inexhaustible; this is not so."

Roosevelt didn't accomplish all of this alone.
Turn to page 170 to learn about the men
who helped turned his ideas into policy.

THE GARBAGE VORTEX

*A lonely plastic bag blows across a parking lot. It tumbles down a hill
and into a creek, where the water carries it downstream to a river.
Down the river it goes until it's swept out to sea. Day after
day it floats in the expanse until, there in the distance—
another plastic bag! And another, and another…and
millions of others. What is this strange place?*

ALARMING DISCOVERY

In the late 1990s, a sea captain and ocean researcher
named Charles Moore entered a yacht race in Hawaii.
As he was sailing back home to California, he came upon an odd
sight: "There were shampoo caps and soap bottles and plastic
bags and fishing floats as far as I could see. Here I was in the
middle of the ocean, and there was nowhere I could go to avoid
the plastic."

Around the same time, oceanographer Curtis Ebbesmeyer was
researching ocean currents by tracking debris that had washed up
on beaches around the world. When he heard of Moore's discovery, he named it the Eastern Garbage Patch (EGP).

Moore put together a team to survey the area in August 1998.
Onboard the research ship *Alguita*, they pulled all sorts of strange
objects out of the ocean: an inflated volleyball dotted with barnacles, a picture tube for a 19" TV, a truck tire on a steel rim, and
even a drum of hazardous chemicals. But most of what they saw
was plastic…and something else. Moore described it as a "rich
broth of minute sea creatures mixed with hundreds of colored
plastic fragments—a plastic-plankton soup." But there was six
times more plastic than there was plankton.

TROPIC OF PLASTIC

Just how large is the Eastern Garbage Patch? No one knows for
sure—it's growing all the time; and the translucent plastic floats
just below the water's surface. "It's one of the great features of
the planet Earth, but you can't see it," said Ebbesmeyer. Estimates, however, say that it's larger than the state of Texas. And
that's just on the surface. Much of the debris—up to 30%—

"If you tell a joke in the forest, but nobody laughs, was it a joke?" —Steven Wright sinks to the ocean floor and lands on top of animal and plant life.

Just how fast is the EGP growing? In a survey conducted in 2007, Moore found that in less than a decade the "patch" had become a "superhighway of junk" running between San Francisco and Japan. He believes that the amount of plastic could now be 10 times higher than it was in 1998; some of the samples he gathered have as much as 48 parts plastic to 1 part plankton.

IN THE DOLDRUMS

How did all that garbage accumulate there? The answer is ocean currents. The EGP is located in an area known as the North Pacific Subtropical Gyre, about 1,000 miles from any landmass. The Gyre is formed by air and water currents that travel between the coasts of Washington, Mexico, and Japan. The clockwise currents form a vortex in the center, just as if a giant soup spoon were constantly stirring it or, as Moore says, "the same way bubbles gather at the center of a hot tub."

The Gyre is part of the Doldrums—an area named by ancient sailors for its weak winds. For centuries sailors avoided it for fear of stalling there, and fishermen knew there was nothing there to catch but plankton or jellyfish. The Gyre has always accumulated marine debris such as driftwood, as well as "flotsam and jetsam"—stuff that washes offshore from beaches or falls overboard from ships and is caught by the currents and pulled into the middle, where it swirls continuously. But the difference in the last century is that the never-ending influx of trash has made it larger and larger. A plastic bag that flows into the ocean from a California river will ride the currents for up to a year before finally making it to the EGP. And because ocean currents travel only about 10 miles per day, depending on where a object enters the ocean, it could float for much longer—even decades.

REVENGE OF THE NURDLES

Most garbage breaks down over time, but plastic is different. No one really knows how long it takes for plastic to biodegrade because, so far, none of it has. Instead of biodegrading, plastic *photodegrades*—the sun's UV rays cause it to become brittle, which breaks it down into small pieces…and then into minute particles that resemble tiny confetti.

Sailors call these plastic bits "mermaid tears," but the technical term is *nurdles*. They're light enough to float in the air (think of tiny packing peanuts and how impossible it is to keep them from spilling everywhere). Everything made out of plastic is made out of nurdles, and every year 5.5 quadrillion of them are manufactured around the world. Just how many end up in the oceans is anyone's guess, but it's a huge amount.

Moore has another name for nurdles: "poison pills." They absorb oily toxic chemicals called *persistent organic pollutants*, or POPs, which include DDT and PCBs. Though many of these chemicals were banned in the 1970s, they still linger in the environment and attach themselves to plastic debris. Japanese environmental researchers found that nurdles can absorb one million times their weight in POPs from surrounding water.

Even more troubling: The "poison pills" resemble plankton in how they seem to "swim" near the surface. Jellyfish and "filter feeder" fish that strain their food out of the water—and who have been eating plankton for eons—are now eating the nurdles instead. And then fish eat the nurdle-eaters. And then those fish are caught by fishing boats…which means there's a good chance you're getting more plastic in your diet than you realize. And not just plastic, but all of those toxic chemicals it absorbed.

NO END IN SIGHT

The problem might not be so severe if the EGP were the only garbage patch in the world. But each major ocean has its own gyre, and each gyre has its own vortex of swirling garbage. There are five major patches in all, covering 40% of the world's oceans. "That corresponds to a quarter of Earth's surface," Moore says. "So 25% of our planet is a toilet that never flushes."

The question now becomes: How do you get rid of millions of tons of tiny bits in the middle of the sea? "Any attempt to remove that much plastic from the oceans—it boggles the mind," Moore says. "There's just too much, and the ocean is just too big." So chances are that the garbage patches will be here for a very long time. About the only thing we can do right now is to stop adding to them.

ODES TO NATURE

Some thoughts on that faraway place known as "outside."

"Nothing is more beautiful than the loveliness of the woods before sunrise."
—George Washington Carver

"A perfect summer day is when the sun is shining, the breeze is blowing, the birds are singing, and the lawn mower is broken."
—James Dent

"To me, a lush carpet of pine needles or spongy grass is more welcome than the most luxurious Persian rug."
—Helen Keller

"In wilderness I sense the miracle of life, and behind it our scientific accomplishments fade to trivia."
—Charles Lindbergh

"For me, another definition of God is 'great outdoors.'"
—Johnny Cash

"That's the thing about Mother Nature—she really doesn't care what economic bracket you're in."
—Whoopi Goldberg

"Nature does not hurry, yet everything is accomplished."
—Lao Tzu

"I am at two with nature."
—Woody Allen

"Live in the sunshine, swim the sea, drink the wild air."
—Ralph Waldo Emerson

"When you take a flower in your hand and really look at it, it's your world for the moment."
—Georgia O'Keefe

"You will find something far greater in the woods than you will find in books. Stones and trees will teach you that which you will never learn from masters."
—St. Bernard

"It seems to me that we all look at Nature too much, and live with her too little."
—Oscar Wilde

"The mountains are calling and I must go."
—John Muir

GO GREEN:
A STARTER KIT

So maybe you haven't had the opportunity to build that 100% green home that provides all of your power and food and creates no waste. Don't fret—there are still lots of things you can do in your regular old house to save energy...and money.

POWER DOWN

PThese days, modern conveniences like electricity and running water are such an integral part of life that we've lost sight of how they're created. The authors of *The Better World Handbook* put it this way: "Our grandparents knew a time when electricity was a luxury. Today, electricity is so convenient that it's easy to forget it is often produced by the burning of nonrenewable, heavily polluting fossil fuels." But that's the big picture—the global reasons to conserve energy. On a smaller scale, there's another way to look at it: How much money can you save by not leaving a light on in an empty room? The answer is: When added to other unnecessary power drains, you can save enough power to make a difference in your life. It's a win-win scenario: Conserve energy, and you help both the environment *and* your bank account. Still, it takes some discipline and a bit of creativity to learn new habits. But it's worth it.

LIGHTS OFF

The average family spends 25% of its home energy budget just to keep the lights on. But it doesn't have to be that much. The big new fad is compact fluorescent light bulbs (CFLs), which are still a work in progress. While they do last longer than incandescants, they contain harmful mercury and cost much more to dispose of (and to purchase). And the jury is still out on whether CFLs will save you enough money over incandescent bulbs to make much of a difference. Some studies have shown the savings are minimal; others put it as high as $45 per year per bulb.

But no matter what kind of bulb you use, the best way to conserve energy is to turn it on only when you absolutely need it. Every

Freezers and fridges are more energy efficient when they're full.

time you *don't* turn it on, you add to its life span. And halogen lights are the biggest energy drainers, so either take yours to Goodwill or turn them on only when you need especially bright light. Train yourself, your family, even your dog (if you can) to always turn off the light when you leave the room. It's the single easiest way to save money on energy bills.

TURN DOWN THE HEAT

The good news: Lowering your thermostat by three or four degrees can save you up to $100 per year. The bad news: You'll be colder in the winter. Here are a few tips on keeping warm.

• First, go for the obvious: Wear a sweater, warm pants, and thick socks at night. Try flannel sheets for extra warmth.

• Cuddle up—the human body maintains an average temperature of 98.6°F, so staying close to a loved one under a blanket is a great way to stay toasty.

• Exercise. After 10 or 20 minutes of aerobic movement—even a walk around the block—you won't be as cold (but you will be healthier).

• Get warm from the inside out with hot tea or cocoa. Make it a nightly ritual, shortly before you go to bed.

KNOW YOUR OUTLETS

What is your toaster doing right now? Your printer? Your blender? Even if they're not toasting, printing, or blending, they may still be costing you money…but only if they're plugged in. For instance, one study found that almost half of all microwaves use more energy just to run the clock than they do to heat food, since the clock is always running. Keeping dozens of appliances plugged in for months at a time can really add up. So take an "outlet walk": If your cordless drill, cell phone, or camera has a full charge, unplug the charger from the wall. That lava lamp that you only turn on during parties? Unplug it. Also, when you shut off your computer at night, turn off the power strip.

KEEP THE FLOODWATERS AT BAY

• The same principles apply with faucets: If you don't keep the water running constantly while you're brushing your teeth or doing the dishes, you'll save bucketloads of water and money.

There are more cars in southern California than there are cows in India.

- Check for and repair leaky faucets—not just inside the house, but outside as well. If it's leaking, you're paying for the water.
- For a few dollars, faucet aerators and low-flow showerheads can reduce water usage by as much as 75% without sacrificing water pressure.
- Irrigate your yard with care. Turn off automatic sprinklers if rain is coming, and don't water in the middle of the day, when much of the water will be lost to evaporation.
- What uses the most water in the house? Sadly, Uncle John's favorite appliance. Here's one tactic from *The Better World Handbook*: "Fill a slim milk jug with water and place it in the toilet tank. This will displace some of the water, reducing the amount required to fill up the tank. Keep adding bottles until there is just enough water to effectively clean the bowl." (They also warn not to block the mechanism of the toilet or displace the water with a brick, which may disintegrate and damage your plumbing.) And don't forget the old adage: If it's yellow, let it mellow; if it's...well, hopefully you know the rest.

TELECOMMUTE

This is becoming a more viable option as employers look to cut energy use at the office. Although you will be using a little more home energy, working from home a day or two each week has many benefits, especially gasoline savings. Added bonus: You'll eat out less (saving you money) and spend less time in stressful traffic jams (saving your sanity). So if you can swing it, let your fingers do the working.

RECYCLED READING

- To reduce the need for new paper, check out your local used bookstore (Uncle John's second-favorite place to visit). Buying used books online is another option, but keep in mind that the books have to be shipped to you, which uses resources.
- Buy books—such as this one—that are printed on recycled paper.
- Read books digitally. Each passing year brings new gadgets that promise paperless books.
- Go to your library and check out some books for free.

• Keep books in circulation as long as possible. Give old books that you've already read to friends and family, donate them to your local library, or make a few bucks by selling them to a used-book store.

REENERGIZE

Here are some "big-picture" things you can do to *really* start making a difference.

• When you buy new major appliances, research them thoroughly and choose only models that are designed to cut costs and save energy. (Check out our article about shopping for and using washing machines on page 87.)

• Find a green energy company. Several U.S. states offer this option. If yours does, shop around. Some companies use renewable energy and give customers rewards for saving power.

• See if your current energy company will come to your home to do an "energy walk" and find out where most of your energy money is going. They'll tell you how to efficiently heat and cool your home, and how to insulate walls and windows. Then you can really get to work greening up your house.

*   *   *

CANADIAN LOONS

The "loonie" is the nickname for the Canadian silver dollar that depicts a loon (a large waterbird) floating on a pond. In 2009 the Canadian environmental group Dogwood Initiative created 200,000 decals that fit perfectly over the loonie and adhere by static cling. The decal makes the loon and the pond look like they're covered with oil. The prank was designed to bring attention to a government plan to lift a 40-year-old ban and allow oil tankers to pass near British Columbia's north coast. (In addition, plans for a "supertanker port" and a pipeline are in the works.) Officials at the Canadian Mint are not happy about the decals, which many businesses have promised to stick onto any loonies they receive. But Dogwood Initiative spokesman Charles Campbell says the decals are perfectly legal as they easily come off without damaging the coin. The Canadian Mint, however, argues that it is "using currency for purposes other than legal tender."

Truffles (edible fungi that grow underground) sell for as much as $3,000 per pound.

THE POWER OF POO

Q: What's brown and sounds like a cowbell? A: DUNNNG!

FIRE STARTER

The Bible may have been way ahead of its time. One line in the book of Ezekiel says, "Lo, I have given thee cow's dung for man's dung, and thou shalt prepare thy bread therewith." It's perhaps the earliest written mention of what we now refer to as *biomass*—any biological material that can be used as fuel, including waste that can be burned. The most plentiful form of biomass on Earth is animal excrement, which, in its basic dried form, is known as *dung*. And humans have been using it for centuries.

The most popular fuel dung comes from members of the bovine family: cattle, bison, yaks, and water buffalo, due to both their large size and the high content of undigested plant matter in their droppings. When dried, these piles of manure are easy to pick up, carry, and toss into a fire. In the mid-19th century, that's what American settlers traveling west did with the massive buffalo chips scattered along the way. Luckily for them, buffalo dung has 50%–75% the heating power of wood, which was much harder to come by on the prairie.

Today dung is still used as a heating source in much of the world. In India, with its millions of impoverished people and millions of cattle, dried dung is known as *gobar* and is used to fuel ovens built in the ground. In the mountains of Tibet, yak dung is used for both cooking and heating. In the Middle East, camels (which are not bovines) provide chips for fuel. And while it's not as common today as it was during the Incan empire, llama dung is used in many mountainous parts of South America.

THE NUMBER TWO PROBLEM

But using dung as a heating source has some disadvantages. For one thing, stored droppings can generate heat as they decompose, spontaneously igniting a fire that's difficult to extinguish. Burning dung—whether by accident or on purpose—also generates a lot of acrid smoke, so indoor ovens must have good ventilation. Finally, dung *is* fecal matter, which means that extreme cleanliness is

---

Locusts are a type of grasshopper.

required to avoid illness. Still, handled properly, dung can provide vital fuel for cooking food and keeping warm. But those aren't the only uses for biomass.

WHAT CAN BROWN DO FOR YOU?

There's another way to convert dung into fuel—and it doesn't involve burning. The process, called *anaerobic digestion*, speeds up the decay of the dung inside a device called a *digester*. Digesters, like your intestines, produce a gas byproduct containing methane, except that digesters produce a lot more of it than you do—and it's about 60% methane, commonly referred to as *natural gas*. Anything that rots (sewage, garbage, dead things) can produce this methane bio-gas. And the gas can be used to heat homes and provide electricity.

By far, the most abundant source of biomass comes from the world's billions of farm animals—just one cow can produce up to 100 pounds of manure per day. Currently, most of that waste lands on the ground to rot on its own. As it does, it releases methane straight into the air—not a good thing, since methane is up to 21 times more harmful to the atmosphere than carbon dioxide. But when methane is collected and used as natural gas, it burns much cleaner than gasoline. Recently there's been a concerted effort on the part of dairy farmers to utilize this poo-power...and not just from cows.

PERSONAL FOWL

Experts say that before long, we may be filling our cars with fuel made from chicken poop...or pig poop, or even human poop, at a cost of about 10 cents per gallon and with better mileage. In recent years, large poultry and pig farms have begun to use dung for power. A plant in western Minnesota converts 700,000 tons of turkey droppings per year into electricity. Another plant in the Netherlands is expected to power 90,000 households by converting 440,000 tons of chicken waste per year. Hog farmers in the U.S. are building converters to tap their waste lagoons for methane. And dozens of waste treatment plants and landfills are taking steps toward utilizing this abundant power source.

So while dung may not solve all of our energy needs, there's certainly a place for it as we search for alternative forms of fuel. And, since poop is a fact of life, it's an energy source that won't be going away anytime soon.

Jimmy Carter was a nuclear engineer in the Navy.

NOT-SO-GREEN STARS

Sometimes even the world's most "trusted" environmental advocates (movie stars, rock stars, politicians) can send mixed messages.

DRIVE MY CAR

Paul McCartney is well known as an environmental (and animal-rights) advocate. He selected Lexus as a sponsor for his 2005 concert tour because he believes they make "environmentally responsible" cars. The tour was lucrative for both, and in 2008 Lexus gave McCartney one of their LS 600h cars, a $150,000 gas/electric hybrid. One problem: Lexus chartered a cargo plane to send the car from Japan, where it was built, directly to McCartney in England. The carbon emissions from that single flight are the equivalent of 300 around-the-world trips in the car it carried. In other words, McCartney can never drive the car enough to make up for the pollution its delivery created.

THE ONE WITH THE IRONIC WATER STORY

Friends star Jennifer Aniston's personal eco-crusade is water conservation. She contributes by taking three-minute showers (and brushing her teeth at the same time). Yet in 2007, after Aniston became the celebrity endorser of Smartwater, a line of bottled water, several environmental groups lashed out at her for the waste created by plastic water bottles. The organization Food and Water Watch said in a press statement: "With 86% of bottles being tossed rather than recycled, Aniston is making a political statement, whether she knows it or not."

ROYAL PAIN

After many years spent participating in environmental charities, Britain's Prince Charles was awarded the Global Environmental Citizen Prize in 2007. Rather than accept the award with a brief speech via a video linkup (an option), Charles flew from London to the awards ceremony in New York City, a round-trip voyage of 7,000 air-polluting miles. He also brought along 17 staff members at a cost (to British taxpayers) of $200,000. This was just a month after Charles announced plans to make the royal family's travel more environmentally sound, including reduced air travel.

WHAT A WENNER

Rolling Stone founder and publisher Jann Wenner frequently uses his magazine as a soapbox, penning editorials about global warming and the need for sweeping environmental-policy change. But Wenner, who lives 15 blocks from the *Rolling Stone* offices, takes a chauffeured car to work every day. During his free time he drives his full-size, gas-guzzling SUV, a Yukon Denali. Wenner commutes by private jet (the single most polluting form of transportation) to his vacation home in Sun Valley, Idaho. There he unwinds by driving a snowmobile, which chugs out even more carbon emissions than his Denali. Back at work, the *Rolling Stone* office lacks recycle bins because Wenner "hates clutter."

WINDBAG

Robert Kennedy, Jr. has made a career out of environmental protection. He's founded a water conservation charity called Waterkeeper Alliance and worked as a lead attorney for the Natural Resources Defense Council. But in 2006, Kennedy vigorously fought a plan to build a windmill farm that would generate extremely cheap, clean, renewable power for thousands. One reported reason for his opposition to the windmills: They would interfere with the work of hundreds of local fishermen. Another possible reason: The windmills were to be built near the Kennedy family compound in Hyannisport, Massachusetts, and would have hindered his family's pristine view of the ocean. "There are appropriate places for everything," said Kennedy in his defense.

*   *   *

HUH?

From a letter to the editor in the Arkansas Democrat *(2007).*

"As you know, Daylight Saving Time started a month earlier this year. You would think that members of Congress would have considered the warming effect that an extra hour of daylight would have on our climate. Or did they?"

EAT LIKE CAVEMAN

Proponents of the Paleolithic diet, or "caveman diet," claim it's one of the healthiest and most environmentally sustainable lifestyles out there. And why not? It worked for the earliest humans.

OGA BOOGA!
In 1975 a gastroenterologist named Walter L. Voegtlin published the book *The Stone Age Diet*. In it, he claimed that people could not only end indigestion, but also reduce the occurrence of stomach ailments such as colitis and Crohn's disease—just by eating nothing but meat, nuts, leaves, roots, and berries.

Here's how it works: The average Neanderthal traveled long distances throughout the day looking for food. He had neither the time nor the know-how to domesticate animals or crops—the agricultural age was still tens of thousands of years away. So he hunted animals and gathered birds' eggs, berries, fruits, and nuts. Seasonings, if any, were raw herbs.

If you want to eat like a caveman, here's what you *can't* eat:

• Dairy products. No cheese, milk, yogurt, ice cream…

• Any food with sugar in it (not counting naturally occurring sugars in fruit)

• Bread, bread products, or pasta

• Salt, beans, cultivated fruits and vegetables, oils, and, of course, Hungry Man Salisbury Steak and Mashed Potatoes

While the Paleolithic diet may appear similar to other low-carb, high-protein fads such as the South Beach and Atkins plans, those diets incorporate processed meals. Paleo-proponents point out that their plan is natural and environmentally sustainable, and generates minimal packaging waste.

But make no mistake—the Paleolithic diet is not easy. People who have tried Dr. Voegtlin's plan report that their first week made them weak, disoriented, and in major need of sugar. But those who stuck with the diet reported healthier blood-sugar levels, higher energy, improved digestion, and less-frequent mood swings (except for the occasional impulse to run out and club a saber-toothed tiger).

The average American uses enough gas in a lifetime to drive around the world 25 times.

MOST ENDANGERED

We'll never get the chance to see an Atlantic gray whale, a Puerto Rican flower bat, a Falkland Islands wolf, or a Caribbean monk seal. Why? Because they all went extinct in the last 200 years. Here are a few more mammals that—if current trends continue—will soon vanish from the Earth.

T**HE WAY OF THE DODO**
A London-based conservation group called Evolutionarily Distinct and Globally Endangered (EDGE) focuses on the protection of animals that "represent a unique and irreplaceable part of the world's natural heritage, yet an alarming proportion are currently sliding silently toward extinction unnoticed." Here, then, are the world's top 10 unusual endangered mammals.

10. Sumatran striped rabbit (*Nesolagus netscheri*). This small rabbit species is found only in the forests of the Barisan Mountains on the Indonesian island of Sumatra. So rare is this rabbit that it's been photographed only three times since 1916. Biologists don't know for sure how many of the rabbits are left—or, for that matter, much about them at all. And rapid deforestation in Sumatra means that the species could disappear before anybody does.

9. Northern hairy-nosed wombat (*Lasiorhinus krefftii*). These Australian marsupials look a bit like hairy pigs: They have short, powerful legs, grow to three feet long, and weigh up to 80 pounds. The wombats have sharp claws for digging burrows, which is why their marsupial pouch opens to the rear—so it won't fill up with dirt. (They also have hairy noses, hence their name.) It's one of just three wombat species existing today, and while it once lived over a large area of eastern Australia, habitat loss now restricts it to about 50,000 acres in central Queensland. There are only an estimated 115 northern hairy-nosed wombats left.

8. Bactrian camel (*Camelus bactrianus*). These are the two-humped camels, and they're one of only two camel species alive today, the other being the one-humped dromedaries of North

Coral reefs cover less than 1% of Earth, but are home to 25% of marine fish species.

Africa and the Middle East. Bactrians once roamed all over North America, where they first appeared, and even inhabited parts of South America. They first crossed the land bridge from present-day Alaska to Asia about three million years ago and have been gone from the Americas for about 10,000 years. Today they survive in the wild in just four regions of the brutally harsh Gobi Desert of northern China and southern Mongolia. Fewer than 1,000 are thought to exist in the wild.

7. Black rhinoceros (*Diceros bicornis*). Rhinos first appeared on Earth around 60 million years ago and branched into several different species, including a now-extinct one that stood 18 feet at the shoulder and weighed more than five tons. There was even a woolly rhinoceros that lived alongside humans in Europe and Asia. Today just five species exist, and they're all endangered. These include black rhinos, which are native to eastern and central Africa. In 1900 there were several hundred thousand of them, but by 1992, poaching and habitat loss had reduced that to about 2,100. Conservation efforts have recently raised that figure, but it still sits at a dangerously low 4,000 or so.

6. Sumatran rhinoceros (*Dicerorhinus sumatrensis*). Also known as the "hairy rhino" for its hairy body, the Sumatran is the smallest and most endangered rhino species. They once thrived from India to Indonesia, but today are found only in tiny, protected pockets on the islands of Sumatra and Borneo, and on peninsular Malaysia. There are fewer than 300 left.

5. Hispaniolan solenodon (*Solenodon paradoxus*). These small, shrewlike insectivores are of great interest to evolutionary biologists—extremely primitive, they have characteristics of mammals that existed alongside dinosaurs. In addition, they're one of only a few mammals that can deliver a venomous bite. For millions of years, these solenodons were the dominant predator on the Caribbean island of Hispaniola. Then the Europeans arrived, and with them dogs, cats, and mongooses. The slow, small solenodons had no chance. They were thought to be extinct in the 1800s, but were rediscovered in 1907. It's not known how many exist today…but there are very few.

4. Cuban solenodon (*Solenodon cubanus*). This species has gone

In one hour, Earth receives more energy from the sun than human beings use in a year.

through the same plight as its Hispaniolan cousin. It was discovered in 1861 and believed to be extinct by 1890...until one was captured in 2003. Just a few more have been found since.

3. Riverine rabbit (*Bunolagus monticularis*). This primitive rabbit species lives only in the floodplains of seasonal rivers in the Karoo Desert of South Africa. Over the past 50 years, more than two-thirds of that habitat has been turned into farmland. In addition, these rabbits are still being hunted illegally for food and pelts, and many have been killed by feral dogs. They also breed very slowly, unlike most rabbits. There are fewer than 250 surviving today.

2. Long-beaked echidna (*Zaglossus bruijni*). Echidnas are covered in coarse hairs and spines, like porcupines, grow to about the size of a housecat, and use their long snouts to forage for earthworms. The echidna is one of only two types of *monotreme* mammals (the platypus is the other): Among other odd characteristics, they don't give live birth, but lay eggs. Long-beaked echidnas live only on the island of New Guinea, and there are believed to be as many as 300,000 of them, but because their habitat is diminishing rapidly, and because they're not receiving the protection conservation groups insist they need—and because locals consider them a delicacy—they are considered to be in imminent danger of extinction.

1. Yangtze River dolphin (*Lipotes vexillifer*). According to EDGE, this is *the* most endangered mammal in the world...that is, if it's still here. Dolphins, like all *cetaceans* (whales, porpoises, and dolphins), evolved from sea creatures that ventured onto land and then went back into the sea. Fossil evidence suggests that dolphins first reentered the oceans around 25 million years ago. River dolphins, however, left the oceans a second time to become full-time freshwater animals. Five species exist today: two in the Amazon River in South America; one in the Indus River and another in the Ganges River in India; and one in the Yangtze River in eastern China, where it's thrived for 20 million years. However, in the 20th century, the Yangtze became one of the most polluted rivers in the world and choked out its native dolphin. A confirmed sighting hasn't been made in years, and many biologists believe the species may already be extinct. There are none in captivity.

Worst air polluter in the state of Washington: Mt. St. Helens. (It's a volcano.)

NO DEPOSIT, NO RETURN

In many states, we take it for granted that a soda or beer costs an extra five cents for a container deposit. Here's the story of how that began...and why it's one of the most successful recycling and litter-reduction programs in American history.

TIME IN A BOTTLE

At the beginning of the 20th century, soda and beer were sold only in glass bottles. When the bottles were empty, you took them back to the local company that bottled the drink, and they gave you a few cents back. It wasn't a law, and the word "recycling" hadn't been invented yet—it was just how bottlers conducted business. They washed the bottles, refilled them, and sent them back out to stores, bars, and restaurants. And the cycle would continue, with the average bottle being reused about 30 times. Back then, soda bottles rarely littered the landscape—they had cash value. (And beer was sold almost exclusively in bars that could easily collect and return their empties.)

Until the 1940s, most soda and beer bottling was done locally, with more than 3,000 bottling plants in the United States. It had to be done that way—the thick glass bottles were too fragile and expensive to transport long distances. But as the American economy soared after World War II, hundreds of bottlers merged (or were purchased by Pepsi or Coca-Cola) and combined their territories.

CAN IT

With fewer bottling companies serving larger areas, refilling and transporting bottles would cost more; a cheaper option had to be found. Coincidentally, American aluminum and steel companies were just beginning to offer an alternative to glass bottles: thin metal cans. They were so cheap to make—far less expensive than collecting and washing bottles—that once the drink was gone, they could simply be thrown away. Cans were a hit with consumers, and by the mid-1950s, half of all beer sold in the U.S. was in cans. Refillable bottles began to die out.

But the lightweight, nearly worthless cans had a big downside: They ended up in the garbage and, worse, littered the sides of

---

The Massachusetts Institute of Technology utilizes stormwater runoff to flush its toilets.

roads and rivers. By 1953 it was already such a problem in Vermont that the state legislature passed a law requiring beer to be sold only in refillable bottles.

Beer and soda companies grew concerned. Vermont's law threatened to lead other states to pass similar container laws. It was just the kind of government regulation the industry didn't want.

KEEP AMERICA CORPORATE

To head off the threat of federal interference, several beverage companies formed a lobbying group under the guise of a litter-prevention nonprofit organization called Keep America Beautiful. In print ads and on billboards, KAB reminded Americans that "every litter bit hurts" and that trash should be thrown away instead of left on the ground, especially in scenic outdoor locations.

While encouraging people to stop littering was a noble aim, Keep America Beautiful actually served the interest of bottlers: If litter was controlled, there would be less demand for container-recycling laws. And without those laws, the industry could continue to use cheap, disposable cans.

Vermont's "bottle bill" was not renewed when it came up for a vote in 1957, and its failure is credited to the convincing lobbying of Keep America Beautiful. The organization went on to spearhead the anti-littering movement through the '60s and early '70s (it produced the famous "crying Indian" television ad). In all that time, no other state adopted a container law.

THE OREGON TRAIL

In 1968 an outdoorsman named Richard Chambers from Salem, Oregon, decided he wanted to climb every mountain, hike every trail, and kayak every river in Oregon. But he was shocked to find that nearly every place he visited was strewn with litter. After routinely filling bags with discarded trash—the majority of which was beer and pop cans—Chambers decided to take action. He did some research and read about the short-lived Vermont bottle bill and the beginnings of another measure to ban nonreturnable containers in British Columbia, Canada.

Chambers wrote to his friend Paul Hanneman, a member of the Oregon state legislature, and in 1969 Hanneman and Chambers drafted Oregon House Bill 1157, nicknamed "the Bottle Bill."

Instead of repeating Vermont's ban on single-use containers, Oregon's version took inspiration from the cash-value bottle days of the early 20th century: By law, soda and beer containers—cans or bottles—would carry a five-cent deposit payable at the time of purchase. Once empty, the container could be returned to grocery stores and the nickel refunded. The empties would then be recycled.

Hanneman and Chambers brought in several people to testify before the State and Federal Affairs Committee about the need to reduce beverage litter. One was a river guide who described the masses of cans and bottles in rivers and streams. Another was a farmer who had lost four cows after they ate metal and glass shards from cans and bottles littering his land. The committee approved the bill 5–4, sending it the House floor for a vote. It failed, 27–33.

GETTING McCALLED OUT

Surprisingly, Oregon's governor Tom McCall, a well-known conservationist and environmentalist, refused to publicly back the Bottle Bill. He also turned down Hanneman's request to help him drum up support for it in the legislature. Instead, McCall backed SOLV (Stop Oregon Litter and Vandalism), a nonprofit anti-littering group similar to Keep America Beautiful. It was later revealed that, in fact, 75% of SOLV's budget came from Keep America Beautiful and similar beverage-industry lobbying groups. Essentially, Keep America Beautiful and the beverage industry had killed another bottle bill.

But in 1970, McCall reversed his opinion. Public pressure to pass the Bottle Bill was mounting, and McCall was accused of betraying his own record of environmentalism. (He first came to prominence in Oregon in 1956 as a TV reporter, producing stories about the pollution of Portland's Willamette River, the cleanup of which he would spearhead in one of his first acts as governor in 1967.) Perhaps sensing an opportunity to win back the public in a big way, McCall reintroduced the Bottle Bill to the state legislature with his full endorsement.

This time, grocery stores were among the bill's fiercest opponents. They feared being buried under a mountain of cans and bottles, and facing the financial strains of having to process returns. More than 20 soda and beer companies sent representatives to Oregon to fight the bill and, reportedly, bribes were offered to some members of the legislature. The pressure tactics backfired—the bill passed and, in 1971, went into effect. Oregon became the first state in the U.S. to institute a five-cent deposit on soda and beer containers.

YES WE CAN

Here's how the deposit system works. Say you buy a six-pack of beer for $5 at a Portland, Oregon, grocery store. At the register, you'll pay $5.30—the additional 30 cents is for a five-cent deposit on each of the six cans. When you return the empty cans, the store gives you back the 30 cents. The store then turns over the cans to a distributor/recycler, who reimburses the store for all the deposit money it paid out. It doesn't matter if you return the cans to the store where you bought them or to a different one, since all containers go back to the same local distributor.

After Oregon led the way, 10 other states adopted container-deposit laws: Vermont (1972), Maine (1976), Michigan (1976), Connecticut (1978), Iowa (1978), Massachusetts (1982), New York (1982), Delaware (1982), California (1986), and Hawaii (2002). As of 2009, four more states have laws in the works.

Has it worked? Undeniably, yes. In states with deposit laws, an average of 70% of qualifying containers get returned and recycled. Those states also report a 64% reduction in beverage-container litter. But in Oregon, where it all started, it's been the most successful. In the state today, just 6% of all litter is bottles and cans, far less than in states without container laws.

BOTTLING IT UP

In the last decade, the fastest-growing sector of the beverage industry was bottled water. It's sold in plastic bottles, which create mountains of trash and litter the way aluminum soda cans did in the 1950s. By 2009 Oregon, California, and Hawaii will have amended their bottle bills to include water containers. In Oregon alone, 125 million plastic bottles of water are sold each year. The recycle rate before the amended law: 32%. If the new law follows the pattern of the old one, that rate could increase to as much as 82%. Considering the other problems associated with plastic bottles (see page 190), let's hope it works.

NATURALLY CLEAN

Here are three "miracle" cleaners that you probably already have.

HAZARDOUS MATERIALS AREA

Look under just about any kitchen sink in America, and what will you see? Bottles and bottles of the latest cleaners, detergents, deodorizers, and stain removers. Most are packaged in nonrecyclable plastic, and many contain caustic chemicals, were tested on animals, and can pollute streams and rivers after they're washed down the drain. But what's the alternative? As it turns out, three items that are in most people's kitchens already—baking soda, vinegar, and lemons—have just as much cleaning power as those name brands.

• **Baking soda:** Here's a laundry tip from *The Better World Handbook*: Replace half of the detergent in each clothes-washer load with baking soda to get whites whiter and colors brighter. For pans with tough, cooked-on stains, add some water and baking soda and boil for a few minutes, then clean with a sponge. For stains on sinks or countertops, sprinkle some baking soda on them, wait a few minutes, then rinse with hot water.

• **Vinegar.** Not only does it clean, but it disinfects and deodorizes, too. And don't worry about that vinegar smell; it dissipates pretty quickly. For most surface-cleaning jobs, mix equal parts vinegar and water in a clean spray bottle, then spray and wipe away. But beware—if you use too much vinegar in the solution, it can damage some surfaces. (You might want to test your solution in an out-of-the-way spot—and never use vinegar on marble.) Vinegar also makes a great fabric softener, especially for those with sensitive skin. Just add a half cup to the rinse cycle.

• **Lemon juice.** Use it to shine brass and copper. It's also great at dissolving soap scum. Want a new sponge? Cut a lemon in half and sprinkle some baking soda on the exposed fruit, then clean your dishes and counters. And if you mix a little olive oil with lemon juice, it makes a great polish for hardwood furniture.

Another alternative is to buy eco-friendly cleaning brands. You may still get the plastic bottles, but at least you'll keep the nasty chemicals out of your house.

How much water is there in a cubic mile of fog? Less than a gallon.

WORD ORIGINS

Who knew the word "pollution" was so sexy?
(Besides oil company executives?)

CARBON FOOTPRINT: In 1992 Canadian ecologist Bill Reese came up with the concept of an "ecological footprint" to refer to the amount of land, in acres, needed to support a given population, in terms of resources and waste disposal. The idea came to Reese, he said years later, while admiring the "smaller footprint" that a new computer made on his desk. That concept evolved into the "carbon footprint," a measurement not of acreage but of greenhouse gas emissions linked to human activity. Its earliest known use was on the BBC television show *Vegetarian Good Food* in 1999.

BIODEGRADABLE: The term "biodegradation" was first used in 1953 to describe the breakdown of materials by bacteria and other microbes. Less than a decade later, the Soap and Detergent Association—a "trade organization which represents North American manufacturers of household, industrial, and institutional cleaning supplies"—began describing soap products as "biodegradable" to ease fears that they were polluting rivers.

FOSSIL FUEL: In 1757 Russian scholar Mikhail Lomonosov first proposed what later became known as the "biogenic theory" of the formation of oil and coal, which says that they are organic in origin, and formed from the fossilized remains of tiny plants and animals. That led to the term "fossil fuel," first recorded in 1835 in the *The History and Description of Fossil Fuel, the Collieries and Coal Trade of Great Britain*, by English geologist John Holland.

ECOSYSTEM: Coined in 1930 by English botanist Roy Clapham, it originally denoted the biological and nonbiological components of a given area of Earth. It has since evolved to mean, as per *Merriam-Webster's Collegiate Dictionary*: "the complex of a community of organisms and its environment functioning as an ecological unit."

GLOBAL WARMING: This phrase was coined in 1975 by environmental scientist Wallace Broecker, now a professor at Columbia University, in a paper entitled "Climate Change: Are we on the Brink of a Pronounced Global Warming?" It referred to what climatologists view as the current period of warmer overall temperatures on Earth due to human activity. Many scientists regret that this phrase has become so popular and prefer to use "climate change," as the overriding belief is that some parts of Earth will actually become colder during this period.

POLLUTION: The Latin word *polluere* meant "to soil, defile, or contaminate." In Late Latin, the word changed to *pollutionenem* and took on a very naughty connotation, meaning (cover your children's ears) "a discharge of semen other than during sex." It entered English as "pollution" in 1340, but didn't take on its modern meaning—polluting the environment—until the 1950s.

PLANNED OBSOLESCENCE: This is the practice of making a product in such a way that it will break, or simply not be desirable, after a certain amount of time so that the consumer will have no choice but to go out and buy another one. American industrial designer Brooks Adams came up with the phrase in 1954 as a title for a speech. To him, planned obsolescence was a great way for companies to stay competitive, as it "instills in the buyer the desire to own something a little newer, a little better, a little sooner than is necessary." Within a few years, the phrase had taken on the negative meaning it has today.

GREENWASHING: A combination of the words "green" and "whitewashing," this describes the practice of a company promoting itself as environmentally friendly, even when it isn't. The term was coined by New York environmentalist Jay Westerveld in an essay he wrote in 1986 about hotels that placed placards in their rooms asking guests to reuse their towels "for the benefit of the environment." Westerveld noted that since the hotels in question had no other "eco-friendly" policies, the goal was actually to save money on towel-washing.

It's estimated that 50 million birds a year die from flying into cell-phone towers.

DRILL, BABY, DRILL?
PART I

Environmentalist: "Wow, look at that beautiful landscape."
Industrialist: "Bet there's lots of beautiful oil under that landscape."
Environmentalist: "You're an idiot!" Industrialist: "No, you're an idiot!"

SLICK DEBATE

Every time the price of gas goes up, the same old questions dominate the airwaves: Should Americans start looking for more oil on their own soil? Or should they renew their efforts at finding renewable forms of energy? Making this debate even muddier is the fact that many of the most oil-rich areas in the United States happen to be located in fragile and protected ecosystems. The two that get the most press are the Outer Continental Shelf (known as the OCS) along the nation's coastlines, and the Arctic National Wildlife Refuge (ANWR) in Alaska. Drilling proponents argue that it's unwise to leave these domestic oil resources untapped while environmentalists argue that it's unwise to risk damaging these sensitive areas. Here's the lowdown on the history of oil exploration in these places and how it became such a sensitive issue.

THERE'S GOLD IN THEM THAR WATERS

As the 19th century was nearing its end, "black gold" became increasingly precious. When oilmen came to realize that their treasure could also be found on the ocean floor, the race was on to figure out how to extract it. The first offshore well was built in Summerland, California, in 1897. Back then, offshore rigs were erected at the end of a long pier or wharf. That first well was only 300 feet from the beach, but as the years went by, rigs were built farther and farther out until one was actually erected at the end of a quarter-mile-long pier; the technology required to build one without connecting it to the land just wasn't there yet. So most oil exploration remained land-based until after World War II when the U.S. government lifted wartime gasoline rationing and the nation began its love affair with the automobile in earnest.

The first known oil wells were drilled in China...in 347 C.E.

With 1947 technology, the Kerr-McGee Corporation built the first modern freestanding offshore well in just 14 feet of water off the coast of Louisiana.

More offshore rigs popped up, and then even more. And they kept getting larger and larger. Today, very few man-made objects are visible from Earth's orbit. One is Shell Oil's massive offshore drilling platform, Troll, which rises 1,000 feet above the North Sea off the coast of Norway. These massive platforms are capable of extracting hundreds of thousands of barrels of crude oil every day. They're also capable of creating catastrophic oil spills.

OOPS

In 1969 disaster struck off the coast of Santa Barbara, California, when an offshore drilling rig, Platform Alpha, accidentally spewed more than three million gallons of oil into the ocean. The spill contaminated 800 square miles of sea, and 35 miles of coastline were coated with a layer of sludge six inches thick. The accident killed at least 3,600 seabirds, plus an untold number of seals, dolphins, and other wildlife. As similar spills kept happening, environmental organizations such as Greenpeace staged protests and demonstrations. Meanwhile, the oil companies kept on drilling as much as possible. Americans needed their oil, they argued.

But offshore drilling hit a major snag in 1982 when Congress issued a limited moratorium that took 736,000 acres along the California coast off the table. In 1990 President George H. W. Bush went a step further, issuing an executive order forbidding the Interior Department from providing offshore leases to oil companies, except in certain parts of the Gulf of Mexico and off the Alaskan coast. President Clinton extended Bush's executive order until 2012.

ACROSS THE WORLD

So, with fewer options at home, U.S. oil companies have steadily purchased more and more of their product from the oil-rich reserves of the Middle East. That hasn't worked out so well in a region infamous for its volatility, and simultaneous wars in Iraq and Afghanistan have led to even more instability. And America has found itself in a precarious position as it has become dependent on not just oil, but on Middle Eastern oil. In 2008 the issue took center stage in the U.S. when gas prices topped $5 per gallon in some states. In response, President George W. Bush reversed his father's executive order banning offshore drilling, and Congress allowed its moratorium to expire as well. The nation's coastlines are once again open for business. But is it safe?

SIGNIFICANTLY INSIGNIFICANT

The Minerals Management Service (MMS), the arm of the government that regulates offshore drilling, noted in its 2002 "OCS Safety Fact Sheet" that "Outer Continental Shelf operations are generally safer now than in the past" and that "the number of blowouts since 1968 shows a gradual decline." Nonetheless, accidents still happen. In fact, according to the MMS, at least one spill of 1,000 barrels or more is likely to occur each year in the Gulf of Mexico. And every three or four years, the government expects a much larger spill of at least 10,000 barrels. After hurricanes Katrina and Rita tore through the Gulf in 2005, the MMS reported that of the 600 offshore rigs in the region, 113 were either partially or severely damaged.

In lieu of major spills, environmentalists argue that even "safe" offshore drilling methods extract more than oil: Pollutants such as mercury and arsenic are brought to the surface as well. Though the MMS assures that these pollutants are generated in "insignificant" amounts, Athan Manuel of the Sierra Club testified to Congress in 2008 that the levels are indeed "significant." As is the case with most of these environmental squabbles, each side seems able to find facts that support its agenda.

However, the Sierra Club and other groups claim that there's more to it than mercury contamination: The infrastructure required to transport and refine oil extracted by offshore rigs is environmentally harmful in and of itself, irreversibly damaging fragile coastal habitats. Ports and pipelines must be built to support a never-ending flow of ship traffic. But where the environmentalist sees damage, the industrialist sees jobs—lots of jobs that would be lost if these rigs went away.

Even if offshore drilling were completely outlawed, at least there are untapped oil reserves up in Alaska, right? Turn to page 186 for that part of the story.

On average, it costs $30 to recycle a ton of trash and $50 to put it in a landfill.

BEER POWER

With more energy needed and less oil to provide it, people are getting desperate for alternative power...very desperate.

Power Source: Tornadoes
Details: Canadian engineer Louis Michaud has patented what he calls a "vortex engine." The simple concept is based on the property of *convection*, where air rising above heated water forms a vortex—a tornado-like column of spinning air. Michaud's vortex engine, which exists only on paper for now, consists of a large container of water with turbines above the surface. As the water is heated up, a vortex forms above it, causing the turbines to spin and generate electricity. And how big will the vortex be? A whopping 200 meters in diameter and between 1 and 12 miles high—essentially, a controlled tornado. Michaud says a vortex engine that size could power 200,000 homes.

Power Source: Beer
Details: Since 2005, California brewer Sierra Nevada has had its own fuel-cell-based and ultra-clean electric power plant right inside its brewery. It originally ran on piped-in natural gas, but as of 2006, it runs on a mix of natural gas and methane, a by-product of the water-treatment process that the brewery uses. So the more beer they brew, the more methane they produce and the less natural gas they use. The facility has been such a success that in 2006 *Power Magazine* named it one of the "Top 12 Plants" in the world.

Power Source: Miniature nuclear power generators
Details: A company called Hyperion Power Generation markets a nuclear reactor approximately the size of a hot tub. It's designed to be buried underground, where it can produce enough power to fuel 20,000 homes for up to a decade. Hyperion recently was contracted to build 18 of them in the Czech Republic, and estimates they will have more than 4,000 mini-reactors in use by 2025.

Power Source: Lasers
Details: Solar power is limited by the fact that the sun goes away

---

Hot stuff! The inside of a compost pile can reach temperatures of 150°F.

for about half of the time (also known as "night"). Japan Aerospace Exploration Agency and Osaka University plan to solve that problem by building solar collectors (made out of chromium) that they'll place in orbit 22,000 miles above Earth. The collectors will then beam the heat energy via a laser back to receiving stations on the surface, each of which will receive a gigawatt of energy, roughly the same as that generated by a small nuclear power plant. The agency hopes to have these solar laser satellites in orbit by 2030.

Power Source: Trees

Details: In 2006 scientists at the Massachusetts Institute of Technology Center for Biomedical Engineering discovered that there's a slight pH imbalance between a tree and its surrounding soil. This causes a small flow of electrons...or electricity. A *bioenergy harvester module* is implanted in a tree's roots, where it collects a constant current with which to charge batteries. The company Voltree plans to use this power source to run an "Early Wildfire Alert Network" in association with the U.S. Forest Service.

Power Source: Japanese commuters

Details: In 2008 the East Japan Railway Corporation tested a power-generating floor in one of the ticket gates at its Tokyo station. The floor contains discs made of *piezoelectric* material that converts vibrations into electrical energy. Based on the millions of people who use the rail stations, the process has the potential to generate enough free energy to completely power the stations' computer displays and ticket machines.

* * *

MY BIG FAT GREEK LANDFILL

The first known official landfill opened in Athens, Greece, around 500 B.C.E. A law was passed requiring garbage to be disposed of two miles outside of the city limits. Reason: defense. The garbage had previously been thrown right outside the city walls, which allowed invaders to climb up the pile and over the walls.

HAPPY ARBOR DAY

For Christmas, millions of people cut down trees. For Arbor Day,
they plant them. Here's the story of an original American holiday.

TREE-MENDOUS PLAN

After graduating with an agriculture degree from the University of Michigan in 1854, Julius Sterling Morton moved to a small settlement called Nebraska City in what would a few months later be called the Nebraska Territory.

Morton faced a problem shared by many settlers in the territory: It was a treeless plain. That meant no trees for building materials, to burn for fuel, or to use as shade for crops. But Morton was one of the New World's first "tree huggers," stating, "We ought to bequeath to posterity as many forests and orchards as we have exhausted and consumed." So he started bequeathing trees, beginning with his own land. By 1860 Morton boasted a lush orchard of more than 300. A few years later, he had more than 1,000.

TREE-DING BOLDLY

As the orchards grew, so did Morton's influence in Nebraska, which became a state in 1867. Morton was the founder and editor of the *Nebraska City News*, the state's first newspaper, in which he frequently wrote editorials about the benefits, practical and aesthetic, of tree planting. He also organized the Nebraska State Horticultural Society and served on the Nebraska State Board of Agriculture.

While serving on the Board, Morton came up with an idea to spread his belief in tree planting statewide (and eventually, worldwide). On January 4, 1872, Morton drafted a resolution that April 10th be "set apart and consecrated for the planting of trees in the State of Nebraska, and to urge upon the people of the State the vital importance of tree planting." Morton called the special event Arbor Day (*arbor* is Latin for "tree").

The state legislature agreed and on April 10, 1872, the first unofficial Arbor Day was celebrated throughout Nebraska. Prizes were awarded to counties, cities, and individuals who planted the largest number of trees. That day, an astounding one million trees took root in Nebraska—an average of more than six for every man, woman, and child in the state. Since 1885, Nebraska has planted more than 700,000 acres of trees, earning it the nickname "the Tree Planters State."

Arbor Day became a legal, civic holiday in the state in 1885. It was held on April 22—Julius Morton's birthday. In addition to a parade in Nebraska City, Morton introduced what has since become a long-standing Arbor Day tradition: Schoolchildren went outside and planted trees together. Morton left Nebraska in 1893 when he was appointed Secretary of Agriculture by President Grover Cleveland.

HAPP-TREE HOLIDAYS

In 1970, nearly a century after Arbor Day was first celebrated, President Richard Nixon declared the last Friday of every April to be observed as National Arbor Day. The day often coincides nicely with Earth Day, which is held every April 22.

All 50 states recognize the April observance, although many hold an additional state Arbor Day in a month more suited to local tree planting. For example, Florida and Louisiana have theirs in January, Hawaii's is in November, and South Carolina's is in December. Countries the world over, including Australia, Brazil, China, Iceland, Japan, Scotland, and Yemen, also observe civic tree-planting day.

Today, tree-planting events are organized and promoted by the National Arbor Day Foundation, which was created in 1971. In addition to increasing the number of thriving trees in the United States, it saves older trees around the world with its charity, Rain Forest Rescue. To date, the foundation has saved more than two billion square feet of rain forest land in North, South, and Central America.

Morton nicely summed the unique nature of his creation: "Arbor Day is not like other holidays. Each of those reposes on the past, while Arbor Day proposes for the future."

*   *   *

"There are no passengers on Spaceship Earth. We are all crew."
—**Marshall McLuhan, 1964**

Arbor Day founder Julius Morton's son, Joy, founded Morton Salt.

DOOOOOOOOOOOOOM!

The phrase "You're destroying the planet!" is all too common (especially when a plastic bottle gets thrown in the trash). In reality, destroying the planet is very difficult. But not impossible. You could...

• **Blow it up with hydrogen bombs.** In order to split apart a planet, you have to apply enough force to overcome its *gravitational binding energy*. To overcome the Earth's GBE, you'd need a force of 224,000,000,000,000,000,000,000,000,000,000 Joules (units of energy). A hydrogen bomb generates a tiny fraction of that, so you'd need to simultaneously set off about 107 trillion of them in order to obliterate Earth.

• **Build a black hole.** Black holes are super-dense vacuums that suck in and absorb whatever happens to be near them. You could make your own black hole by cramming together a bunch of neutronium atoms (although you'd need far more than exist on Earth). Your black hole would then systematically devour the planet, and anything else in the vicinity, until nothing was left.

• **Use an antimatter collision.** *Star Trek* was right: Antimatter is the most explosive substance in the universe. It's the opposite of matter (i.e., *everything*), so when the two collide, they explode, vaporizing both. You can create a small amount of antimatter in a particle accelerator, but to make enough to destroy Earth (using current technology), it would take you roughly 500 years.

• **Dig and shoot.** This involves breaking off chunks of the planet and shooting them into space with enough force to break the planet's *escape velocity*, to ensure the chunks don't start orbiting the planet. Even so, and at a rate of *only* a billion tons of materials shot into space per second, it would take about 100 million years to dispose of Earth.

• **Boil it.** First, intercept thousands of asteroids. Then turn the raw materials—aluminum, nickel, and iron—into gigantic reflective surfaces. About two million square miles' worth should do it. Train them on the sun and redirect enough heat toward Earth to boil it into a cloud of gases. Bwa-ha-ha-ha!

ECO-PIRATES

We're not condoning their behavior, just their cojones.

CLIMATE MAN

In 2008 the Kingsnorth power station in Kent, England, suddenly shut down. Security cameras later revealed what happened: A man had scaled two 10-foot razor-wire fences that protected the facility—the most heavily guarded coal-burning plant in England—then walked across the parking lot, calmly went through an unlocked door, found his way into the room housing the turbines, entered some commands into a computer, and shut down a massive 500-megawatt turbine. "It was running at full capacity," a station spokesman said, "and the noise it would have made as it shut itself down is just incredible." The intruder, dubbed "Climate Man" by the press, then calmly left the way he came…leaving behind a bedsheet with "No New Coal" written on it in duct tape. The station was down for four hours—and about 2% of the United Kingdom's electricity output was stopped by the single intruder.

AUCTIONERROR

In December 2008, the outgoing George W. Bush administration made a controversial move when it hastily set up an auction for oil and gas companies to buy portions of 360,000 acres of public land in Utah—located next to such natural wonders as Arches National Park, the White River, Desolation Canyon, and Canyonlands National Park. Tim DeChristopher, a 27-year-old University of Utah economics student, attended the auction and made several bids, driving up the prices of the parcels by $500,000 and winning 13 of them, an area covering 22,500 acres and costing $1.7 million. But DeChristopher had no intention of actually buying them…he had no money. He was just there to disrupt the auction and bring publicity to the issue. "Once I started buying up every parcel, they understood pretty clearly what was going on," DeChristopher said later. "They stopped the auction, and some federal agents came in and took me out." In February 2009, incoming Secretary of the Interior Ken Salazar cancelled the controversial land sales—and DeChristopher's legal case was put in limbo.

THE ELECTRIC CAR
IS BORN

*Gas prices go up, gas prices go down, and as we try to guess
how much the next tank of gas will cost, a lot of us can't
help but wonder, why don't we all have electric cars?
A look into their history may tell us why.*

HORSE POWER

If you were living in an American city toward the end of
the 19th century and you wanted to get from one place
to another, your choices were limited to walking, riding a bicycle
or a horse, or riding in a horse-drawn vehicle. The wealthy had
private carriages; everyone else had to pile into "horsecars"—
streetcars pulled by a team of horses. A person would pay 5¢ to
climb aboard a vehicle built to hold 40 people—but which might
be jammed with 70—and was rolled to his destination only about
twice as quickly as if he'd saved the nickel and walked.

These early streetcar systems left a lot to be desired. Aside from
being slow, they were expensive to run, thanks to the cost of sta-
bling, feeding, and caring for hundreds or even thousands of horses.
In the 1880s, as the first power-generating plants were being built
in American cities, streetcar company owners began to wonder if
streetcars powered by the new electricity might be a lot cheaper
than a system dependent upon horses.

THE FIRST ELECTRIC VEHICLES

The question was put to the test in 1887, when America's first
"electric railroad" opened for business in Richmond, Virginia. Laying the 12 miles of tracks and accompanying overhead wires took
more time and money than expected, but the electric streetcars
were twice as fast as horsecars and cost so much less to operate
that towns and cities all over the country began putting their
horsecars out to pasture. By the turn of the century, they had all
but disappeared from American towns and cities.

As nice as the new streetcars were, riding in them could still
be an ordeal. They were often overcrowded, and with so many

people getting on and off at each stop, it could still take forever to get where you wanted to go. And with so many people packed into the car—some of whom hadn't bathed recently—you never knew if people would keep their hands, comments, and catcalls to themselves, or if you'd arrive at your destination with your possessions, body, and dignity intact. It was the Victorian era: Many respectable ladies were loath to ride a streetcar for fear of the kinds of people they might meet on one. And in an age when deadly epidemics were commonplace, and the discovery of antibiotics still more than 40 years away, a trip on a crowded streetcar might be the last trip a person would ever make.

DOWNSIZING

Ordinary city dwellers had long dreamed of having their own personal vehicles, just as the wealthy had their carriages. And almost as soon as electric streetcar technology was developed, hopeful inventors began adapting the electrical components to much smaller vehicles. Many of the first electric "horseless carriages" were just that—ordinary carriages fitted with batteries and electric motors designed for streetcars. The sight of one moving down the street without horses pulling it was as startling at the turn of the century as a car without a driver would look today.

In 1897 the Pope Manufacturing Company, makers of the popular Columbia bicycle, became the first American company to manufacture electric vehicles in significant quantities. Called the Columbia Electric Phaeton, it was silent, clean, very simple to drive, and could travel at speeds of up to 15 mph for up to 30 miles before the batteries needed recharging. Starting it was as easy as flipping a switch.

THE COMPETITION

While Pope and other electric-car manufacturers were bringing their vehicles to market, other inventors were working on cars powered by steam engines or internal combustion engines powered by gasoline. Francis and Freelan Stanley built the first Stanley Steamer in 1897, and Ransom Eli Olds, father of the Oldsmobile, built his first gasoline-powered car in 1901.

Each technology had its advantages and disadvantages: Steam-powered cars were faster than electric cars and had a longer range, but they were more expensive to both build and purchase than electrics. Because the engine operated at very high pressures, it required a lot of maintenance. And it could take a half hour to "start" a steamer: You had to light the fire, bring the water to a boil, and build up steam pressure in the engine to move the vehicle. If you drove too far or too fast and let too much steam escape, you lost power and had to pull over and wait for the pressure to build up again. Someone had to keep a close watch on the fire and the water level while driving; many wealthy owners hired fire stokers—called *chauffeurs* in French— so they wouldn't have to bother with these chores themselves.

Gasoline-powered cars could also drive long distances (assuming they didn't break down), but on top of being noisy, dirty, smoky, and unreliable, they were also difficult to operate: You had to turn a hand crank that stuck out from the front. If you were careless and forgot to manually retard the spark before turning the crank, the engine could backfire, causing the crank to kick back with enough force to break your arm. As was the case with steam cars, many early gasoline car owners left the dirty and dangerous work of starting and operating the vehicles to hired drivers.

HIT THE ROAD

By 1900 nearly 40% of all cars sold in the United States were electric. They were so easy to drive—no crank starter, no spark plug to advance, no clutch to operate or gears to shift, no noise, no smoke or fumes—that they were advertised as vehicles that anyone, even the most cultured of high society ladies, could operate themselves without a chauffeur.

But 1900 turned out to be the peak of the electric car's share of the automotive market. Just five years later, fewer than 7% of cars sold in the U.S. were electric. For all their comfort and ease of use, electric cars fell rapidly from public favor because of one major drawback: their batteries.

One of the biggest problems with the lead-acid batteries of the era was that they required regular maintenance: The acid/water mixture inside the batteries had to be carefully checked with a device called a *hydrometer*, and if the reading was even slightly off, either water or caustic sulfuric acid had to be poured in to restore it to balance. This dangerous chore was required every few days, or the batteries would lose their ability to hold a charge. Less diligent owners soon found that their vehicle's range had dropped to 10 miles or less, forcing them to spend a fortune on new batteries for a car that might be only a few months old. And who knew how long the new batteries would last?

SHORT TRIPS ONLY

But what really killed enthusiasm for turn-of-the-century electric cars was that even when the batteries were working perfectly, their range was extremely limited compared to steam or gasoline cars. And that was quickly becoming more of a factor to people who were trying to decide which kind of car to buy.

In modern times, a person in San Francisco can just jump into a Honda Civic and drive 300 miles to Los Angeles in a few hours. So it's hard to imagine what owning a gas- or steam-powered car symbolized to a person living at the beginning of the 20th century. Back then, if you didn't take the train, the distance you could travel in a day was limited to how far your bicycle or your horse could carry you, usually no more than 25 miles, after which you or the horse needed to take a long rest before starting out again. Life had always been that way—traveling any farther in a single day wasn't just impossible, it was inconceivable.

AND AWAY WE GO

Then, with the invention of cars like the Stanley Steamer and the first Oldsmobiles, all that began to change. Suddenly it became possible to drive 20 miles in an *hour*, and then keep right on going, hour after hour, for as long as you wanted. When you ran low on gasoline, water, or fuel to heat the steam boiler, refilling the fuel tank took only a minute or two and you were off again.

Electric cars couldn't compete. Yes, you traveled faster than you could on a horse, but only about the same distance. After that, your batteries died and you were stuck for several hours until they recharged enough for you to continue on your way, much as it would have been with a horse. And where would you recharge the batteries? Only major cities and towns had electricity. If your steam or gasoline car ran out of fuel in the countryside, you could hitch a ride on a farmer's wagon back to town for more fuel, which was readily available. But if your electric car died in the middle of nowhere, you were *really* stuck. "The lack of proper charging facilities outside of the larger cities and towns is discouraging to those who are fond of touring," *Electrical World* magazine complained in 1902. "Gasoline is available everywhere, and the supply can be promptly replenished, while charging a battery is always a slow job." Few people could even charge their vehicles at home: As late as 1910, fewer than 10% of American homes were wired for electricity.

THE ORIGINAL RVs

People didn't buy these early automobiles to get to work, run errands, or drop the kids off at school; they already lived within walking, riding, or streetcar distance of virtually everywhere they needed to go, because they'd never had any other choice. So the first cars were largely for recreational purposes, or as Henry Ford would soon put it, to enjoy "the blessing of hours of pleasure in God's great open spaces."

Electric cars failed in the early 1900s because their inefficient batteries made them unsuitable for the one thing that people wanted most from their automobiles: the opportunity to travel as far out into the countryside as they wanted to go. As people began to realize this, they abandoned the electric car and bought a steam-powered car or, increasingly, a gasoline-powered one.

OUT OF JUICE

But what if a better battery could be invented? Over the next decade, many inventors, including Thomas Edison, set their sights on achieving that. In 1901 Edison founded the Edison Storage Battery Company and promised that better batteries were just around the corner. But he had a history of promising things well in advance of his ability to deliver them, and this was no exception. His "improved" nickel-iron batteries didn't appear until 1903, and even then they cost more than twice as much as comparable lead-acid batteries, produced just over half the voltage, and were prone to leaks and explosions. Poor sales sent Edison back to the drawing board in 1904. Five years, $1.7 million and nearly 50,000 experiments later, he finally did produce a better nickel-iron battery. This battery, and other improved models sold by competitors, did help to increase interest in electric vehicles—

Underwater ocean noise has increased by 300% since 1969.

they were now capable of traveling up to 40 mph. Or they could go as far as 100 miles on a single charge…but only if the driver slowed down to 14 mph. At that speed, a 100-mile trip took more than seven hours.

ELECTROCUTED

Sales of electric cars peaked at about 6,500 vehicles in 1912, though they still made up only a small fraction of automobile sales. And in 1913 they began to decline. The problem wasn't that electric cars hadn't improved; in addition to having a better range, their batteries had become more reliable and somewhat easier to maintain. The problem was that steam-powered and especially gas-powered cars had also made improvements—ones that dwarfed the gains made by the electrics.

Gasoline cars had become larger, faster, more powerful, more reliable, and in the case of Henry Ford's Model T, much more affordable. Introduced in 1908, the Model T had originally sold for $850, but high volume had enabled Ford to lower the price to $550 by 1913. That year he sold more than 200,000 Model Ts, while sales of electric vehicles (which ranged in price from $850 to $5,500) stalled at about 6,000.

Ironically, the invention that proved to be the death knell for the electric car was another electric device: the automatic starter, introduced by Cadillac in 1912. In a single stroke, the last major disadvantage to owning a gasoline-powered car—the difficulty of starting it—was swept away. Gasoline cars could be started with the push of a button, or the turn of a key…just like an electric. *Anyone* could drive one, no chauffeur required.

LIGHTS OUT

With the advantage clearly on the side of the gas-powered cars, sales of electrics went into a long, slow decline. By the time the Great Depression wiped out the handful of surviving electric car companies in the 1930s, electrics had become stigmatized as slow-moving cars for rich little old ladies. More than 40 years would pass before the public took another look at the electric car.

Part II of the story is on page 136.

GREEN GADGETS

*What do you get for the concerned citizen who seems
to have everything? Here are some odd and
nifty items we found online.*

N ON-ELECTRIC "FOOD PROCESSOR" ($179.95).
At last, a device that lets you reduce your carbon footprint while making your own junk food—mini French
fries, potato chips (plain *or* ridged!), hash browns, and grated
cheese for quesadillas—at home. The Non-Electric Food Processor
is actually more like a hand-cranked salad spinner than an actual
food processor; it fastens to your countertop with a suction-cup
base strong enough to hold it in place in a hurricane. It also makes
healthy snacks like apple slices and shredded carrots (for when
you run out of junk food).

HAND-CRANKED MINI CLOTHES WASHER ($50). This
simple but effective washer is a plastic jug that's small enough to
sit on a countertop, yet large enough to hold a pair of jeans, five
adult T-shirts, or the equivalent in socks and underwear. You fill
the jug with laundry, hot water, and soap, seal the watertight lid,
and then suspend the jug within a special frame. A hand crank
turns the jug over and over until your clothes are clean. It uses no
electricity and 90% less soap and water than an ordinary washing
machine, and it cleans clothes in just a few minutes.

WIND-POWERED MOLE CHASER ($20). Tired of moles and
gophers ruining your lawn and garden? Instead of using poisons
and traps to kill them, you can *annoy* them off your property with
the Mole Chaser. It looks like a weathervane or windmill mounted
on a long metal pipe that you hammer into the ground. The spinning blades vibrate in the wind, sending vibrations down the pole
and into the soil—which drive the underground varmints nuts,
forcing them to move elsewhere. The idea may sound far-fetched,
but the devices have been around for years, and gardeners—
including Uncle John's next-door neighbors—swear by them.
Each Mole Chaser is effective over 10,000 square feet of ground.
And if there isn't a lot of wind in your area, you can buy battery-
and solar-powered versions for $25 to $40.

HEATED ERGONOMIC FOOTREST ($90). Have you ever turned up the thermostat on a cold day just because your feet were cold? Instead of heating up the entire house, you can save money and energy with this 90-watt foot warmer that sends the heat directly where it needs to go—your feet—while using only as much electricity as a single standard light bulb.

SOLAR UMBRELLA ($199). It looks like any other patio umbrella, except for a small solar panel at the top of the pole. During the day, the panel charges batteries that power 24 LED lights built into the ribs of the umbrella; they can be set to turn on automatically when the sun goes down.

THE BUGZOOKA ($29). This humane alternative to a fly swatter uses suction power to pull insects into a sealed chamber so that they can be released outdoors unharmed. Compress the spring-loaded bellows at the end of the stick to "load" the weapon, then point it at the fly, spider, bee, or other bug you want to catch. Pressing a red button releases the bellows, which sucks the bug into the device. It's safer than poison and kinder than a fly swatter, and the 24-inch telescoping arm even lets you suck spiders off the ceiling. Kids love it—they'll take over the bug-busting chores so that you don't have to do them yourself.

DOGGIE DOOLEY PET TOILET ($90). The Doggie Dooley, which resembles a small trash can with an attached lid, is like a septic tank for your dog. You bury it in your lawn with the lid flush with the ground. Then, whenever you're picking up after your dog, just step on the lid to open it and deposit your dog's "business" inside. The occasional addition of pre-packaged enzymes and water from a garden hose will allow the dog doo to dissolve and soak easily into the ground; one Doggie Dooley can dispose of the waste of up to four dogs.

COMPOSTABLE PICNIC & PARTYWARE ($10). Why *wash* the dishes when you can *bury* them? These dishes and cutlery look like ordinary plastic picnicware, but the "plastic" they're made of contains no petroleum-based products and is 100% biodegradable. When the party's over, just throw them on the compost pile.

Foreign import: Pigs were introduced to North America by Christopher Columbus.

LET IT ALL HANG OUT

Here's a tale of two countries—one that rallied around a simple device that considerably curbs greenhouse gases, and another that shunned the same device because it was deemed "unsightly." What's the device? Read on.

ROUND AND ROUND

It was 1945, and Lance Hill had just returned from World War II to his home in Adelaide, Australia. An unemployed motor mechanic, Hill needed something to do. When his wife started complaining that their clothesline kept getting tangled in their fruit trees, Hill had his project. He gathered some scrap metal and set about making a new kind of clothesline.

What he came up with was a rotary clothesline—a metal "tree" that resembled a large umbrella. The basic design had been around since the 1890s, but Hill added his own touch: a crank on the center pole that allowed the frame to be raised and lowered. Hill's frame had four sides with several rows of rustproof wire on each one. The outside wire on each was long enough to hold four cloth diapers. Result: the Hills Rotary Hoist. The rotary design not only allowed the clothesline to spin in the breeze, but also let the user stand in one place while hanging clothes.

Hill began manufacturing the clotheslines in 1946. Even though a Hills Hoist cost £11 (twice the average weekly wage back then), he could barely keep up with the demand. To say that Hill's invention became popular in Australia is an understatement—it became a national symbol of ingenuity. Even now, more than 80% of Australians hang their clothes outside to dry. And in 1994, the nation celebrated the sale of the five millionth Hills Hoist. Its crowning glory came when it was honored during the closing ceremonies of the 2000 Olympic Games in Sydney.

THE COST OF DRYING

Hills Hoists became popular because they're easy to use, but there's an added bonus: Using a clothesline prevents greenhouse gases from entering the atmosphere—and it saves energy, while electric clothes dryers are notorious energy suckers. After the refrigerator (which runs constantly), the dryer is the second-largest energy consumer in the average home…even if it's used for only a few hours per week. A whopping 6% of U.S. domestic power consumption is attributed to electric clothes dryers. And over an average dryer's life span, you'll pay more than $1,500 in energy costs to operate it.

NO, THANKS

So with all the concern about energy conservation in the 1990s, the U.S. would seem like a perfect fit for a Hills Hoist invasion. But when Hills tried to introduce the brand to America in 2000, retailers weren't interested. They cited reasons such as the lack of year-round warm weather in much of the nation, or that the electric dryer was better suited to Americans' busy lifestyles. But the reasons went deeper than that.

In recent years, there's been a focused effort in the U.S.—mostly among the nation's 300,000 homeowners associations—to ban backyard clotheslines. The reasoning? Clotheslines supposedly drive down property values. In fact, homeowners associations report that the number-one complaint they hear from their members—owners of condos, co-op apartments, and houses in planned communities—is about clotheslines. Some people just don't want their neighbors' underwear hanging there for all to see.

And the clothesline taboo is nothing new. At the same time that Lance Hill was designing his rotary hoist in Australia, newly returned U.S. soldiers were chasing the American Dream. As families moved from the cities to the suburbs, they left behind the myriad clotheslines strewn haphazardly between apartment buildings, and by the 1950s, the electric clothes dryer had become a status symbol. By the turn of the 21st century, the stigma against clotheslines was so firmly entrenched that the Hills Hoist sales pitch for a product that had already sold more than *five million* units was promptly turned down.

THE RIGHT TO DRY

But since 2000, things have changed. The environmental movement has gone mainstream, and energy-sucking appliances like electric dryers have come under fire for their role in accelerating climate change. The clothesline's greatest champion has been the "Right to Dry" movement—a grassroots campaign throughout the U.S. to convince homeowners associations to ease up on their clothesline rules. Organizations such as Project Laundry List have even lobbied lawmakers to draft legislation that will effectively ban the associations from banning clotheslines. Some restrictions have already been lifted.

Result: When Hills reintroduced the Hoist to the U.S. in the summer of 2008 (with Aussie celebrity Olivia Newton-John promoting its benefits), initial sales were strong. So there's a good chance you'll see Hills Hoists all across North America over the next decade, as well as in Europe and Asia.

YOUR DRYER AND YOU

In the meantime, what do you do if you're one of the millions of Americans who live in a no-clothesline neighborhood? One option is to hang your wet clothes in your house or garage. Another strategy is to go greener with your dryer. Here's how:

Buying Your Dryer

• If you have a choice between electric or gas, choose gas—it costs only 15 to 20 cents per load, compared to 30 to 40 cents for an electric dryer. The extra $50 that a gas dryer costs up front will pay for itself within a few months.

• Every dryer model is assigned its own "energy-factor number," which indicates how many pounds of clothes it can dry per kilowatt-hour of electricity. Again, it's worth spending a little more on a dryer with a higher energy-factor number.

• Most dryers have a sensor that measures either moisture or temperature to determine when to shut down. Choose one with a moisture sensor—it's more accurate, so you won't be drying dry clothes.

Using Your Dryer

• Your dryer's lint trap and outside exhaust vent should always be clean of lint and other debris. This is not only more efficient, but safer: A clog may cause the dryer to run too long and overheat, creating a serious fire hazard.

• The less it runs, the more you'll save, so dry only full loads. When doing multiple loads, put a batch in right after removing the previous one. Your already-warm dryer will dry more quickly.

• Skirts, socks, and underwear take only a few minutes to dry, so dry them together. Better yet, pull the towels, jeans, and sweatshirts out of the mix altogether and hang them to dry. Added benefit: Without the repeated tumbling in a dryer, they'll last longer.

BARK! VROOM! BANG! RING RING! WAHH!

One definition of noise pollution: "human-created noise that is harmful to health and/or welfare." It's everywhere—and some people are up in arms about it.

COMMON PROBLEM

Noise pollution affects everybody for one simple reason: Noise travels through the air, a "common space" that no one owns. Sick of the constant clamoring, several organizations are lobbying for more regulation of this common space. One is the group Noise Pollution Clearinghouse, who put it this way: "People, businesses, and organizations do not have unlimited rights to broadcast noise as they please, as if the effects of noise were limited only to their private property."

But what, if any, are the legal ramifications of being too loud? And how can noise laws be enforced? Before we get ahead of ourselves, let's look at the fundamentals: how we hear sound, and how sounds affect everyone—and everything—on the planet.

SAY WHAT?

It's a common myth that as we enter our golden years, our hearing naturally begins to go. While hearing loss often does occur, it's not due to any natural aging process—it's simply that, after enduring decades of loud noises, our ears become physically damaged. It's called noise-induced hearing loss, and about 10 million Americans suffer from it to varying degrees—from a constant ringing in the ears to complete deafness. How does sound damage hearing? Basic science: When a sound wave enters the ear, it sends vibrations across microscopic hair cells that trigger electronic signals to the auditory nerves, which our brain then translates into sound. The louder the noise, the more intense the vibrations. If the sound waves are intense enough and occur repeatedly over a long enough period of time, they can damage the hair cells and nerves, a bit like a shock wave from a bomb blast that lays waste to a forest.

Sound is measured in decibels (dB). It's a logarithmic scale, meaning that each 10-dB increase represents sound waves that are perceived as three times *louder*, but are actually 10 times *more intense*. More than volume, it's the intensity of the waves that cause the damage. So even if a noise doesn't cause discernable pain, the sound waves can still be strong enough to harm hearing.

For example, the voice level of a typical conversation is about 60 dB. Raise that 25 dB to 85, and that's the level of city traffic as heard from the sidewalk. Now, it doesn't "hurt" your ears to stroll through Times Square as a tourist, but if you spend many years there selling souvenirs, those 85-dB sound waves will slowly damage your ear cells, resulting in partial hearing loss. If you increase the decibel level another 15 to reach 100, it only takes *15 minutes* of exposure to create damage. What's a typical 100-dB situation? Listening to loud music through headphones.

Increase the level to between 110 and 120 dB, and you're in the territory of leaf blowers, chain saws, ambulance sirens, and rock concerts—all of which can begin to cause hearing damage after only a few minutes. Jet engines, gunshots, and close-range lightning strikes begin at around 130 dB and can damage the ears instantly.

CRAZY-MAKING

Hearing loss is only one result of noise pollution; it may also have far-reaching effects on the mental health of society as a whole. The human brain is capable of taking in dozens of noises at a time and sorting through them all, making us aware of only those sounds we need to pay attention to at that moment. But the brain can only do so much; it becomes much more difficult to concentrate on a task when we're constantly bombarded with unwanted noise. This causes mental fatigue, which leads to irritation, making tasks more difficult and, in some cases, more dangerous— especially at work.

Noise pollution, according to some sources, is now the most common occupational hazard. An estimated 30 million American workers are exposed to potentially harmful sounds on the job, and many don't wear, or are not provided with, ear protection. Noisy workspaces aren't limited to factories; offices suffer as well, from noise within the office—phones, air conditioners, computer fans, music, and even chatty co-workers—and from sounds that enter through the floors, windows, and walls, such as traffic and construction noise. They all lead to higher stress and lower productiv-

Trees have "veins," too—tissue called *phloem* that circulates nutrients through the trees.

ity. Students also suffer: Studies show that people studying in noisy surroundings have a much harder time concentrating than those in a quiet setting. The bottom line is that most humans require a calm and controlled environment in order to work at their best.

Yet as our cities and towns grow more crowded, life only gets louder. Even our hobbies can be loud: off-roading, snowmobiling, going to sporting events, nightclubs, and concerts, or just staying home and listening to music. Add to that the kids screaming and the neighbor mowing his lawn and the car alarm honking...so you turn up the stereo to drown out the rest of the noise.

At least you can escape it all by going on a quiet hike in the woods, right? Not so much, anymore. And wildlife can't escape it, either.

MUTED NATURE

Nearly all animals rely on their sense of hearing to detect predators, prey, and mating calls, and to keep track of their young. Human-made noises can throw all of this off. Not only has airplane noise become more prevalent and louder in forested areas, so have off-road vehicles. According to Noise Pollution Clearinghouse, "ATVs produce a loud, throaty growl that carries due to the low frequencies involved. The traditional two-stroke engines on dirt bikes have gotten larger and can propagate the sound for a mile or more. The noise produced by these vehicles is particularly disturbing due to the wide variations in frequency and volume." The effects of these engines and other man-made sounds (factories, fireworks, gunshots, highways, etc.) on wildlife are far-reaching—and alarming.

Numerous studies have shown that loud noises, either sustained or in short bursts, can cause panic and disorientation in animals. For example, imagine a fighter jet performing a low flyby over a stand of trees. Not able to decipher where the noise is coming from, mammals nervously trot away from their dens, their hearts racing, leaving their young at risk to predators. (In severe cases, a flyby can cause a stampede in which the young are trampled underfoot.) At the same time, birds nesting in the trees react to the jet by flapping their wings, which may dislodge eggs. When the birds fly off to investigate the noise, this also leaves their young at risk. The vibrations felt underground can even disrupt burrowing species and insects. And when one animal is affected, it can also affect others...and so on. That puts the entire ecosystem at risk.

SHHHHH!

So what's being done to quiet down this noisy world? At the moment, not a lot. The modern movement began in the late 1960s and culminated with the passing of the EPA's Noise Control Act of 1972. Describing noise as a "controllable pollutant," the law set noise emission standards for transportation, construction, and electrical equipment. In addition, it recommended regulations to curb the noise for the millions of Americans who live near airports. A few years later, the Occupational Safety and Health Administration (OSHA) began to regulate and control workplace noise. But when Ronald Reagan became president in 1981, he quietly cut the funding of these programs, maintaining that noise control should be dealt with by state and local governments. Result: Noise regulations have, for the most part, gone unenforced ever since.

SOUND REASONING

Taking up the slack are organizations and activist groups that petition governments and spread information about noise pollution. The primary battle for these groups is to re-establish noise pollution as an environmental hazard. Without strict regulations, though, it's difficult for municipalities to enforce noise restrictions, if they even have them. Generally, individual citizens have to complain about a loud party or a noisy highway before the cops are called or a sound barrier is erected.

So what can you do?

• **Protect yourself.** If you work with power tools or near heavy machinery, use earplugs or headphones with a noise-reduction rating of 29 to 32 dB. If you work in a loud office, see if your managers and co-workers can help to keep things quiet. Consider soundproofing the walls and floors to keep outside noises outside.

• **Cut it out.** Fix the muffler or squeaky fan belt on your car, take your incessantly barking dog to obedience school, don't play a loud boom box while picnicking in a quiet meadow, and so on.

• **Protect your children.** Hearing damage is increasing among kids, whose world is filled with blaring TVs and video games, beeping toys, and scream-filled playgrounds. Just as you would with their

What's *saxicolous*? Something that lives or grows on rocks.

sugar intake, try to reduce their noise intake. Turn down the volume, encourage talking instead of yelling, and set aside some "quiet time" in the house, especially when they do homework.

• **Use people power.** Tidy your yard with rakes and a push mower instead of a leaf blower and a power mower. You'll use less gasoline, get more exercise, and keep the neighborhood more peaceful.

• **Tread lightly.** If you're an ATV enthusiast, join one of the growing number of rider organizations that are working with local municipalities to adhere to noise regulations, and only use designated off-road trails.

• **Get organized.** Without serious intervention on the part of the government to curb noise pollution, it may take a unified popular movement to lobby at the local, state, and federal levels to enact new noise-restriction laws and ensure that they're enforced. Check online for any organizations in your area.

A QUIET FUTURE

But people are getting wise. Some companies have heard the message loud and clear, and have started to:

...build quieter. Increased pressure on residential construction sites is resulting in barriers around noisy generators, regular maintenance on heavy equipment to keep it running quietly, and restrictions on the use of loud machinery (in some areas) to regular working hours.

...develop smarter developments. By necessity, housing developers must take into account all environmental concerns—a major one being noise pollution. Result: Developments are being built farther from industrial areas with noise-blocking walls which, while unsightly, greatly reduce highway noise inside.

...use alternate power. As new forms of energy steadily take over, most will be much quieter than what we're used to. One standout is the nearly-silent electric engines of hybrid and electric cars. (Ironically, this silence has proven to be dangerous, as bikers and pedestrians have a much harder time hearing these vehicles over regular traffic noise.)

But, realistically speaking, it may take a century or more before the "commons" is as quiet as it was a century ago. Hopefully we all won't have gone completely bonkers by then.

If everyone who could telecommute did, it would save 10 billions gallons of gas each year.

SILENCE IS GOLDEN

Shhhhhh…

"There is always music amongst the trees in the garden, but our hearts must be very quiet to hear it."
—**Minnie Aumonier, poet**

"God is the friend of silence. Trees, flowers, grass grow in silence. See the stars, moon, and sun, how they move in silence."
—**Mother Teresa**

"I lived in solitude in the country and noticed how the monotony of a quiet life stimulates the creative mind."
—**Albert Einstein**

"Nowadays most men lead lives of noisy desperation."
—**James Thurber**

"Let us be silent, that we may hear the whispers of the gods."
—**Ralph Waldo Emerson**

"Not merely an absence of noise, real silence begins when a reasonable being withdraws from the noise in order to find peace and order in his inner sanctuary."
—**Peter Minard, Benedictine monk**

"A happy life must be to a great extent a quiet life, for it is only in an atmosphere of quiet that true joy dare live."
—**Bertrand Russell**

"A quiet mind cureth all."
—**Robert Burton, author**

"Do not shout to a person standing far; go near him or beckon to him to approach you. Loud noise is sacrilege on the sky, just as there are sacrilegious uses of earth and of water."
—**Sri Sathya Sai Baba, guru**

"Only in quiet waters do things mirror themselves undistorted. Only in a quiet mind is adequate perception of the world."
—**Hans Margolius, author**

"There is a way that nature speaks. Most of the time we are simply not patient enough, quiet enough, to pay attention to the story."
—**Linda Hogan, author**

"Lie down and listen to the crabgrass grow."
—**Marya Mannes, critic**

In the U.S. alone, McDonald's sells about 17 Big Macs every second.

JOIN THE PARTY

The Green Party wasn't the first environmentally themed political party in the United States. Here are some others from the dustbin of history.

MOUNTAIN PARTY. This party was formed in West Virginia in 2000 to protest against "mountaintop removal coal mining," a common practice in the state in which the tops of mountains are blasted off, exposing the coal beneath. The process instantly eradicates forests and pollutes streams and the air. (It's still legal.) The Mountain Party became part of the Green Party in 2007.

AMERICAN VEGETARIAN PARTY. Founded in 1947, the party was, for the most part, politically moderate, and even supported military actions. There was one big difference, though: They advocated for the then-obscure practice of not eating meat. Formed by an international collection of vegetarian groups, the AVP ran candidates for president in every election between 1948 and 1964.

CITIZENS PARTY. Barry Commoner, a biologist and author of *Science and Survival* and *The Closing Circle*, spoke out against the U.S.'s postwar industrial boom, blaming it for the problems of radiation, lead poisoning, and nuclear waste. In 1979 he formed the Citizens Party to bring together environmental organizations frustrated by President Carter's moderate, pro-corporate environmental policies. Commoner thought he could do better, so he ran in 1980. Despite airing an ad on national radio (which used profanity, generating lots of press), Commoner received only 200,000 votes. The Citizens Party disbanded in 1987.

NATURAL LAW PARTY. Their leader, John Hagelin, believed that all social problems could be solved through meditation. A physicist who lectured on the dangers of genetically modified food, he ran for president in 1992, 1996, and 2000. From his stump speech: "The scientific knowledge is now available to end terrorism and conflict, to achieve indomitable national strength and security, and to create permanent world peace." Hagelin received just 0.1% of the vote in 2000. The party folded soon after.

The main ingredient in chewing gum, *polyvinyl acetate*, is also used for glue on postage stamps.

UNSUNG HEROES

*For every John Muir, Rachel Carson, and Al Gore out there, there are
dozens of important environmental pioneers that most people
have never heard of. Here are some of their stories.*

H UGH HAMMOND BENNETT (1881–1960)

Claim to Fame: The father of soil conservation

Life Story: After spending two decades as a surveyor and
scientist in the U.S. and South America, in 1928 Bennett
authored a USDA bulletin called "Soil Erosion: A National Menace." He warned that irresponsible farming techniques were allowing soil to erode and be swept away by wind.

In April 1935, as Bennett was testifying before Congress,
nature provided a frightening visual aid to prove his point: A massive dust storm that had started in the Great Plains had now
reached all the way to Washington, where it blacked out the midday sun. "This, gentlemen," said Bennett as he pointed out the
windows, "is what I have been talking about." Shortly after, Congress passed the Soil Conversation Act and Bennett spent the
next 17 years as chief of the USDA's Soil Conservation Service—
now known as the Natural Resources Conservation Service.

At first, farmers were apprehensive about someone from Washington telling them how to farm, but Bennett toured extensively,
giving lectures on how conserving the soil would save their farms
from a future dustbowl. Today, farmers consider him a hero.

Environmental Statement: "Almost invariably, conservation
farming—which, after all, is common-sense farming with scientific
methods—begins to show results the very first years it is applied."

CHICO MENDES (1944–88)

Claim to Fame: Gave his life to save the rain forest

Life Story: Raised in the Brazilian rain forest surrounding the
Amazon River, Mendes was the oldest of 17 siblings, only 6 of
whom lived to adulthood. At just eight years old, Mendes began
work as a rubber tapper, extracting latex from the trees so it could
be processed into rubber. When he was 13, Mendes met a political
prisoner named Euclides Fernandes Tavora, a Communist revolu-

tionary who taught Mendes about philosophy and labor unions, inspiring the boy to begin writing letters to the Brazilian president about the incredibly difficult life that rubber tappers endured.

That set Mendes down the path to establishing a labor union for tappers. To fight for one of their main objectives—preventing further destruction of the rain forest—Mendes and other union supporters traveled to areas where the forest was scheduled for clearing and destroyed the crews' shacks. Some of his companions were killed in the attacks.

During the 1980s, Mendes organized the Rubber Tappers of Amazonia to alert the world to these "defenders of the rain forest." Just as his plans were taking shape, Mendes was murdered one week after his 44th birthday. After his death set off a media firestorm, Brazil passed new laws to protect the rain forest and replanted 2.5 million acres of forest that had been destroyed.

Environmental Statement: "At first I thought I was fighting to save rubber trees, then I thought I was fighting to save the Amazon rain forest. Now I realize I am fighting for humanity."

FRANK SHERWOOD ROWLAND (b. 1927)

Claim to Fame: Discovered the hole in the ozone layer

Life Story: In 1973 Rowland was the chair of the chemistry department at the University of California, Irvine, when he and a postdoctoral student named Mario Molina made a startling discovery: Chlorofluorocarbons from aerosols and propellants were damaging Earth's ozone layer, allowing large amounts of the sun's ultraviolet radiation to penetrate the atmosphere. This could lead not only to dangerous climate change, they theorized, but also to a massive rise in skin cancer. Rowland published the findings the following year in the science journal *Nature*. The response: Few of his colleagues believed such "alarmist" claims—how could people spraying deodorant burn a hole in the sky? Manufacturers of aerosol cans asked the same question...and fought Rowland's findings.

An investigation was opened, and when the National Academy of Sciences reached the same conclusion as Rowland's team, changes were implemented throughout the chemical industry and all ozone-depleting gases were banned in 1987. Rowland's work earned him the Nobel Prize for Chemistry in 1995; the award panel stated that he may have "saved the world from catastrophe."

Rowland's discovery had another impact: It proved that politi-cians shouldn't ignore scientists when it came to deciding policy.

Environmental Statement: "One of the messages is that it is possi-ble for mankind to influence his environment negatively. On the other side there's the recognition on an international basis that we can act in unison."

RUSSELL E. TRAIN (b. 1920)

Claim to Fame: The "Conservative Conservationist"

Life Story: Train began his professional life as a government attorney. But it wasn't until he was in his 40s that the lifelong Republican realized his true calling as a conservationist. He found-ed the African Wildlife Leadership Foundation in 1961, and in 1968 was appointed to the National Water Commission by Presi-dent Johnson.

The following year, President Nixon gave Train a challenging job: dealing with the growing number of controversial environ-mental issues, including the highly debated Trans Alaska oil pipeline. Train persuaded Congress to create the Council on Envi-ronmental Quality, which focused on identifying the most impor-tant environmental problems and creating federal policies to find solutions. While Train headed the CEQ, he helped standardize the catalytic converter in automobiles to reach the Clean Air Act's emission reductions. He also spearheaded the Toxic Substances Control Act, which regulated new and existing chemicals, and the National Pollutant Discharge Elimination System, a part of the Clean Water Act. Often disagreeing with Nixon's opinions, Train pushed for increasing government involvement in conserving energy and reducing water pollution. He was head of the EPA from 1973 to '77 before going on to serve as the president and chairman of the World Wildlife Fund. Later, he was named Chair-man of the National Commission on the Environment. And he's still speaking out for conservation.

Environmental Statement: "The Golden Rule says, 'Thou shalt do unto others what you would have them do unto you.' To my way of thinking, those others include the whole community of this Earth, all the living things—and inanimate as well—and we dam-age that extraordinary structure at our peril."

For more Unsung Heroes, turn to page 279.

LANDFILLS: TODAY AND TOMORROW

When you throw something in the garbage, where does it go?
And what happens to it when it gets there?

TRASH TALK

The average American generates 4.6 pounds' worth of garbage every day. That adds up to nearly one ton of garbage per person per year. Multiply that by the number of people in the United States, and it's enough to bury more than 82,000 football fields six feet deep...every year.

The technical name for all of this trash is *municipal solid waste* (MSW), which consists of everything from candy wrappers to banana peels to disposable cameras. Not included in the definition of MSW: hazardous materials, industrial and construction waste, computers, refrigerators, and tires, all of which are dealt with separately.

Humans have been burying their trash for centuries, but it wasn't until the advent of massive cities in the Industrial Age that the pollution and stink from these sites became a serious problem. In fact, the first "modern" landfill—one in which the ultimate goal is to not let any MSW infiltrate the ecosystem— wasn't built until 1937 in Fresno, California. By 1980 there were nearly 8,000 landfills in the U.S., but today there are fewer than 2,000. What happened to them all? Many filled up, while others were closed because they didn't meet tougher environmental standards imposed by the government in recent years. Most large cities now have their garbage taken to transfer stations, where it's loaded up and sent to other states. Most new landfills—the largest of which contain from two to four million tons of garbage, spread out over several hundred acres—are located in rural areas.

A MULTILAYERED STORY

What exactly *is* a landfill? Basically, it's a giant bathtub into which

---

In 2008 Ankeny, Iowa, de-iced roads with expired garlic salt, keeping it out of landfills.

the trash is placed, then crushed, then covered up. Most modern landfills are made up of three parts:

• **Cells.** Each day sanitation trucks bring the trash in and dump it on top of a layer of soil, which itself is covering an older layer of garbage. Then bulldozers and graders compact the garbage into a tightly packed cell, typically a 50-by-50-foot square about 15 feet deep. The trash is packed so tightly that one cubic yard may weigh as much as 1,500 pounds. After the cell is complete, a *daily cover*, or layer of soil (and sometimes other material) is spread over the top of the cell, then graders compact it even more. The goal: to keep pests and rainwater out, and gases in. The next day, a new cell is added next to the previous day's until an entire layer is complete. Then a new layer of cells begins on top of that. This system ensures that only one "working face" will be exposed to the air at any given time.

• **Leachate Collection System.** Compressing the garbage so tightly squeezes out most of the liquids, which then mix with rainwater to create a highly toxic juice called *leachate*. The leachate sinks down into a sloped layer of gravel below the cells, then drains into a series of pipes called the *leachate collection system*. This "garbage juice" is then pumped into a waste treatment pond similar to those found at sewage plants, or it's held in a storage tank and then delivered to an off-site waste-treatment facility.

• **Bottom Liner.** This is the only part of the landfill designed to come into direct contact with the ground. Made of plastic or clay, or a composite of both, these bottom liners are subject to damage (and up until the 1930s, they weren't used at all). Result: An alarming amount of leachates and other contaminants has infiltrated groundwater systems near landfills all over the United States. And whatever garbage doesn't leak out is compacted so tightly that it takes a very long time—perhaps even thousands of years—for it to decompose. If you were to excavate the layers of an old landfill, you'd find newspapers from the 1960s in nearly the same condition as when they were first printed. The tight compaction is by design—landfills are simply designed to bury MSW, not to decompose it.

HOLES IN THE SYSTEM

Damaged bottom layers aren't the only threat to public health.

The top covers are also subject to leakage, which releases chemicals into the air and surrounding ground. Air pollutants—equal parts methane and carbon dioxide—are released into the air as the top cover is weakened over time due to exposure to sunlight, tree and vegetation roots, and weathering and erosion caused by seasonal freezing and thawing. And not only is this methane/CO_2 mixture a pollutant that stinks up the surrounding area, it's highly combustible as well. According to the National Fire Incident Reporting System, each year an average of 8,400 fires are reported at U.S. landfills. (This statistic also includes industrial waste dumps as well as sites that contain larger waste, such as mattresses, appliances, and tires.)

BUILDING A BETTER LANDFILL

However bleak this all sounds, there is a concerted effort around the world to minimize the impact of landfills…and, in some cases, to use them to our advantage. There are two main strategies: building new sites that function properly, and fixing the old ones that are leaking. As it becomes more and more expensive to build a new landfill—most cost taxpayers between $10 and $20 million—the pressure is on to build them more responsibly. Before ground is even broken, a proposed site must endure rigorous legal, environmental, engineering, and public scrutiny. The first order of business:

• **Place them better.** Some sites are better suited to a properly functioning landfill than others. For example, soil with high clay content makes it much more difficult for contaminants to reach the groundwater. Other factors include accessibility by truck, proximity to the community being served, and public approval by those who will have to live near it.

• **Build them better.** The science of building a new landfill is among the greatest technological feats of our time—particularly the engineering of bottom liners, leachate collection systems that don't clog, and storm drainage systems that keep most of the rainwater out. In addition, in order to prevent the top cover from eroding, new and existing sites are now adding a top layer of vegetation specifically designed to keep gases, solids, and liquids from breaking through the surface.

• **Add groundwater monitoring stations.** Just in case the leachates

Since the 1950s, the average size of a new home has doubled from 1,000 to 2,000 sq. feet.

do leak out, monitoring stations are being added to new and existing sites to check for contaminants.

BUILDING A NEW KIND OF LANDFILL

But there are even better options: What if, instead of pumping that highly toxic leachate out of the landfill, it was collected and pumped back into it? That's the premise behind landfills known as *bioreactors*, which use the leachate—along with air, water, and other liquids—to create an ideal environment for breaking down the organic waste. Bioreactors require much less space than landfills (because all of the organic waste eventually breaks down), and the leachates don't need to be treated or trucked away. While bioreactors do emit more methane and carbon dioxide than traditional landfills, they're less apt to contaminate groundwater.

There are fewer than 20 true bioreactors in the world today, but short-term studies of their effectiveness have shown promise; they could become the standard for waste-disposal sites in the near future. But that still leaves the task of figuring out what to do with old, leaky landfills that are no longer in service.

MAKING LEMONS INTO LEMONADE

When a landfill is closed, the standard practice is to completely seal all of the cells and then cover the surface with clay, soil, and vegetation. Many communities then reclaim the land, turning the old dump into a park, golf course, ski slope, or parking lot. (The ground is too unstable to support any large structures.) In accordance with strict federal laws, the groundwater is closely monitored to detect any contaminant seepage, and any leaking methane must be contained and safely incinerated.

A recent innovation is to convert gases produced by landfills into power. For example, the methane from San Diego's defunct Jamacha Landfill powers a nearby plant that converts sewage into irrigation water. As the technology to separate and pump out methane develops, more and more cities plan to utilize these old landfills for power. The Jamacha methane pipeline will completely pay for itself in about four years, and should provide power for decades. In addition, nearly 400 *active* U.S. landfills are converting methane into heating fuel.

ALL FULL

Most experts agree that the best way to make landfills more efficient is to reduce the need for them—in other words, to significantly reduce the amount of waste that gets dumped into them. The broad term for this is *source reduction*: "altering the design, manufacture, or use of products and materials to reduce the amount and toxicity of what gets thrown away." There are several ways to recycle and reduce waste (many can be found in this book), leading to the ultimate goal of 21st-century garbage disposal: no landfills at all. That will come from achieving "Zero Waste," and you can read about it on page 207.

*   *   *

A DARKER SHADE OF GREEN

"It isn't pollution that's harming the environment. It's the impurities in our air and water that are doing it."

—**Dan Quayle**

"We've got to pause and ask ourselves: How much clean air do we need?"

—**Lee Iacocca**

"A tree's a tree. How many more do you need to look at?"

—**Ronald Reagan**

"The whole global warming thing was created to destroy America's free enterprise system and our economic stability."

—**Jerry Falwell**

"Let's just call global warming 'science fiction.'"

—**Orrin Hatch**

"Goodbye from the world's biggest polluter."

—**George W. Bush, to other world leaders at a meeting**

Since WWII, more than 53 million acres of wetlands have been converted to farmland.

GREEN TECH

Innovative advancements from science and industry.

POLLUTION-EATING ROADS

In 2006 an Italian company called Italcementi invented a new kind of cement that eats air pollution. Called TX Active, it's laced with titanium dioxide, which, through a natural process called *photocatalysis*, transforms hazardous pollutants such as carbon monoxide, nitrogen oxide, and benzene into harmless substances like nitrates and water. (It also makes the cement bright white, so it kind of looks like marble.) Bonus: The cement is self-cleaning—after it has absorbed and transformed the pollutants into harmless by-products, they wash off with rainwater. Pre-liminary tests of a TX Active-paved street in the town of Segrate showed a significant reduction of air pollutants—up to 60%. Italcementi has big plans for their cement to cover the streets and buildings of the world's dirtiest cities.

E = REFRIGERATOR SQUARED

In 2008 scientists at Oxford University built an eco-friendly refrigerator...originally designed by Albert Einstein in 1930. Rather than using freon—which creates ozone-harming chlorofluorocarbons—Einstein's fridge used ammonia, butane, and water; had no moving parts; and needed no electricity. It never made it in the marketplace because it was inefficient compared to the electric freon refrigerators that took over in the 1950s. But the Oxford team improved on Einstein's design, and say they will soon have a viable model that will be perfect for areas with no electricity—or for people who simply want a really cool Einstein fridge.

SUGAR BATT'Y

In 2008 Sony announced that they had designed a battery that runs on sugar. The science behind it is complicated; suffice it to say that the battery takes advantage of electrons freed during the breakdown of sugars by enzymes. It's still a prototype—four of the one-and-a-half-inch-square batteries provide only enough power

There are more roads in national forests than in the national interstate system.

to run a small MP3 player—but that's the most power ever produced by a "bio-battery," and it's hailed as a sign that eco-friendly
batteries will be a thing of the not-too-distant future.

ASH-TACULAR

In December 2008, a "fly-ash" spill occurred near a coal-burning
power plant in Tennessee. Fly ash is the very fine ash produced by
burning coal. It's nasty stuff—high in mercury content, for
starters—and coal plants capture as much of it as they can in
chimney stacks and store it in slurry ponds, one of which spilled
billions of gallons of ash in this spill. But there may be hope for fly
ash: In 2007 Dr. Henry Liu of Columbia, Missouri, invented a
process to safely turn it into bricks. This means that brick-building
plants could be built right next to coal plants, and the ash could
be carried by conveyor belt into them, eliminating the need for
trucks to ferry materials. The bricks are made of 100% fly ash, so
no other materials would need to be shipped in, and they're made
at room temperature, so no energy for kilns is required. And for
reasons that aren't fully understood, fly ash bricks don't leach mercury—they actually absorb ambient mercury from the air, thereby
acting as pollution eaters.

THE ECO KETTLE

Millions of people around the world use electric kettles for boiling
water, and most of the time they boil more water than they actually need, thereby using more energy than necessary. In 2005 retired
engineer Brian Hartley of Chesterfield, England, invented the
ECO Kettle: It looks like a standard kettle, but has one large
reservoir for water—and another where the boiling is done. That
means you can keep it full and simply press a button to send
exactly as much water as you need, from one to eight cups, to be
boiled. The ECO Kettle not only saves water, it also uses a third
less energy than normal kettles. Tens of thousands of the kettles
were sold to environmentally minded tea drinkers, with amazing
results: The British Department for Environment, Food and Rural
Affairs estimated that in just two years, use of the kettles had
resulted in a reduction of more than 1,000,000 pounds in CO_2
emissions from U.K. coal-fired power plants.

In 1988 there were 600 curbside recycling programs in the U.S. Today: more than 9,300.

NUCLEAR HISTORY-235

Get ready to start splitting some atoms!

MATTER OF FACTS

The theory that all matter can be broken down into tiny parts that can't be broken down any further has been around for millennia. The ancient Greeks called the tiniest theoretical parts "atoms." The history of nuclear energy, however, is short: Until recently, no one knew what an actual atom was composed of. But once scientists figure that out, things started happening quickly. A few milestones on the road to modern nuclear technology:

• In the early 1800s, English scientist John Dalton proposed that each element—oxygen, gold, uranium, etc.—has a unique kind of atom. This began the modern era of atomic theory.

• In 1895 German physicist Wilhelm Roentgen performed experiments with electric vacuum tubes—including one in which he "took a picture" of the inside of his wife's hand (scaring the wits out of her). Roentgen had discovered x-rays.

• A year later, French physicist Henri Becquerel began looking for x-rays in nature. Although he didn't find any, he did find a similar type of energy ray emitting from uranium…all by itself.

• In 1898 Marie Curie, also a French physicist, discovered other elements that emitted invisible rays. She named the phenomenon *radioactivity*. And, in what's been called her most important gift to science, Curie proposed that radioactivity was an "atomic property," meaning that the rays were emanating from *inside* atoms.

A GLOWING FUTURE

Over the next few years, the idea of exotic materials full of unexplained energy caught the public's imagination. In 1903 the *St. Louis Post-Dispatch* wrote:

> The most wonderful and mysterious force in the universe—the atom's power—will be inconceivable. It could revolutionize the illumination system of the world. It could make war impossible. It is even possible that an instrument might be invented which at the touch of a key would blow up the whole Earth and bring about the end of the world.

Over the next couple of decades, experiments with radioactivity led to the discovery of the structure of the atom, the "planetary model" most of us are familiar with: a tiny, dense nucleus packed with protons and neutrons, and tiny wisps of energy—the electrons—orbiting the nucleus like planets around a star.

The next step for nuclear physicists was to attempt to tap into the atom's energy. But how? In 1934 Italian scientist Enrico Fermi shot a beam of neutrons (a form of radiation) at uranium. The atom broke into two parts—and created an astonishing amount of energy. Fermi had become the first person to "split the atom."

Fermi didn't understand exactly *what* had happened, but over time the process became better understood after atomic experiments by such noted physicists as Niels Bohr, Otto Hahn, Fritz Strassmann, Lise Meitner, and Otto Frisch. In 1938 Frisch coined the term for splitting the nucleus of an atom: *nuclear fission*.

WORKING ON THE CHAIN GANG

Nuclear fission is one thing, but getting usable power out of it was another. That required a *chain reaction*, an idea formulated by Hungarian scientist Leó Szilárd:

• A neutron smashes into a nucleus of an atom, splits it in two, and in the process frees two neutrons from the split nucleus.

• Those two neutrons hit two more atoms, which eject two more neutrons each.

• Those four neutrons hit four more atoms, which eject eight neutrons—and he process goes on and on, escalating until millions of neutrons are splitting nuclei.

• With enough material, this process produces a self-sustaining chain reaction, known as a *critical mass*, that keeps making its own neutrons to keep the reaction going until the fuel runs out—a very long time.

• Because neutrons travel so fast—millions of meters per second—the process is capable of producing a lot of energy.

At Columbia University in Manhattan in 1939, Fermi joined Szilárd to combine their respective work with fission and chain reactions. Were they thinking about new and exciting ways to generate electricity? Perhaps. But another, much more sinister use for nuclear power was becoming more and more obvious.

THE MANHATTAN PROJECT

By the start of World War II in 1939, the thinking that nuclear fission and a chain reaction could be used to create potentially devastating weapons had already spread throughout the scientific community, including in Nazi Germany. Several prominent scientists, most notably Szilárd and Albert Einstein, wrote to President Franklin Roosevelt, warning of the danger. They urged him to secure sources of uranium for the Allies and begin a program to develop nuclear weapons before it was too late. Result: the Manhattan Project. By 1942 Fermi, Szilárd, and many other scientists created the first controlled nuclear chain reaction, using uranium. Three years later saw the first test of a nuclear weapon at Alamogordo, New Mexico. In August 1945, the Japanese cities of Hiroshima and Nagasaki were devastated by them, bringing the war to a sudden end.

BACK TO AN ENERGY SOURCE

Nuclear weapons remained a dangerous threat to the world, but with the war over, scientists concentrated on turning nuclear power into electricity. It didn't take long.

• In 1951 the Experimental Breeder Reactor I (EBR-I) in Arco, Idaho, became the first electricity-producing nuclear power plant. It produced enough energy to power four light bulbs.

• Five years later, the Calder Hall Nuclear Power Station in England became the first in the world to generate electricity on an industrial scale. It produced 50 megawatts of power, enough for about 20,000 homes.

• In 1957 the Shippingport Atomic Power Station in Pennsylvania became the first commercial plant in the United States.

CAKE, PELLETS, AND RODS

A nuclear power plant works pretty much the same way a nuclear bomb works—except it has a controlled, or *critical*, chain reaction, whereas in a bomb there's an uncontrolled, or *super-critical*, chain reaction. The technology has changed over the years, and there are many kinds of nuclear power plants, but the basics are the same. Here are the elements of the most common process, starting after uranium ore is mined from the ground.

The atomic bomb that destroyed Nagasaki generated heat above 7,000°F.

Yellowcake: The ore is chemically treated in order to extract the uranium; the end product is *yellowcake*. (The original process turned it bright yellow. Today it's actually khaki colored.)

Enrichment: Uranium comes in different forms, called *isotopes*. One of them, uranium-235, is the form needed to create chain reactions. U-235 makes up only about 0.7% of uranium; *enrichment* is the process of increasing that content level. For nuclear-power purposes, the U-235 must be increased to about 3%, whereas nuclear weapons need to be enriched to as much as 97%.

Pellets: Enriched uranium is processed into powder form and pressed into pellets about the size of a fingertip.

Fuel rods: The pellets are stacked one on top of the other inside metal tubes about 12 feet long. Up to 300 of these fuel rods are bundled together into fuel assemblies.

Control rods: Because a chain reaction consists of freed neutrons smashing atoms and freeing more neutrons, if you take away those neutrons, the chain reaction ceases. That's what the control rods do. Made of materials such as silver and cobalt, their job is to absorb neutrons. When the control rods are fully inserted between the fuel rods, they stop the reaction. Pull the control rods out, and the reaction begins again.

POWERING UP

Nuclear power plants then utilize the heat created by the fuel assembly to boil water and create steam, which then turns turbines that generate electricity. That's the same way that traditional power plants which use coal, oil, or natural gas, generate their electricity. Nuclear chain reactions, however, are capable of creating enormous amounts of heat. And they're much more effective than traditional sources for two reasons: 1) it only takes a small amount of nuclear fuel to create a remarkably large amount of energy; and 2) the process creates very few greenhouse gases.

So why haven't we gotten rid of all those messy traditional power plants and created a nuclear-powered paradise?

Split on over to page 270 to read about the nuclear debate.

MORE SUGAR, HONEY?

If you eat something sweet, it's usually sweetened with sugar,
honey, or corn syrup. They're all the same, right? Hardly.

SUGAR VS. HONEY

"Table sugar" and honey—for many years, the two sweeteners of choice in American homes—are both combinations of two different types of sugars: simple glucose and the more chemically complex fructose. Other than the obvious variation in texture, the main difference between sugar and honey is that honey is easier for the human body to digest than sugar. Honey is 31% glucose, the simplest form of sugar, so every cell in the body can readily and instantly absorb it and use it as energy. It's helped along by an enzyme naturally present in honey that speeds up this digestion. Table sugar, however, has a high fructose content—as much as 50%. To convert that into energy, the body must first generate its own enzymes in the stomach and then process the enzyme-treated fructose in the liver before it can be turned into energy.

THIS NEXT SECTION IS A LITTLE SYRUPY

But the most prominent sweetener in use today is neither honey nor sugar; it's a processed substance called *high-fructose corn syrup*. HFCS is present in as much as 80% of all processed food products. It's the primary sweetener in many sodas, cereals, cookies, crackers, juices, candies, even tomato sauces and soups.

HFCS was first developed in the mid-1970s. Agribusiness conglomerates such as Archer Daniels Midland were dealt a huge financial blow with the rise of the soybean industry, which had introduced cheap, high-quality, shelf-stable, soy-derived margarine. Traditionally, that butter substitute had been made of corn and was one of the corn industry's biggest moneymakers. Seeking a new, lucrative market, scientists at several corn processors worked together to come up with HFCS, basically a modern adaptation of corn syrup, a corn-based sweetener created in the 1920s.

The difference is that *high-fructose* corn syrup, as the name implies, has high amounts of fructose, and the way it's made allows

"We cannot command Nature except by obeying her." —Francis Bacon for very tight control of the proportion of ingredients. Basically, HFCS is enzyme-treated cornstarch. The enzymes break down complex corn sugar molecules into simpler ones, a process that isolates the glucose and then converts it to a mixture which is made up of exactly 55% fructose. In its final state, HFCS is a clear, viscous, sweet syrup with a long shelf life. And it brings in $3 billion a year for the four companies that make it.

Despite the lengthy manufacturing process and the chemicals involved, HFCS is cheaper for food production than sugar. There's far more corn grown in the continental U.S. than sugar (most sugar has to be imported from Hawaii and the Caribbean), and corn production is even subsidized by the government.

MEDICINE HELPS THE SUGAR GO DOWN

It's long been known that too much sugar isn't good for you, but researchers are finding that fructose may be much worse, specifically when consumed in large amounts in a highly concentrated form like HFCS.

Large doses of fructose can delay or block *insulin*, a hormone produced in the pancreas that converts food (like fructose) to useable energy. Too much fructose over a long time makes the body insulin resistant. In other words, the pancreas has to produce more and more insulin to keep up with all of the sugar coming in.

Eventually, this can wear out the pancreas to where it stops producing insulin altogether. Left unmetabolized, the dietary fructose spills into the urine and the bloodstream, or gets stored in the body as fat. And excess body fat can lead to even more insulin resistance. These factors can lead to *type 2 diabetes*, a condition that affects more than 15 million Americans. Many people with type 2 diabetes must take daily insulin injections to replace what their bodies no longer make, or to assist what insulin is still produced. And long-term complications of poorly managed diabetes are circulatory damage, blindness, limb loss, and kidney failure.

AW, RATS

Again, HFCS wouldn't be so detrimental if it weren't consumed in such large amounts. Americans consume three times more HFCS today than they did in 1980, when the sweetener first gained

U.S. federal subsidies to corn growers amount to $40 billion per year.

widespread use. That's also when obesity and type 2 diabetes rates started rising in the United States.

In a 1999 study led by Dr. Meira Fields at the U.S. Department of Agriculture, researchers fed high amounts of common table sugar (sucrose) to rats. The animals developed a number of health problems, such as anemia, high cholesterol, weight gain, infertility, liver damage, and even early death. Curious to pinpoint if it was the fructose or glucose component of the sugar that was causing the damage, Fields conducted a new experiment: One group of rats was fed just glucose, the other only fructose. The rats that ate the glucose were fine (except for the malnutrition that comes from an all-sugar diet). But the rats that ate high concentrations of fructose—not unlike a diet with a moderate amount of HFCS— developed all of the same severe health problems as the rats in the first experiment.

A 2008 study at the University of Florida College of Medicine linked HFCS overconsumption to another disorder: *leptin resistance*. Leptin is a hormone that, along with insulin, helps convert food into energy. Researchers discovered that when rats were fed a diet high in HFCS, their bodies couldn't keep up with the leptin demand, and eventually their systems stopped acknowledging the leptin they did produce. Since the hormone turns food into usable energy, the unprocessed food got stored in the body as fat. In short, HFCS leads to leptin resistance, which leads to a greater likelihood of obesity.

A CORNY ENDING

So if high-fructose corn syrup has proven to be harmful, why is it so prevalent? Again, it's cheap to make, it's subsidized by the government, and it's one of the most profitable uses for corn.

But is it really so bad? A Web site operated by the nonprofit "HFCS Facts" cites a 2008 American Medical Association study that found that "HFCS does not appear to contribute more to obesity than other sweeteners." This fact should be taken with a grain of salt (or sugar) for two reasons: First, HFCS can't really be compared to other sweeteners because it's used so much more. Second: HFCS Facts is operated by the Corn Refiners Association…a group of companies that make high-fructose corn syrup.

According to a CDC study, 148 toxic chemicals are present in virtually all Americans' bodies.

SUZUKI SAYS...

As the 30-year host of CBC's documentary series The Nature of Things, *Canadian environmentalist David Suzuki has become one of the most revered scientists of our time. Here's a bit of what he's learned.*

"People think of 'Mother Earth' as a metaphor. Aboriginal people mean it literally. And I, as a scientist, have come to understand, they are absolutely right in the most profound scientific way."

"Every bit of our food was once alive. We take another creature, plant, animal, microorganism, tear it apart in our mouths, and incorporate those molecules into our own bodies. We are the Earth in the most profound way."

"Never in the four billion years that life has existed on this planet has a single species been able to transform the physical, chemical, and biological makeup of the planet as we are doing now."

"Education has failed in a very serious way to convey the most important lesson science can teach: skepticism."

"We now have access to so much information that we can find support for any opinion."

"Ecology and economy have the same root word, 'eco,' which means 'home.' But what we have done is elevate the economy above ecology."

"People in positions of power have invested a tremendous amount of effort and time to get to where they are. They really don't want to hear that we're on the wrong path, that we've got to shift gears and start thinking differently."

"For the first time in human history, we now have to ask what are all six billion people on the planet doing? What is the collective impact of humanity? And because we've never had to do that, we're not used to thinking this way."

"We must reinvent a future free of blinders so that we can choose from real options."

"I've got to do everything I can to make sure that my grandchildren don't say to me, 'Grandpa, you could have done more.'"

Which is the most populous mammal species? Humans. (The common house mouse is #2.)

THE AMISH WAY

Because the Amish prefer to keep to themselves, most "English" (that's what they call us) know little about their daily lives. But as it turns out, they have a lot to teach us when it comes to living green. Here's an inside account from BRI member Michele Tune, who lived on an Amish farm in Missouri in the autumn of 2008.

FROM WHENCE THEY CAME

In the 1700s, fleeing persecution, a group of religious people emigrated from Switzerland to Pennsylvania. Though to this day they call themselves "Dutch," we know them as the Amish, named after their first leader, Jakob Ammann. In 1693 he formed a faction that split from the Mennonites, believing they weren't adhering to one of the basic traditions outlined in their faith: isolation from the outside world.

And even as that world has modernized around the Amish over the past 300 years, they have changed little. Today, there are more than a quarter million of them living in the U.S. east, midwest, and Ontario, Canada. Although there are different sects, some more rigid than others, all Amish live "off the grid," without cars or electricity. Why? To them, modern technology is not evil in and of itself, but having it around can lead to the deterioration of church and family life. For example, each Amish community has a phone—it's not in anyone's house, but rather in a shed where it's only used for emergencies. Still, that doesn't mean that the Amish don't *have* technology—it's just not plugged in.

So if you're thinking of utilizing Amish methods to start greening up your own life, here are answers to some frequently-asked questions, such as...

How do the Amish get water? They use windmills to pump drinking water from a well into a large tank. No wind? The mechanism can also be pumped by hand. Either way, the water gets piped into a wash house.

• For other purposes—watering livestock, washing, etc.—gutters on the barn catch rainwater and direct it into a large tank. Pipes run from there to a faucet that's used for watering the chickens, turkeys, horses, cattle, gardens, etc.

A single run of the Sunday *New York Times* consumes 75,000 trees.

• The house gutters catch rainwater, too, and send it to another tank connected to the kitchen sink. So in effect, the Amish do have running water, just no water bills.

How do the they take care of heating and eating? Though most Amish homes are heated with kerosene (and lots of wool clothing in winter), some now use propane as well for cooking, heating, and lighting.

• Whenever possible, the Amish prepare and eat their food fresh to eliminate the need for storage. This includes meat, poultry, vegetables, milk, eggs, butter, and cheese—all from their farm.

• On the occasions they do have leftovers, or if they want to store up for the winter, the Amish have perfected the art of canning.

• Indoor food pantries are built on stilts, allowing air to circulate and keep the pantry cooler than the rest of the house in the summer. In the winter, food is stored on the cold basement floor.

How do they wash their clothes? The Amish make their own version of the washing "machine." First, a barrel is sawed in half. Then a tumbler is set inside the half-barrel and connected to a lever. The clothes (also homemade) are added to the machine, followed by a few pots of boiled water and some lye soap. The lever is pulled forward and pushed back by hand, tumbling the clothes until they're clean. No electricity, no chemical cleaners, and no dryer (except, of course, a "solar dryer"—the sun).

How do the Amish...uh, go? Most Amish bathrooms consist of a three-seater outhouse. It's not usually "out," though, but connected to the house. When the receptacle is full, they flip open the hatch door in the back and scoop it out with a shovel.

• Waste disposal has been a tricky legal issue of late within Amish communities, with a few high-profile cases concerning groundwater contamination calling attention to the issue. A new trend among some Amish families is to build composting toilets, which turn waste into fertilizer.

• Many Amish families rip the pages out of the Sears and J. C. Penney catalogs and use them as toilet paper (just like your great grandparents did).

Do they ride in cars? Yes, but only if someone else is driving, and only to get to a job or a hospital. Otherwise, they use horse-drawn carriages. Although a carriage's carbon footprint is smaller than that of a gas vehicle, there is the unfortunate trail of horse manure left behind.

• Some less conservative Amish groups ride bicycles that they purchase from the English. Although a bike was made using modern technology, it only requires human power to ride.

Do they recycle? Yes, pretty much everything. Structures aren't "torn down," but carefully taken apart so the materials can be used again. To avoid wasting food, the Amish make a dish invented in Pennsylvania called scrapple—leftover parts of a slaughtered animal are boiled with cornmeal, formed into a loaf, and then fried.

Do they use power of any kind? There's no way to completely isolate themselves from the laws of the land in which they live, so some compromises have been necessary. Amish stores now use refrigeration, mostly due to safety concerns regarding raw milk. If possible, they use solar power, but some Amish sects have resorted to diesel generators to power their coolers and to charge batteries for their carriage lights (mandatory by law).

COME TOGETHER

Not surprisingly, many environmentalists have latched on to the Amish way as a guide for green living. And many in the Amish community have found environmentalism as a way that they can share *their* technology with us. For instance, you can purchase sustainable furniture made by hand on Amish farms. One Amish farmer is even making and selling solar panels. While that may seem at odds with their beliefs, according to Don Kraybill, a professor at Elizabethtown College in Pennsylvania, it makes perfect sense. "They selectively use technology that fits into their philosophy and their religious way of life. In a sense, with solar, they are tapping into God's grid."

So if you think you could never survive without life's modern conveniences, remember that there are people who have been living just fine without them for centuries. As the Amish saying goes, "We don't want to stop progress, just slow it down."

THE TOXIC TOP TEN

*The Blacksmith Institute in New York City issues an annual
list of the world's top 10 pollution problems. Here's 2008's.*

• **Lead Acid Battery Recycling.** Most car batteries contain lead
plates submerged in sulfuric acid. Over time, these plates deterio-
rate until the batteries can't hold a charge anymore. The lead,
however, is still valuable, and in developing countries unregulated
acid battery recycling has become so lucrative that many people
do it in their homes and often develop lead poisoning. The metal
also contaminates local groundwater, vegetation, and wildlife.

• **Urban Air Quality.** Toxic amounts of pollutants float through
many of the world's cities. What's to blame? Coal-burning power
plants, automobiles, airplanes, factories, as well as natural pollution producers such as volcanos and wildfires. Some of these toxins include carbon monoxide, ground-level ozone, nitrogen oxide,
sulfur dioxide, particles of ash, and soot, and heavy metals like
lead. The World Health Organization estimates that urban air
pollution is the direct cause of 865,000 deaths per year.

• **Untreated Sewage.** This is a huge problem in impoverished
places, where sewage often spills into local waterways. It not only
endangers the plants and animals living in those waterways, it's
also a huge health risk for humans who rely on these rivers, streams,
and lakes for their drinking water.

• **Radioactive Waste and Uranium Mines.** There are more than
430 nuclear power plants worldwide, with hundreds more planned.
Those plants need uranium, which is often mined using very low-
tech, unsafe methods. The process affects the miners directly, but
also pollutes the surrounding land. And when the uranium has
outlived its usefulness, it's still toxic but is often stored unsafely
…which can lead to even more pollution.

• **Industrial Mining Activities.** Aside from the direct damage
caused by digging up huge amounts of earth, mining also produces
enormous amounts of pollution. An example is *acid mine drainage*:

When rain drains through coal or metal mines, it picks up acids in the exposed ore and carries them into the ecosystem. A notorious example of that is the Berkeley Pit, a former copper mine in Butte, Montana, that closed in 1982. The pit is 1,700 feet deep and holds a small lake of highly acidic water. In 1995 a flock of migrating snow geese landed in the water—and died.

• **Metal Smelting.** Metals such as copper, nickel, lead, and zinc are extracted from ore through heating and melting—either by burning coal or by treatment with highly toxic chemicals. A few smelting byproducts: smog, ozone, sulfur dioxide, lead, arsenic, chromium, cadmium, and carbon dioxide.

• **Indoor Air Pollution.** Unhealthy air exists inside many schools, workplaces, and homes. The biggest concern: homes in developing nations where people burn wood or dung for cooking and heating, most often using poorly ventilated ovens. The toxic air leads to heart disease, lung cancer, and tuberculosis—and 90% of the world cooks and heats this way.

• **Groundwater Contamination.** About 97% of the world's accessible freshwater lies just below Earth's surface, where it's easily contaminated by nearby landfills, factories, and mines. Toxic groundwater wells provide water to many communities, and they lead to a host of health problems—from diarrhea to cancer—in millions of people around the world every year.

• **Contaminated Surface Water.** Oceans, lakes, and rivers are even more easily contaminated than groundwater. For millions of people, local rivers are their primary source of drinking water—and most of those rivers are polluted.

• **Artisanal Gold Mining.** These small-scale gold mining operations, when added up, supply roughly a quarter of the world's gold. The gold is extracted from the ore via *mercury amalgamation*, which leaks mercury gas into the air, directly affecting the world's 15 million gold miners (many of them children). The mercury that contaminates the groundwater becomes *methylmercury* and accumulates in fish before making its way through the food chain...all the way to us.

MEET MR. AUDUBON

John James Audubon, a 19th-century conservationist, produced some of the most influential nature artwork in American history. But art wasn't the only contribution he made to the science of birdwatching.

THE BIRD MAN

T • In 1827 Audubon published the first of four volumes of *The Birds of America*, a collection of 435 watercolor-and-chalk portraits of 497 different birds—more than half of America's 700 or so known species. He began the project in 1820, and finally completed it 18 years later, in 1838.

• In his research, Audubon discovered 25 new species and 12 new sub-species of birds.

• To track migratory patterns of phoebes, he tied colored yarn to their legs. This is the first known use of what's now called *banding*.

• Yet Audubon's love of birds didn't mean that he was opposed to hunting. His portraits were so stunningly lifelike because for models he used real birds...that he had shot and mounted. Audubon used fine buckshot to keep their bodies intact, then held them in lifelike poses with stiff wires. Because the birds would lose their color and rot before he was done painting them, Audubon would routinely shoot up to a dozen of each bird to ensure he rendered them as lifelike as possible.

THE LEGACY

Today, it isn't for hunting birds that Audubon is remembered, but for his appreciation of them. He actually warned that overhunting and unchecked development could cause many of the species which he catalogued to go extinct—and several have, including the Carolina parakeet, the passenger pigeon, and the Labrador duck.

In 1905, more than 50 years after his death, the National Audubon Society was formed in has name and has since become one of the world's most influential conservation groups. If you'd like to help carry on Audubon's work, you can join the annual "Christmas Bird Count," a census of bird species in the Western Hemisphere. They always need lots of help. Contact your local Audubon chapter for more information.

Don't confuse 'em: Jan. 5 is National Bird Day; Feb. 8 is Draw a Picture of a Bird Day.

LIGHTS, CAMERA, DESTRUCTION

In a world where nothing is at it seems...an incredible journey is about to take place as a determined Hollywood crew descends upon an island paradise. Will it be an uplifting story of hope? Or a tragedy of epic proportions?

BOO-RAY FOR HOLLYWOOD
With all of the outspoken A-list actors driving hybrid cars and preaching about the environment, you'd think that Tinseltown was one of the greener businesses out there. But that's not always the case. For example, here's a typical scene you might come across at an exotic filming location:

The first thing you notice is the fleet of semitrucks—at least three for the production equipment, two for construction materials, and one for the catering services. Many of those trucks' engines are idling. Add to that the noise of the generators, the hum of the massive spotlights that shine down on the action, and the crane whirring as it lifts a huge camera above the fray. Your nose is offended by the exhaust from all of those engines, with occasional whiffs of the Porta Pottis mixed in. Looking down, you see miles of wires crisscrossing the landscape. The "talent," however, is nowhere to be seen...they're lounging in their spacious trailers with the air conditioners blasting. Meanwhile, the caterers are preparing the midday meal for upwards of 100 people, complete with plastic plates and bottles, all destined for the dumpster. A stressed-out producer walks by without even noticing you—he flicks his cigarette butt onto the ground and then yells into his cell phone, "Where the hell are the helicopters?!"

And that's just one day of a shoot that can last anywhere from three months to a year...or more.

A TALE OF TWO BEACHES
But not all big-budget movie productions are created equal. Here are the behind-the-scenes tales of two major shoots—one that got it right, and one that didn't. First, the one that didn't.

The Beach. Produced by Twentieth Century Fox, this 2000 drama

---

How did South America's Black River get its name? Decaying organic matter makes it black.

starred Leonardo DiCaprio as a young American who journeys to Thailand in search of a radical adventure. He finds an island of hippies who frolic like nymphs in an eco-friendly paradise. But this beach has a dark secret...

Filming took place in Thailand on a pristine beach at Maya Bay. But it wasn't pristine enough for the filmmakers. The crew cleared coconut trees and grass to widen the beach, then resculpted the sand dunes to make them more aesthetically pleasing. It still wasn't pristine enough, so the crew planted imported palm trees.

The locals were flabbergasted, but Fox assured them that the beach would be restored to its natural setting. When the film wrapped, a crew stayed behind and moved some sand around, took out a few trees, and left it at that. Thai authorities were not pleased—they claimed that the fragile ecosystem had been destroyed and sued Fox for $2 million.

In an ironic twist, while the case was still pending, the devastating tsunami of December 26, 2004, swept through the area and removed the imported palms and rearranged the already rearranged sand dunes, doing what the crew had failed to do—restore the beach to its original condition. That didn't get Fox off the hook, though: In 2006 Thailand's Supreme Court upheld a court ruling that filming had harmed the environment and that damages should be paid.

And so *The Beach*, a movie with an eco-friendly message, turned into one of the biggest Hollywood eco-disasters to date. One positive side effect: DiCaprio was so appalled by the damage that he became a champion for environmental awareness.

Cast Away. A year later, Fox was given the chance to atone for their Thailand debacle when director Robert Zemeckis chose a pristine beach in western Fiji to film the story of Chuck Noland (Tom Hanks), a man stranded on a deserted island after he survives a plane crash.

Zemeckis called on environmentalist Dick Watling to develop a green plan for the film. After going through the lengthy process of attaining permission from the locals to use the area, which is considered sacred, the crew operated under a leave-no-trace order. For example, for each tree that was cut down (the ones that

Noland burns), the crew planted three new ones in its place. The World Wildlife Fund investigated the island after filming and determined that the studio had fulfilled its promise to keep things green.

REELY GREEN

It isn't that production crews *want* to mess up the environment, it's that film budgets are so tight that keeping things green is often unaffordable. That's where groups such as Reel Green Media (RGM) come in: Formed by environmentalist Lauren Selman, RGM is the "ultimate ecological tool kit" for a film crew.

Selman explains what movie productions are up against: "The difficulty of greening the entertainment industry is that it is so woven into various subcontractors and other industries. In order to green the movie industry, you are essentially greening every contractor related to that industry." So RGM works with production supervisors to provide sustainability assessments, green production training, on-site monitoring, discounts with select green vendors, and help in recycling or donating used sets and props.

TYPICAL HOLLYWOOD ENDING?

Most environmentalists agree that while there's still much work to do, some Hollywood businesses are becoming role models of environmental responsibility—and not just on the set. The famed William Morris Agency, whose agents represent many of Hollywood's A-list actors and directors, has built a new office in Beverly Hills that is certified by LEED (Leadership in Energy and Environmental Design), an environmental regulation council.

In 2007 Twentieth Century Fox, NBC Universal, Paramount, Sony Pictures, Walt Disney Company, Warner Bros., and the West Coast divisions of ABC and CBS collectively diverted 20,862 tons of studio sets and other solid waste from landfills. Also, according to the Motion Picture Association of America, the studios prevented the emission of 65,497 metric tons of greenhouse gases.

So it seems that Hollywood really is learning to keep it green. Now if they could only learn how to *stop* recycling movie plots…

A-maize-ing fact: Corn farmers use 140 pounds of synthetic fertilizer for every acre of crops.

THINKING *INSIDE* THE BOX

*When you got a toy as a kid, did you sometimes think that the box
it came in was more fun to play with than the toy itself? One
recent trend in architecture is based on a similar principle.*

BOXED IN

Like a lot of developed countries around the world, the
United States imports more goods from other countries
than it exports, and this has been the case for decades. This *trade
deficit*, as it's called, is partly due to the fact that high wages in the
U.S. makes it cheaper to manufacture goods in other countries.
But those higher wages also mean that Americans have more
money to spend on imported goods, and that, too, adds to the
imbalance of trade.

U.S. economists are still arguing over whether a consistently
large trade deficit is bad for the economy. But one thing is certain: The containers that all these goods were stored in when
they came over on ships are piling up in American ports faster
than the shipping companies can get rid of them. If you've ever
been near a dock at a large shipping port, you've probably seen
the containers yourself—they're metal boxes, 45' long, 8' wide,
and 9½' high, that are stacked six or eight high in miniature
mountains along the docks. It doesn't make much financial sense
to send the empty containers back to where they came from,
since a brand-new container can be built in the country of origin
for not much more than the cost of shipping the old one back
home. So the containers accumulate in the U.S. by the tens of
thousands until they're reused or sold for scrap. The companies
that are stuck with the containers will part with them for as little
as $1,000 apiece, but until recently, not many people wanted
them. Who has a need, or even the space, for a steel box that's
the size of a long, narrow room?

BUILDING BOX

As long as empty shipping containers have been left on the docks,
people with no place else to sleep have taken shelter inside of
them. But not many people took seriously the idea of using them

to build actual *housing* until the late 1990s, when architects in the U.S., Europe, and other regions began experimenting with ways to put them to use. One of the first companies to embrace the idea was a British firm called Urban Space Management (USM). When they won a contract in the late 1990s to redevelop a section of the London Docklands area into affordable rental housing, they decided to take advantage of the unwanted shipping containers that were stacking up on London's wharves.

USM named the development "Container City." In two phases of construction, the company stacked more than two dozen containers five stories high to create 30 self-contained artists' studios and live/work spaces. It took only a few days to stack each section, and only a few months of additional work to get them ready for occupation. And the cost to build them was less than half what it would have cost using conventional construction methods. The success of the project, which was completed in 2002, led to the construction of a 5-story, 73-container office building nearby three years later. As of the fall of 2008, USM has completed 16 shipping-container projects, including classrooms, youth centers, shops, lakeside cabins, and exhibition spaces. More than a dozen additional projects are in the works.

RACK 'EM AND STACK 'EM

Shipping containers have many qualities that architects and engineers value. Both airtight and watertight, they're easy to insulate and cheap to heat and cool; a single, well-insulated shipping container that has been converted to living space can be kept warm with a heater that uses as little energy as a coffeemaker. When long, skinny spaces are undesirable, multiple containers can easily be joined together to create more conventional rooms.

Shipping containers are strong enough to support more than 10 times their own weight, and they're designed to be stacked on top of each other, like LEGO building blocks. Just as importantly, when they've finished serving one purpose, they can be *unstacked* easily, transported to another location, and converted into something completely different.

THINKING BIG

Tempohousing, a company in the Netherlands, has stretched the

---

First airline to offer an all-organic menu: Song Airlines, owned by Delta (2003–06).

shipping-container concept even farther. The company owns its own shipping-container manufacturing plant in China, where it builds the containers, converts them into housing or office modules at the factory, and ships them to construction sites all over the world. Then they're stacked into any number of different finished buildings—hotels, office buildings, dormitories, etc.

The largest Tempohousing project to date is Keetwonen, a dormitory complex in Amsterdam consisting of 12 five-story buildings that together house more than 1,000 students, each in their own individual shipping container. Each students pays the relatively low rent of about $410 a month for a container apartment that features a full kitchen and bathroom, a balcony, floor-to-ceiling windows at both ends, and separate sleeping and study areas.

Completed in 2006, the development was originally intended as a quick, temporary fix for a student-housing shortage; the original plan was to dismantle the buildings after five years. But Keetwonen has proven so popular that the student organization that owns the complex is putting off the dismantling until 2016.

BOX YOURSELF IN

If you happen to be visiting London and would like to find out what it's like to stay in a shipping container, the Travelodge hotel chain has built what it calls "the first recyclable Travelodge" in Uxbridge, West London. Its 86 steel containers were stacked in place in just nine days. Several countries are also using shipping containers for emergency housing in the wake of hurricanes, floods, and earthquakes.

But you don't have to wait for an emergency or a trip to London to give shipping-container housing a try. A handful of architects in the U.S. and Canada are designing homes using anywhere from a single shipping container to several dozen, depending on the homeowner's budget and space requirements. And unlike any other dream house, if you don't like this one, you always can take it apart and stack it up some other way.

*　　*　　*

"A pessimist sees the difficulty in every opportunity; an optimist sees the opportunity in every difficulty."　**—Winston Churchill**

How about you? The average American uses about 270 aluminum cans a year.

THE OWL OF FAME

Wise up and find out hoo's in the "World Owl Hall of Fame."

BACKGROUND
In the spring of 1984, Robert Nero, an ornithologist for the Manitoba Department of Natural Resources in Canada, found an injured, starving owl nestling. It was a female great grey owl, a species that Nero had been studying since the 1960s. Knowing the bird would die if he left it, Nero took her home and—with the help of his backyard wildlife rehabilitation group, Wildlife Haven—nursed "Lady Gray'l" back to health.

Over the next 21 years, Nero took Lady Gray'l on lecture trips to schools, festivals, and television shows. The large, calm owl fascinated kids and adults alike, and helped raise tens of thousands of dollars for owl protection. Not long after Lady Gray'l died of natural causes in 2005, she became the inspiration for the World Owl Hall of Fame at the Houston Nature Center in Houston, Minnesota. Each year a panel of owl experts search the world to find a recipient deserving of the "Lady Gray'l Award," which honors owls that have been exceptional ambassadors for their species.

2006 Winner: "Fat Broad"
Owl-ography: In 1970 owl biologist Eric Forsman saved a parasite-ridden three-week-old spotted owl he found in northwestern Oregon. Forsman nursed her back to health, and then the two went on the road, educating people about endangered owls and the old-growth forests they live in—for the next 32 years. (Owls, like many birds, can live much longer in captivity than in the wild.) Fat Broad's greatest honor: A photograph of her perched on a logger's shoulder was included in *Life* magazine's "Year in Pictures" in 1990. (The portly owl got her name because she resembled the character "Fat Broad" from the comic strip B.C.)

2007 Winner: "Owly"
Owl-ography: In 1991 a young short-eared owl flew into a floodlight on a fishing boat in the Bering Sea off Alaska, and was taken to the Bird Treatment and Learning Center in Anchorage. The owl's right leg was paralyzed, he was unable to feed himself, and he

---

Anytime your car will be idling for more than a minute, shutting off the engine will save gas.

was blind. Volunteer Barbara Doak took Owly home to raise him. And though he never regained the use of his leg or his eyesight, he's become the "owl ambassador" of Alaska and regularly travels the state visiting people with disabilities. On one visit, a young boy ran up to the front of the classroom and began peppering the teacher with questions about Owly. Everyone in the room was shocked: The boy was autistic…and hadn't said a single word in so long that he'd been deemed unable to speak.

2008 Winner: "Mozart"

Owl-ography: Born in captivity, Mozart, a Eurasian eagle owl, spent his youth at the Royal Academy of Music in England, where he was very popular. Mozart is so patient at the National Birds of Prey Centre, where he's lived for many years, that he allows blind people to "see" him by letting them run their hands over his feathers and beak (owls don't generally like to be touched). Mozart's lasting legacy: He is, according to the Owl Hall of Fame, "the forerunner of trained owls in the United Kingdom and other countries, helping his keeper, Jemima Parry-Jones, to develop and refine owl training and care techniques she later published in two books and a video on owls." It's estimated that the 35-year-old owl has educated—in person, in print, or on television—more than a million people.

2009 Winner: "Georgie"

Owl-ography: Georgie the barn owl was born in 1990, and at just a few weeks old was severely injured in a collision with a car. He was brought to the World Owl Trust in Cumbria, England, and given to Tony Warburton, one of the world's leading owl experts. The two became very close…sometimes *too* close. "It was Georgie's habit to mate with my head whenever I entered his enclosure," Warburton said, "behavior which sometimes necessitated a delicate explanation when the audience comprised young schoolchildren." The vivacious bird became an international celebrity, having been seen by more than a million people in the World Owl Trust's "Meet the Birds" program. In 2000 Georgie's image was chosen to appear on England's first postage stamp of the new millennium. Georgie passed away at the age of 13 in 2003, but lives on as the 2009 inductee to the World Owl Hall of Fame.

Experts say you can add body and shine to your hair with vodka. (Twist of lemon optional.)

UNCLE JOHN'S PAGE OF LISTS

Some random bits from the BRI archive.

6 PLACES WHERE SHEEP OUTNUMBER HUMANS
1. New Zealand
2. Uruguay
3. Mongolia
4. Syria
5. Iceland
6. Mauritania

5 MOST VISITED NATIONAL PARK SITES
1. Blue Ridge Pkwy.
2. Golden Gate Recreation Area
3. Great Smoky Mountains
4. Gateway Recreation Area
5. Lake Mead

7 AREAS OF BIOSPHERE II
1. Rain forest
2. Ocean and reef
3. Wetlands
4. Grasslands
5. Desert
6. Farm
7. Living quarters

5 "GREENEST" CITIES
1. Portland, Oregon
2. San Francisco
3. Boston
4. Oakland, Calif.
5. Eugene, Oregon
(*Popular Science*)

7 MOST AIR-POLLUTED CITIES
1. Pittsburgh
2. Los Angeles
3. Fresno
4. Bakersfield
5. Birmingham
6. Logan, Utah
7. Salt Lake City
(*Amer. Lung Assoc.*)

6 STRANGELY NAMED EXTINCT ANIMALS
1. Gilbert's potoroo
2. Pig-footed bandicoot
3. Bubal hartebeest
4. Syrian onager
5. Black mamo
6. Slender-billed grackle

4 THINGS THAT ARE ILLEGAL TO THROW AWAY
1. Motor oil
2. Car batteries
3. Tires
4. Air conditioners

5 MOST POLLUTING CARS
1. Volkswagen Touareg
2. Bugatti Veyron
3. Mercedes GL 320
4. Jeep Grand Cherokee
5. Mercedes R320

5 LEAST POLLUTING CARS
1. Honda Civic GX
2. Toyota Prius
3. Honda Civic Hybrid
4. Nissan Altima Hybrid
5. Toyota Yaris

1 PERSON WHO CAN PREVENT FOREST FIRES
1. You

GLOBAL WARMING, PART I

Here it is...your ultimate guide to deciphering this whole climate-change thing that everyone keeps talking about.

OBJECTIVELY SPEAKING

Global warming is either the biggest threat to humanity since the end of the last ice age or the greatest hoax ever perpetrated. It depends on who you talk to: climate scientists (who, according to their critics, are secret socialists out to destroy the capitalist system) or oil executives (who, according to *their* critics, are concerned only with profit and don't care about the environment). This kind of name-calling has distracted a lot of people from the seriousness of the debate. After all, if the worst does happen, it will alter our world forever.

There are two questions at the center of the global-warming issue: Is the atmosphere heating up? And if so, are humans to blame? To find out, in 2008 the University of Illinois polled 3,146 members of the American Geological Institute's Directory of Geoscience Departments in hopes of getting the answers from some of the nation's top scientists in the field. Results: 90% of all scientists polled agreed that global temperatures have been rising since the 1800s, and 82% agreed that human activity has been a significant factor. Among the actual *climate* scientists, who study this exclusively, there was a 97% agreement that humans play a role. The biggest doubters were petroleum geologists, whose job it is to find underground oil reserves, and meteorologists, who study minute daily fluctuations (in other words, weather), but aren't involved in big-picture climate research.

WHAT EXACTLY IS CLIMATE?

Climate is the flow system that moves energy around Earth's surface and throughout its atmosphere. That energy comes from sunlight, which only hits half of the Earth at a time. So half of the planet is always warmer, the other half is always cooler, and energy flows from the hotter places to the cooler ones. Add the seasons into the day-night cycle, and things get even more complicated. And, of course, the sun hits more directly near the equator, and less directly at the poles.

The climate in any one particular place—say, Las Vegas—is extremely variable. In general, it'll be hotter in summer and cooler in winter, but because of the chaotic way energy gets moved around, you can get cold snaps in June and warm weather in November. Earth, however, is a much larger system. When you're talking about climate, it makes no sense to ask about whether Norway had a heat wave in winter, or whether Topeka got a cold snap in June. You have to take into account the entire global system. And for the entire global system, 2008 was the eighth-hottest year on record. And all 10 of the top 10 hottest years have happened since 1997. The leader: 1998, which has caused some climate skeptics to claim that, looking at the past 10 or so years, the temperature has actually been dropping.

COMPROMISING THE SCIENTIFIC METHOD

Of course, looking at only a single decade to make your point isn't good science. A true scientist examines all the evidence and then attempts to come up with a theory that explains the data. People spend their entire lives examining tree rings or drilling cores deep into Arctic ice, ending up with reams of tedious measurements. Only then do they draw their conclusions.

And then what happens? Some politician, or pundit, or even a scientist from a completely different discipline who has an axe to grind, spends 15 minutes looking over the data and declares, "Actually, you're completely wrong, and if you look you'll see that these 15 numbers over here prove my position."

So who do you believe?

MEASURED RESPONSES

Most scientists, by necessity, are very careful about what they say. Good scientists will never say "X definitely caused Y" unless they're 100% sure, which is almost never the case; instead, they prefer to use phrases like "extremely likely" or "there is a good chance that." So when scientists say, "We expect the Arctic Ocean will be ice-free by 2100"—as many scientists have been saying recently—they don't say it lightly. And "by 2100" doesn't mean we can relax until then—it could happen in 88 years...or next year.

PART OF THE NATURAL CYCLE

One of the most common arguments used by those who claim global warming is a hoax is that our climate regularly goes through cyclic shifts, and we happen to be in a warming trend. It's true that the climate works in shifts—more than 30,000 years ago, Europe, Asia, and North America were covered with mile-thick glaciers and the world was 4–8°F colder than it is today. Over time, the planet warmed up, the glaciers melted, trees grew where alpine meadows once thrived, and our *Homo sapiens* ancestors wandered north, setting the groundwork for agriculture, cities, empires, and Starbucks.

So climate change *is* natural. But what's happening today is different: The climate is changing more rapidly than at any time in known history (for more on that, see page 216). Is this just some strange coincidence? Or is it because human industry and population have both skyrocketed over the past century?

THE GREENHOUSE EFFECT

Why is Earth getting warmer? Think of a car in a parking lot on a hot day with the windows rolled up tight. As sunlight pours in, the heat inside starts rising. That's because glass easily lets in light-energy, which turns into heat inside the car. But that same glass lets out heat-energy slowly. Same thing for the planet: Sunlight pours in through the atmosphere readily, turns to heat, and then radiates back out through the atmosphere more slowly.

It's a good thing that it does, because otherwise none of us would have been born. Scientists have evidence that the early years of Earth's history were very cold—they call it the "Ice Cube Earth" or "Snowball Earth" phase. It took hundreds of millions of years for the early "greenhouse effect" to heat the planet up to the point where it became warm enough to support life.

Three gases are responsible for this effect: water vapor, carbon dioxide (CO_2), and methane. The one that gets the most attention is CO_2, because it's the one we're directly responsible for—we pump it into the atmosphere every time we start up our car or lawnmower, and indirectly every time we use the electricity generated by a coal-fired, oil-fired, or natural gas-fired power plant. When we add more CO_2 it acts like the glass on that hot car—it traps more of the sun's energy as heat, and Earth's global temperature rises. The bad news: A warmer Earth means that more water evaporates from the oceans, and more methane is released from Arctic permafrost. Both of those gases are added to the atmosphere, multiplying the effects.

BUT WHAT ABOUT 1934?

Some global-warming deniers are quick to point out that 1934, not 1998, was the warmest year on record. Technically, 1934 was very warm for the U.S. Northwest. But the Northeast was cooler than usual (and Alaska wasn't even a state yet, so its temperatures aren't included in the data). Again, that's weather, not climate.

John Mashey is a member of the Union of Concerned Scientists, a nonprofit alliance of more than 250,000 scientists and citizens. He uses a football analogy to describe the difference: Defensive players are instructed to "watch the belt buckle, ignore the head-fakes." Translated into climate terms: Don't watch the yearly weather, which can and will wiggle every which way; watch the overall trend. So what if the hottest year in the U.S. was 1934? In the global data, 1934 doesn't stand out at all. What climatologists are reporting is that the overall warming trend has been getting steeper—worldwide—especially since the mid-1970s. And so far, every year of the 21st century has been among the top-10 warmest ever...in spite of the occasional snowfall in Las Vegas.

Experts who have spent decades studying our planetary climate system have a sobering message: The debate is over, and humanity is faced with a potential catastrophe unlike any in recorded history. Our actions can make it much worse, or we can work now to start minimizing its effects. But first, let's look at what those effects might be.

For more on climate change, go to page 248.

*   *   *

"I think having land and not ruining it is the most beautiful art that anybody could ever want to own."
                                                        —**Andy Warhol**

Though CFCs were banned in 1996, the ozone layer won't fully recover for another 50 years.

EPA'S MOST WANTED

Like the FBI, the Environmental Protection Agency has its own list of most-wanted fugitives...only these are environmental criminals.

CRIMINAL: William Morgan
COMPANY: Hydromet Environmental
STORY: Morgan was CEO of this Illinois-based hazardous-waste management and disposal company. Other companies—attempting to responsibly dispose of their own toxic and chemical waste—paid Morgan's company to do it for them. One problem: Hydromet wasn't always equipped to safely or legally handle the waste. The EPA alleges that between 1995 and '98, Morgan allowed his company to accept more than 3.8 million pounds of cyanide, arsenic, and lead. Instead of doing what they were hired to do, Morgan ordered his workers to either store the stuff in warehouses or dump it in municipal landfills, potentially exposing thousands of people to hazardous materials. After the waste was traced back to Hydromet, Morgan denied any involvement. He was indicted in 2006 for making false statements to the Illinois state EPA, illegal transportation of hazardous waste, and conspiracy. He fled to Canada, where he lived until his death in 2008.

CRIMINAL: John Karyannides
COMPANY: Sabine Transportation
STORY: Karyannides, a Sabine VP, received an urgent call in 1999 from the crew of one of the company's cargo ships. They were in the middle of the South China Sea carrying about a million pounds of wheat to aid in humanitarian efforts in Bangladesh, but a diesel fuel leak had contaminated their cargo, rendering it useless. What should they do? Karyannides's answer: Dump all of the tainted wheat into the ocean. The company's lawyers later claimed that the crew cleaned the wheat before dumping it overboard, which investigators ruled was "impossible," given the limited equipment on board. Sabine was ordered to pay a $2 million fine; Karyannides, however, disappeared and is still at large. Among other charges he faces are illegal oil dumping and conspiracy. His last known whereabouts: Athens, Greece.

CRIMINAL: Bhavesh Kamdar
COMPANY: Industrial Site Services
STORY: In 2001 Kamdar won a $12 million contract with the state of New York to replace underground storage tanks for oil and gasoline at police stations, prisons, and other public buildings. But by 2004 it had become all too evident to state officials that Kamdar's tanks were prone to leaks. As a result, an unknown amount of groundwater in upstate New York had been contaminated. In addition, Kamdar overbilled the state by $1.1 million for contractual expenses that actually totalled only $59,000. With the investigation heating up, Kamdar fled to his home country of India but was arrested by an Interpol agent in 2006. If he's ever extradited to the United States, he'll stand trial on more than 30 charges, for which he could receive prison time and as much as $5.9 million in fines.

CRIMINAL: Denis Feron
COMPANY: Chemetco
STORY: Illinois-based Chemetco, one of the nation's largest copper processors, produced a *lot* of toxic industrial waste in its day-to-day operations of refining lead, zinc, and cadmium—which, in high concentrations, are deadly to humans and animals. Rather than dispose of it responsibly (or legally), Chemetco CEO Denis Feron ordered a secret pipe be built from the company's smelting plant to Long Lake in Illinois. For a decade, from 1986 to '96, that pipe dumped potentially fatal concentrations of waste into the lake. After the pipe was discovered, Feron was indicted for conspiring to violate the Clean Water Act but fled (reportedly) to Belgium before his trial began. If captured, Feron faces a five-year prison sentence and a $250,000 fine. Chemetco, meanwhile, went bankrupt, and the facility is likely to become an EPA Superfund toxic cleanup site, meaning it's one of the most polluted places in the United States. Feron remains at large.

*　　*　　*

"The biggest corporation, like the humblest private citizen, must be held to strict compliance with the will of the people."
—**Theodore Roosevelt**

Sweden has set a goal of being completely oil-free by 2023.

THE ELECTRIC CAR, PART II: R.I.P.

When the gasoline-powered automobile revolutionized the American way of life, it also condemned the electric car to an exile that lasted for decades. (Part I of the story is on page 79.)

LONG-DISTANCE LOVE AFFAIR

Even after the invention of the electric starter in 1912 made gasoline-powered automobiles as safe and convenient to operate as electric cars, the manufacturers of electric cars held out hope that the novelty of long distance touring would wear off over time, and when it did, consumer interest in electrics would return. But it didn't: The coming of the automobile changed the way Americans lived their lives, and in the process it sent the electric automobile even further into oblivion.

In the past, Americans had had no choice but to live close to their jobs; companies built their factories near urban population centers to ensure a steady supply of workers. Now automobiles made it possible for people to live on the other side of town from their jobs, or even 20 or 30 miles out in the countryside, well away from streetcars and train stations. In the past, suburban growth had followed the railroads and been limited to areas within walking distance of train stations; on a map these communities looked like beads on a necklace. But by the 1920s, this traditional growth pattern was beginning to give way to suburban sprawl that spread out from city centers in *every* direction, not just along the railroad tracks.

A TRIP TOO FAR

As more and more Americans moved farther away from their jobs, they also moved outside the operating range of electric vehicles, which remained frustratingly stuck at around 50 miles per charge, and limited to a top speed of about 35 miles per hour. (The gas-powered Model T had a top speed of 40–45 mph and could travel 200 miles or more on a single tank of gas.) Electrified delivery trucks were among the last holdouts among electric vehicles, but

---

The 1908 Ford Model T got better gas mileage than the 2008 Ford Explorer.

they too began to disappear as customers moved further away from city centers. And with a top speed of 15 mph, the delivery trucks were soon the slowest vehicles on the road, which pressured business owners to dump them in favor of larger, faster and—just as importantly—*modern*-looking gasoline-powered delivery trucks.

A BREATH OF FRESH AIR

People understood from the very beginning that gasoline vehicles produced pollution—one sniff of the fumes streaming out of the tailpipe was proof of that. And the poor quality of the gasoline and complete lack of emissions controls in the early 1900s made the exhaust of that time even darker, dirtier, and smellier than it is today. But the public didn't take much notice, partly because cars were still few in number in the 1910s and '20s, and partly because much less was known about the harmful effects of air pollution and its impact on human health and the environment. But there was another reason why people didn't mind exhaust: The automobile was replacing another polluter, the horse.

BLACK BEAUTY?

Today the horse is regarded as a symbol of unspoiled grace and beauty; nearly a century after these creatures were the main source of urban transportation, it can be difficult to see them as anything other than majestic. But the people who depended on horses for transportation at the turn of the 20th century saw things differently. Hundreds of thousands of horses trod the streets of America's cities, and every one of them deposited as much as 50 pounds of manure on those streets each day—about nine tons of manure from each horse each year. That's a lot of mess to step over and around when you're trying to cross a busy street while watching out for traffic.

And manure was more than an eyesore. It was also the breeding ground for billions of disease-carrying flies. On rainy days, the soupy mess was everywhere and unavoidable. On hot, humid days, the stench of the city streets could be unbearable. And on hot, *dry* days it was even worse: The manure dried to a fine powder that billowed up into great clouds of dust with the slightest gust of wind. If you were walking on the street, the filthy, disease-bearing dust got into your clothing, hair, eyes, nostrils, and lungs. And if your house was on a busy street, the dust seeped under the doors and through windows that, in the days before air conditioning, were usually kept open on hot days. There was no way to keep it out.

The people who drove horse-drawn vehicles had it even worse—they had a front-row seat for the sights and smells of manure every single day. So a few sniffs of fumes from the tailpipe of an internal-combustion engine seemed like a small price to pay to be rid of all the filth and disease associated with horses. As soon as gasoline cars were reliable and cheap enough that ordinary people could afford them, they said good riddance to the age of the horse and never looked back.

WHERE THERE'S SMOKE

By the time the public became aware of the damage that gasoline exhaust could do to health and the environment, so many years had passed that few people even remembered that the automobile had once been thought of a *solution* to an environmental problem, not a problem in and of itself. But the growing awareness of the hazards of automobile pollution, combined with the rising price of gasoline, caused policy makers, the public, and eventually even the auto companies to take another serious look at electric cars.

Part III of the story is on page 200.

*   *   *

LIPO-TRUCTION

Taking the concept of recycling to a new level, a Beverly Hills plastic surgeon named Craig Bittner saves the fat that he removes from his patients and turns it into biodiesel fuel. (Fat contains triglycerides, which can actually be extracted and turned into diesel.) "Not only do they get to lose their love handles or chubby belly," he says, "they get to take part in saving the Earth." But however eco-friendly the practice may be, it is illegal in California to use human medical waste to power vehicles, and Bittner is being investigated by the state's public health department. In the meantime, he drives his SUV to work every day…powered by his former patients.

EARTHLY PROVERBS

Proof that going green is not a new concept.

All earthly goods we have only on loan.
—**Arabian**

Nature without effort surpasses art.
—**Latin**

The Earth produces all things and receives all again.
—**Spanish**

It is better to work in your own land than count your money abroad.
—**Croatian**

When a man moves away from nature, his heart becomes hard.
—**Lakota**

If you keep a green tree in your heart, the singing bird will come.
—**Chinese**

Every animal knows far more than you do.
—**Nez Perce**

The best time to plant a tree was 20 years ago. The second best time is today.
—**Chinese**

The tiger depends on the forest; the forest depends on the tiger.
—**Cambodian**

All riches come from the Earth.
—**Armenian**

The chameleon changes color to match the Earth, the Earth doesn't change color to match the chameleon.
—**Senegalese**

The Earth is mankind's only friend.
—**Bulgarian**

When elephants fight, the grass gets hurt.
—**East African**

A society grows great when old men plant trees whose shade they know they shall never sit in.
—**Greek**

As the sun's shadow shifts, so there is no permanence on Earth.
—**Afghan**

When the last tree has been cut down, the last river has been polluted, and the last fish has been caught, only then do you realize that money can't buy everything.
—**Amer. Indian**

Man is preceded by forest and followed by desert.
—**French**

No matter how long the winter, spring is sure to follow.
—**Guinea**

WHAT IS "ORGANIC"?

How could such a simple concept be so complex? Here are the best answers we could find to some frequently asked questions.

W**here does the word "organic" come from?**
The word entered the English language in 1517 and has its root in the Greek word *organikos*, meaning "of or pertaining to an organ." In the time since, it has come to describe parts of a system that work together harmoniously, like the organs of a body.

When was the modern organic food movement born?
• Though he never used the term, British botanist Sir Albert Howard is considered the "Father of Organic Farming." He traveled to India in 1905 to teach farmers Western agricultural techniques, but actually found that the Indians knew more about sustainable farming practices than most Western farmers. Howard remained in India for 25 years looking for ways to integrate traditional farming practices into modern technology.

• The term "organic" was first used in reference to farming in the 1940 book *Look to the Land*, by British agriculturalist Walter Northbourne. Building on Howard's methods, Northbourne advocated for treating a farm as if it were a "living organism."

What is the history of the U.S. organic movement?
• The term spread to the United States thanks in part to American author J. I. Rodale's successful magazine *Organic Farming and Gardening*, which got its start in the 1940s. Small-scale farmers and conservationists soon embraced the concept when they joined together to oppose the use of chemical pesticides on large industrial farms.

• In the 1960s, when Rachel Carson's book *Silent Spring* accused the U.S. government of knowingly allowing the widespread use of harmful pesticides, the push for organic farming grew even greater. This led to the formation of farming collectives like the International Federation of Organic Agriculture Movements (IFOAM) in the 1970s, whose efforts came to fruition with the Organic Foods Production Act of 1990 and the subsequent National Organic

---

Solar power provides .02% of electricity in the United States.

Standards, which set the criteria under which the U.S. Department of Agriculture certified a food as "organic."

What is the modern definition of organic food?

• According to the USDA: "Organic food is produced by farmers who emphasize the use of renewable resources and the conservation of soil and water to enhance environmental quality for future generations. Organic meat, poultry, eggs, and dairy products come from animals that are given no antibiotics or growth hormones. Organic food is produced without using most conventional pesticides, fertilizers made with synthetic ingredients or sewage sludge, bioengineering; or ionizing radiation."

• A less technical definition, and one that reflects the general consensus among farmers, comes from IFOAM: "Organic agriculture is a production system that sustains the health of soils, ecosystems, and people. It relies on ecological processes, biodiversity, and cycles adapted to local conditions, rather than the use of inputs with adverse effects."

• The big word in the above definition is "sustains"—a successful organic farm is sustainable, meaning that it renews itself. One of the main methods (as well as an important distinction from industrial farms) is *crop rotation*, planting a different crop in a field each year. Crop rotation keeps the the soil enriched and acts as a natural pesticide by interrupting insect mating cycles. Plus, organic farmers often plant "cover crops," which, when plowed, further improve the soil's nutrients.

• Another major component of the organic movement: human and animal rights. The growers and their communities should be treated fairly, and animals—both those used for consumption and those living in the surrounding ecosystem—should always be treated humanely.

What criteria must farms and foods undergo to get the label?

• According to the USDA: "Before a product can be labeled 'organic,' a government-approved certifier inspects the farm where the food is grown to make sure the farmer is following all the rules necessary to meet USDA organic standards. Companies that handle or process organic food before it gets to your local supermarket or restaurant must be certified too."

• For a farm to be certified organic, it must go three full years without any use of commercial fertilizers or herbicides. Also, a "buffer zone" must be created to keep any contaminants from the surrounding area from infiltrating the organic farm.

Why are organic food products more expensive?

• After World War II, many governments awarded subsidies to farmers to ensure that the food shortages during the war would not be repeated. These subsidies still exist, but are only given to large-scale farming companies, which leaves out nearly all organic farmers. So basically, your tax dollars have already paid for a portion of the conventionally grown food you buy at the store.

• Chemical pesticides and fertilizers are less expensive and less time-consuming to use than organic methods. Also, organic fertilizers made from compost and animal manure are bulkier and more expensive to ship than their chemical counterparts. And for cattle to be considered "organic," they must be given organic feed, which can cost twice as much as conventional feed.

• Whereas organic farmers rotate their crops, conventional farmers grow the same high-yield crop in the same field year after year. As a result, organic farming brings a smaller yield at a higher cost. That cost then gets passed on to grocery stores, since organic farmers can't give grocers the bulk discounts that the big farming companies can.

• Grocery stores, in turn, must charge their customers even more for organic food to maintain the same profit margin they get for conventional food. And some grocery stores that cater to more affluent customers charge up to 100% more for their organic products. Typically, though, the increase ranges from 10% to 40% more than conventional foods—meaning if a box of Kellogg's Corn Flakes is $4.00, then a box of organic corn flakes may cost $5.60.

Is organic food better for you?

• Currently, there are no studies which say unequivocally that organic food is more nutritious. However, in some cases they may be: Researchers at the University of California, Davis, released a report claiming that organic tomatoes have higher levels of beneficial phytochemicals and vitamin C than conventional tomatoes do.

70% of foods in the supermarket contain some kind of genetically engineered ingredient.

• Organic farmers try to emphasize, instead, that their products are safer because they don't include harmful chemicals.

Is the organic food movement all a hoax?

The most outspoken critic of the movement is Alex Avery, director of research and education for the Hudson Institute's Center for Global Food Issues, a conservative think tank that receives much of its funding from companies such as DuPont and Proctor & Gamble. In his book *The Truth About Organic Foods*, Avery calls the movement a "total con", and claims there is not "a shred of science" proving that eating organic is healthier than eating conventional foods. Among the accusations that Avery and other critics level at the organic industry:

• Organic fertilizers and pesticides are not necessarily safer than their conventional counterparts. Some types of organic fertilizers contain high levels of pathogenic bacteria, such as salmonella and *E. coli*. And when it comes to livestock, organic farmers are allowed to combat fungal diseases by using copper solutions that, unlike biodegradable pesticides, leave copper residue in the soil.

• Some organic farms use large amounts of manure from animals that were raised nonorganically, a practice that may release additional chemicals into the soil.

• Recently, some critics have accused organic dairy farms of using cloned or genetically modified animals.

• The USDA's rules for organic farming are so ambiguous that a consumer can never be sure if any given product really *is* organic.

Are the rules regulating organic farms *really* ambiguous?

• Because it's impossible for farmers—organic or conventional— to ensure that their foods are 100% of free of anything deemed harmful, the USDA has come under pressure from lobbyists of both industries to ease their standards.

• This has created several loopholes. Certified-organic food can include nonorganic ingredients under two conditions: if they total less than 5% of the food, and if the organic version of the ingredient is not "commercially available." For example, in 2007 Anheuser-Busch released a certified-organic beer, Wild Hop Lager, even though the hops themselves were chemically treated. The company claimed that they had used as much organic hops as they could, but were forced to add hops from their conventional farms because their demand had exceeded the supply. And hops (which provide beer's bitter taste) totaled less than 5% of the ingredients.

• The USDA has also been under pressure to allow inclusion of other nonorganic ingredients in certified-organic foods. In 2007 the *Los Angeles Times* reported that the USDA was considering 38 of them, including hops. Others: "19 food colorings, two starches, casings for sausages and hot dogs, fish oil, chipotle chili pepper, gelatin, and a host of obscure ingredients."

• USDA enforcement of organic foods and farms is inconsistent. Why? Because USDA agents don't perform the inspections; instead, the agency contracts the service out to private companies. This had led to concerns about the validity of many of these inspections, especially when it comes to how well the organic farm is protected from contaminants in the area.

• Organic farmers have found it impossible to inspect every single seed and fertilizer that enters or surrounds their farm. So in 2004 they successfully lobbied the USDA to pass new rules allowing organic farms to use fertilizers and pesticides that contain "unknown" ingredients.

How big is the organic movement, and where is it headed?

• Despite the controversy, worldwide organic food sales jumped from $23 billion in 2002 to $40 billion in 2006. In the U.S., organic food is the fastest-growing food sector, with sales growing 20% over the past few years (conventional food has only increased by 2%–3%). And it's not just in health-food stores any more; organic food products are now available in 75% of conventional grocery outlets as well. Still, organic food accounts for only about 2% of the world's food sales.

• Basically, the whole organic industry is still a work in progress, and there remain a whole host of kinks to work out to ensure that certified-organic food really is "organic."

What about those other terms, like "natural" and "free range"?

• We attempt to solve the mysteries of reading food labels on page 241.

In 1994 only 1 wild sockeye salmon returned to its Idaho breeding ground. 63 did in 2008.

PAPER OR PLASTIC?

Finally—an answer to the age-old question.

D EAD TREE OR POLYETHYLENE?
You used to hear it every time you went to the grocery store: "Paper or plastic?" But these days, many grocery stores have moved entirely over to paper bags, citing the massive litter problem associated with plastic ones. So which bag is better? Which is worse?

The Evil Plastic Bag

• Since they were introduced in 1977, trillions of plastic grocery bags have found their way into lakes and oceans, where they can harm wildlife that mistake them for food or get trapped inside.

• Plastic bags are made from *ethylene*, a byproduct of oil, gas, and coal production—all nonrenewable resources. The petroleum used to make 14 plastic bags is enough to drive a car one mile. What's more, plastic bags may take up to 1,000 years to decompose.

The Evil Paper Bag

• Nearly all paper comes from trees. Although wood is a renewable resource, it's a slow-growing one: It takes a tree several years to grow from a seedling to harvestable size.

• Paper production is anything but clean. Making one paper bag creates 70% more air pollutants and 50 times more water pollutants than making a plastic bag.

• It takes one gallon of water to produce one paper bag.

• Paper bags are larger and heavier than plastic ones, so fewer can be transported per truck. The result: higher fuel consumption.

The Wonderful Plastic Bag

• According to the American Chemistry Council (they represent the plastics industry), a polyethylene plastic bag requires less energy, oil, and water to produce compared with a paper bag made with 30% recycled content.

• Plastic bag production emits .04 tons of CO_2 per 1,000 bags,

---

The Sludge Boat: A one-week cruise generates 200,000 gal. of sewage and 50 tons of trash.

while paper bag production emits twice that much. A new option—compostable plastic bags—emits .14 tons, or nearly four times as much as polyethylene bags, but the upside is that they break down more quickly in a landfill. The numbers are similar for fossil fuel usage, water usage, and solid waste production—regular plastic bags always use fewer resources than paper ones.

The Wonderful Paper Bag

• It only takes a year for the average paper bag to break down.

And that's about all that's wonderful about the paper bag. Based on how much energy and resources go into making it, paper is as bad as or worse than plastic. And according to the EPA, it takes 91% more energy to recycle a pound of paper than it does to recycle a pound of plastic.

EXCUSE ME, DID YOU WANT PAPER OR PLASTIC?

A better solution is to buy some cloth bags and use them over and over. On those inevitable occasions when you do acquire plastic bags, don't use them as trash bags or to hold dirty diapers or cat litter. Save them up and find out where you can recycle them in your area. Most municipalities don't yet allow for curbside recycling of plastic bags, but many grocery stores can take your plastic bags back. They then ship them to companies that recycle them into more bags, park benches, jackets, kayaks, and even car bodies that weigh far less than steel, requiring less fuel to operate. This kind of *postconsumer* recycling extends the usefulness of plastic bags while keeping them out of the landfills… and out of the oceans.

*   *   *

ETERNALLY NOT YOURS

On Veterans Day 2008, the Medal of Honor Memorial opened at the Arizona Veterans Memorial Park in Bullhead City, Arizona. One feature of the exhibit was an eternal flame to honor Arizonans who'd lost their lives in military conflicts. But the fire didn't stay lit—Bullhead City officials extinguished it when they got their first month's gas bill…for $961. (Thanks to donations from veterans groups, the flame was re-lit in January 2009.)

80% of commonly used pesticides have been found in human breast milk.

GETTING DUMPED

What's sadder than a toy nobody wants? Millions of them.

FLUBBER FLUBBED

"Flubber," introduced in the 1961 Disney film *The Absent-Minded Professor*, was a fictional gravity-defying ball of goop that could bounce and fly. To promote the 1963 sequel, *Son of Flubber*, Disney hired Hasbro Toys to release "real" Flubber. Hasbro's goop wasn't magical—the rubber/mineral-oil mixture was nearly identical to Silly Putty. But when more than 1,600 consumers later complained that Flubber had given them a rash, Hasbro recalled the toy. Thousands of pounds of the stuff were sent to a trash incinerator at a landfill in Rhode Island, but the Flubber wouldn't burn. It melted instead—and produced a giant black cloud over the landfill. What was left of the Flubber was sent back to Hasbro, who, with the government's permission, dumped it into the Atlantic Ocean. That didn't work, either—it floated back into Rhode Island's Narragansett Bay. Hasbro finally buried it on the grounds of a new warehouse in Pawtuckett, Rhode Island. A parking lot was paved over it, but employees say that on hot days, the Flubber still seeps up through the cracks.

ALIEN NATION

In July 1982, Atari paid $20 million for the rights to make a video game out of the year's biggest movie, *E.T.: the Extra-Terrestrial*. But for the game to be in stores by Christmas, it had to be finished by September 1—a deadline of just six weeks. The resulting game has been called one of the worst ever made (as E.T., the player walks around and avoids falling in holes). But based on the popularity of the movie, Atari manufactured more than five million *E.T.* cartridges. Only about a million sold; the rest were returned by stores to Atari and stored in a warehouse in El Paso, Texas. In September 1983, Atari sent 14 truckloads of unsold merchandise, the vast majority of which was *E.T.* cartridges, to a landfill in Alamogordo, New Mexico. To prevent theft, the games were flattened with a steamroller, then covered with a concrete slab.

Wet Christmas: It takes about 4,800 gallons of water to raise a Christmas tree.

WHAT'S THE BEEF?

U.S. beef is the healthiest food in the entire world. Ever. (We were told to say that by our law firm—Flankman, Chuckerson, and Ribeye.)

THE UNITED STEAKS

Americans eat a lot of beef. How much? In 2007 they consumed more than 28 billion pounds of it. That averages out to nearly 70 pounds per person. And the fast-food industry is spending billions of dollars annually in advertising to keep that consumption high. But it wasn't always this way: Before the Industrial Revolution, beef was a luxury that few people could afford. Then the introduction of the refrigerated rail car led to the "Western Cattle Boom" of the 1880s—and the birth of the modern beef industry. By 1900 cow meat was a staple of the American diet.

In the 1950s, the emergence of the fast-food industry—with the hamburger at the forefront—created a huge growth in demand for cattle. With that came the rise of a few large companies that would come to dominate the beef business. The industry has had its share of scrutiny over the years: Upton Sinclair's 1906 best-seller *The Jungle*, a brutal depiction of unsafe meatpacking practices, led to many reforms. It didn't really slow down U.S. beef consumption, though, which remains very high today, in spite of all the environmental and health concerns that activists have been pointing out since the 1970s.

IT'S WASTE FOR DINNER

A huge amount of grain is needed to feed the millions of cattle raised each year for beef. This inefficient process utilizes vast tracts of land to grow food for animals which are themselves going to be used for food. Critics argue that this is a wasteful system, especially in a world where so many people go hungry. Why not just eliminate the middlemen—or middle*cows*, as it were—and grow the grains for *people* in the first place? That would also reduce the use of fossil fuels required to get that grain to the cows. Even the cows themselves are greenhouse-gas emitters—and the more there are, the more they emit. In fact, according to a 2005 University of

About 80,000 edible plants grow on Earth, but only about 150 of them are cultivated.

Chicago study, switching from a standard American meat-based diet to a vegetarian diet can have more of an impact on climate change than switching from driving an SUV to driving a hybrid. Here are a few other beefs with the beef industry:

• Many of the world's cattle farms were, until recently, rain forests. Just how fast these forests are being cut down is uncertain (the statistics vary widely depending on the source), but there's no question that large areas of the world's most lush and diverse ecosystems—most notably in the Amazon—are being lost, perhaps permanently, to the inefficient production of beef.

• The beef industry has nearly wiped out smaller, family-run farms. For decades, a handful of giant beef companies have regularly controlled up to 80% of the market, making it very difficult for these smaller farms to survive. And more small farms go out of business every year.

• Another highly publicized beef issue: the treatment of the cattle themselves. Animal-rights activists have managed to sneak cameras into slaughterhouses. Most are overcrowded, and many cows are still conscious when the butchering process begins. And the beef is often contaminated with cow feces, old meat, insects, machine oil, and other unappetizing items. It's not a pretty sight.

TO BEEF, OR NOT TO BEEF

That brings us to the health issues. For most of the 20th century, beef was considered good for you—the "hearty" part of a well-balanced diet. But now many people are saying that beef is bad for you. So which is it?

• Red meat is higher in dietary cholesterol and saturated fat than meats such as poultry and fish, and numerous studies have connected high levels of both to an increased risk of heart disease.

• A study by the American Cancer Society completed in 2005 found a link between the high consumption of beef (more than three ounces per day for long periods of time) and other red meats to a higher occurrence of colorectal cancers—up to 40% higher for those who ate the most beef.

• Most cattle in the American beef (and dairy) industry are treated with growth hormones to make them grow fatter faster. Many doctors believe the hormones could pose long-term health risks to

On a 1982 "special episode" of Diff'rent Strokes, acid rain turns Kimberly's hair green.

humans, including higher rates of cancer. In fact, the European Union banned the use of hormones in cattle in 1988 because of such concerns—and since 1996 has banned hormone-treated beef from being sold in any of its 27 countries. That includes beef from the U.S. and Canada, and the ban has resulted in a bitter and ongoing trade dispute.

• Does this mean that beef is just all-around bad for you? Not necessarily. Red meat is a great source of many essential nutrients, including protein, zinc, selenium, iron, phosphorus, and B vitamins. Most nutritionist say the key is looking for leaner cuts of hormone-free beef, and limiting how much of it you eat.

MEAT ME IN THE MIDDLE

So what's a thoughtful, environmentally minded, burger-loving person to do? If you're looking for tips on a healthier and more eco-friendly diet, here are a few of the basics:

• There are good sources of proteins other than meat, including eggs, rice, cheese, yogurt, tofu, legumes (soybeans, lentils, and black-eyed peas are especially protein-rich), almonds, and many vegetables, including artichokes, asparagus, corn, peas, and collards.

• A diet based around grains, beans, vegetables, fruits, herbs— rather than meat, meat, meat, potatoes, lots and lots of cheese, and maybe a pea or two—has been proven to have a much lower chance of resulting in a number of serious diseases.

• The old environmental adage "buy local" is followed by millions of people around the world as a means of not only supporting smaller, more eco-friendly farms and ranches, but also cutting down on the fossil fuels needed to transport food from far-away lands.

*   *   *

KITCHEN TIP

If you use Teflon-coated cookware, you might want to reconsider it. According to scientists, at high temperatures, the Teflon breaks down and releases fumes that can be fatal to birds and cause flu-like symptoms in humans. But there is a common piece of cookware that doesn't release any toxins, and can even add small amounts of iron to your food, which is good for you. What is it? The cast-iron skillet.

"If a tree dies, plant another in its place." —botanist Carolus Linnaeus

19 USES FOR RECYCLED TIRES

You're hiking alongside a pretty creek when, all of a sudden, there's a pile of old tires ruining the scene! Wah!

DON'T TREAD ON ME

Old tires are far worse than a mere eyesore; they're a health, safety, and environmental hazard. Rainwater collects and stagnates inside them, creating a perfect breeding ground for mosquitoes...and West Nile virus. Waste-tire piles are also highly flammable and can give off toxic fumes: In 1996 an illegal tire dump caught fire in Philadelphia, creating an inferno so intense that it destroyed part of a bridge on Interstate 95. Tires that don't burn take centuries to decompose, and as they do, they can contaminate the groundwater. And there are *a lot* of them—roughly one waste tire per person per year is generated in the United States. All over the world, there are billions of littered tires.

But a massive cleanup is under way. Law enforcement has started to crack down on catching and prosecuting illegal tire dumpers, and new ways to use old tires are being invented all the time. Those in the best shape can be retreaded and used again, requiring less than a third of the energy needed to make a new tire. For the rest, they can be shredded, ground up, or put through a variety of other processes to find new uses. Here are 19 of them.

1. Mulch. Tires are shredded, then a magnet pulls out all of the metal bits and a blast of air blows away all the fibers, leaving only rubber pieces safe enough for most gardens.

2. Playground padding. The same type of mulch makes the ground softer and safer. And intact tires are used for obstacles and jungle gyms.

3. Sound barrier walls. Rubber is great at absorbing sound waves.

4. Coal substitute. Using special filters, tires are burned in the kilns of metal, glass, and concrete manufacturers.

5. Vulcana. This leather-like material is used for backpacks, purses, wallets, luggage, etc.

There are more than 9,000 man-made objects floating in space...so far.

6. Sidewalks. This alternative to concrete is softer, doesn't crack when frozen, and won't be damaged by tree roots.

7. Landfill coverings. Tires are crushed and then spread over the top of garbage.

8. Footwear. Recycled tires are used to manufacture sandals as well as the rubber soles of shoes and boots.

9. Safety mats. They're great for restaurant kitchens, hospitals, schools, pools, etc.

10. Roads. Rubberized Asphalt Concrete, or RAC, is a road resurfacing overlay that gives more traction on wet roads and reduces traffic noise.

11. Speed bumps. Larger and softer than the asphalt variety, speed bumps made from tires are easier on cars and won't crack over time.

12. Molded landscaping blocks. Used to control erosion, the rubber allows water to seep through but keeps the soil in place.

13. Ag Mats. Designed for livestock stalls, they provide insulation, clean up easily, and reduce the need for other, more expensive, bedding materials.

14. Wheel chocks. You know, for trucks.

15. Tire logs. These are cut tires rolled into large logs for use in construction, retaining walls, and utility poles.

16. Fuel and steel. A process called *pyrolysis* heats steel-belted tires in an oxygen-free environment to extrude the steel. It can also produce carbon, benzene, kerosene, and even diesel fuel.

17. Racetrack safety barriers. Drivers who are burning rubber just might be saved by these stacks of rubber tires.

18. Household items. Anything that can be made from rubber can be made from old tires—mouse pads, coasters, jar openers, key chains, etc.

19. And don't forget about the old-fashioned **tire swing!**

*   *   *

"I may be a living legend, but that sure don't help when I've got to change a flat tire."
—**Roy Orbison**

What's the state flower of Maine? A: The eastern white pinecone. (Technically, it's a flower.)

RACHEL CARSON

One author and biologist was so influential that she's now known as the "Mother of the Environmental Movement." Here's her story.

FLOWER CHILD

On May 27, 1907, in the town of Springdale, Pennsylvania, Rachel Louise Carson was born to Robert and Maria Carson. Her father had a flair for real estate and her mother a talent for teaching, but Rachel soon developed a passion for nature. "I was rather a solitary child and spent a great deal of time in the woods and beside streams, learning the birds and insects and flowers," she later recalled. Encouraged by her mother to read books, Rachel also took to writing early on, her first publishing credit coming at age 10 in the children's literary magazine *St. Nicholas*. (Other writers first published there: F. Scott Fitzgerald, e.e. cummings, William Faulkner, E. B. White, and Edna St. Vincent Millay.)

In 1925, fresh out of high school, Carson enrolled at the Pennsylvania College for Women (now known as Chatham College) to study English. She was awarded a $100 scholarship, but it didn't come close to covering her tuition, textbooks, and room and board. So, showing the tenacity that would later make her famous, Carson went straight to the dean and college president to ask for help. Impressed by her character, they rallied their friends to loan her what she needed. (Carson later sold a piece of her family's land to repay the debt.)

A GREAT TEACHER

Carson's main focus in college was writing and submitting stories to magazines, but even English majors were required to take two semesters of science. One biology teacher, Mary Skinker, often took her class to Cook State Forest to do field research. Those trips reawakened Carson's interest in nature and, in a move that shocked her friends, the college junior switched her major to zoology. She graduated in 1929, magna cum laude.

DREAMS OF THE SEA

While a young girl, Carson had listened to the conch shell her mother kept in the parlor. The sound had sparked a lifelong fascination with the ocean and, thanks to a gift from one of her sponsors, she was able to pursue that dream with a trip to Woods Hole, Massachusetts, to study at the Marine Biological Laboratory. For six weeks she worked in the facility's extensive libraries while rubbing elbows with some of the nation's leading marine biologists.

The following fall, Carson worked on her master's thesis at Johns Hopkins University in Baltimore, and her parents soon joined her in a house near Chesapeake Bay. Although she received a one-year scholarship, Carson had to work her way through the rest of graduate school by assisting Dr. Raymond Pearl and Dr. H. S. Jennings in the genetics department. She also worked as an assistant teacher in the zoology department at the University of Maryland.

Graduating in 1932 with a master's in marine zoology, Carson maintained her part-time teaching position and continued helping her family financially. Money had never been abundant, but it was even more scarce during the Great Depression. The family finances suffered further when her father died of a heart attack in 1935, leaving Carson as the sole provider for her mother.

FISH TALES

With the added strain on her already meager budget, Carson had no choice but to postpone earning her doctorate. To make ends meet, she wrote feature articles for the *Baltimore Sun* and also applied for a job at the U.S. Bureau of Fisheries. Elmer Higgins, who ran the Bureau's Division of Scientific Inquiry, was impressed by Carson's writing skills and hired her to pen scripts for their (then) unpopular *Romance Under the Seas* radio show. Thanks to Carson's storytelling talents, the seven-minute shows about marine biology took on a new life, and ratings improved dramatically.

In 1937 Carson's older sister, Marion, died at the age of 40, leaving behind two young daughters…whom Carson took in to raise as her own. Now, with a 70-year-old mother, two girls in school, and a lengthy commute to work, Carson sold the family home in Chesapeake Bay and moved everyone to Silver Spring, Maryland, to be close to the Bureau's office.

That same year, Carson took the civil service examination required for promotion to full-time junior aquatic biologist. Earning a score higher than any of the other candidates—all men—she made history as the first female biologist hired by the Bureau of Fisheries. Carson was assigned to Elmer Higgins's department, per his request.

AUTHOR, AUTHOR

Higgins put her to work doing what she did best, writing brochures about natural resources and conservation. But Carson's first piece, according to Higgins, was a little too "fluffy" for a government agency, so he asked her for a rewrite. But he also recommended that she submit the original to the *Atlantic Monthly*, a national magazine. The piece, titled "Undersea" and published in September 1937, put Carson on the map, earning high praise from literary critics, naturalists, and scientists. Her reputation now growing, Carson decided to take the next step: writing a book.

That opportunity came about when the author of *The Story of Mankind*, Hendrik Willem van Loon, read Carson's "Undersea" article. At Loon's insistence, Quincy Howe, an editor at Simon and Schuster, met with Carson. They made a deal, and Carson's book of essays about the Atlantic coast, *Under the Sea Wind*, was published in 1941. It received glowing reviews but was the victim of bad timing: Pearl Harbor was bombed later that year, and sales of the book dropped off as the country turned its attention to World War II.

FINDING HER VOICE

During the war, the Bureau, now called the Fish and Wildlife Service, kept Carson writing. She dutifully created four pamphlets from 1943 to '45 with descriptive pages highlighting more than 60 varieties of fish and a dozen types of shellfish. The pamphlets, which found their way into schools and libraries all across the country, brought Carson's writing to tens of thousands of people—even if they didn't yet know her name.

During the '40s, Carson often attended parties in Washington, D.C., hosted by the Fish and Wildlife Service. Though shy, she enjoyed mingling and conversing with her fellow scientists and government employees. But more and more, she also began noticing a discrepancy between what government agencies said and what they actually did.

In the fall of 1948, Carson became a full-fledged biologist as well as editor-in-chief of the Bureau's Informative Division...even as the seeds of dissent were growing inside her. So Carson, described by naturalist Louis Halle as "quiet, diffident, neat, proper, and without affectation," started attacking the establishment, quietly at first. Still a government employee, she couldn't rock the boat too much...yet.

START SPREADING THE NEWS

Though Carson kept the focus of her writing on nature's wonders, she had trouble finding publishers. *National Geographic* decided not to run her second book about the sea's origins in serial form, and other magazines rejected it as well. Eventually, it landed on the desk of William Shawn, editor of *The New Yorker*. He immediately recognized the work as "polished gold" and ran most of it in the magazine as a series called "A Profile of the Sea." This exposed Carson to a wider audience than ever before, and helped the book—published in 1951 as *The Sea Around Us*—become a bestseller. It sold more than 200,000 copies and won the National Book Award.

Thanks to her literary success, Carson was able to retire from the Fish and Wildlife Service in 1952 and focus on writing full-time. She built a small cottage on the Maine coast, where she wrote the final book of her ocean trilogy, *The Edge of the Sea*. It was popular as well, but no one could have foreseen the impact her next work would have.

(D)ON'T (D)O (T)HAT

With each passing year, Carson saw the condition of the environment get worse and those responsible grow more irresponsible. Her biggest concern: the reckless use of synthetic chemical pesticides, including the then-popular dichloro-diphenyl-trichloroethane, or DDT. That and even stronger chemicals, such as malathion, heptachlor, dieldrin, and parathion, were all on the Department of Agriculture's approved list for public and commercial use. But Carson had seen firsthand the damage these pesticides could cause when a friend's birds were all killed in their aviary...after a plane flew over it spraying DDT.

Carson laid it all out in her fourth book, *Silent Spring*. Published in 1962, it pulled no punches in calling on the government

First anti-DDT book: J. I. Rodale's *Pay Dirt*, published 17 years before *Silent Spring*.

and agricultural scientists to ban the use of these substances. She painted a grim picture of the future—a day when crickets and birds would be silenced by extinction. Here's an excerpt:

> The most alarming of all man's assaults upon the environment is the contamination of air, earth, rivers, and sea with dangerous and even lethal materials. This pollution is for the most part irrecoverable; the chain of evil it initiates not only in the world that must support life but in living tissues is for the most part irreversible. In this now universal contamination of the environment, chemicals are the sinister and little-recognized partners of radiation in changing the very nature of the world—the very nature of its life.

With the book flying off the shelves, Carson appeared before Congress in 1963 to testify in favor of new policies that would protect the environment, wildlife, and the health of humans. But her mission was cut short when, on April 14, 1964, she died of breast cancer. At only 56 years old, she passed away at her home in Silver Spring.

LOUD LEGACY

After Carson's death, *Silent Spring* lived on…in a big way. A runaway bestseller, the book opened people's eyes to the fact that both government and big business could and would brazenly lie about public safety. This growing mistrust—spurred by the assassination of President Kennedy and, later, an unpopular war in Vietnam—helped the 1960s to become a decade of social awareness. But *Silent Spring* did more than just start a movement. It had a direct impact on government policy, leading to the formation of the Environmental Protection Agency and the banning of DDT. (For that story, go to page 255.)

In 1966, just two years after her death, the Rachel Carson National Wildlife Refuge opened in Maine. It still protects migratory bird habitats, estuaries, and delicate salt marshes—a fitting tribute to one of the 20th century's most influential environmentalists.

*   *   *

"Those who contemplate the beauty of the earth…find reserves of strength that will endure as long as life lasts."
—**Rachel Carson**

500 million pounds of fertilizer are used on U.S. lawns each year.

THE BIG BOX RE-BOX

Don't be sad when your local megastore goes out of business.
Look for ways to get creative, like these folks did.

NOW THAT'S RECYCLING!
Despite their popularity, stores such as Wal-Mart, Kmart, Target, Home Depot, and larger grocery stores sometimes close, leaving behind a prime location and a building—with ample parking—that's ready for reuse. But many leases specify that a competitor can't move in for at least 25 years, and not too many other businesses require that much space. So what do you do with a building that's basically one big room? Many communities are transforming these big boxes into things their citizens actually want.

• The abandoned Wal-Mart in Bardstown, Kentucky, was converted into the Nelson County Justice Center, which holds a courthouse, county jail, and legal offices.

• Goodbye, Wal-Mart. Hello, RPM Indoor Raceway, a go-kart track located in Round Rock, Texas.

• In Mount Sterling, Kentucky, four doctors pooled $4 million to renovate an old Wal-Mart into the Central Kentucky Comprehensive Medical Center. It houses a cardiovascular center, a physical therapy program, 88 exam rooms, and an urgent-care clinic.

• In Hastings, Nebraska, the Head Start facility, a publicly funded preschool and early education center, is an old Kmart.

• At 52,000 square feet, the Grand Union in Princeton, New Jersey, was one of the largest grocery stores on the east coast. Today, it's the Princeton Fitness and Wellness Center, one of the region's biggest gyms.

• A former Wal-Mart, the Snowy Range Academy is now a private charter school in Laramie, Wyoming. Still in business next to the school is a Staples office store, so pens and notebooks are readily available.

• Uncle John's favorite: the Spam Museum, a 33,000-square-foot former Kmart in Austin, Minnesota, adjacent to the Hormel plant where Spam is manufactured.

GREEN BUSINESSES

*Some companies were green long before the word became a cliché,
and more are jumping on the bandwagon all the time.*

W**HO'S THE GREENEST OF THEM ALL?**
In 2008, after five years of exhaustive research, the Better World Shopping Guide released their list of the "greenest" companies in the world. To compile the list, they investigated more than 1,000 companies and evaluated them on their practices regarding human rights, community involvement, animal protection, and the environment.

The winner: Seventh Generation, famous for their recycled household paper products and nontoxic cleaners. Founded in 1988 in Burlington, Vermont, the company was among the first to join the Green Business Network of Co-op America (now called Green America), an organization set up to support small-to-medium-size businesses that employ green practices. Today, GBN has 4,000-plus members, each of which had to meet strict criteria to join. And all of the top 10 best companies named by the Better World Shopping Guide are GBN members. Here are some companies—large and small, old and new—are truly green, or are working toward that goal.

GREEN ACRES IS THE PLACE TO BE
• **TerraCycle.** Started by two Princeton University students in 2001, TerraCycle manufactures, among other things, plant food made from liquefied worm castings (i.e., poop) that they sell in reused plastic soda bottles. In fact, nearly everything that TerraCycle sells was used before—even their shipping containers and squirt nozzles are "mistakes" that were discarded by other companies. TerraCycle is always looking for garbage—cookie wrappers, drink pouches, yogurt containers, corks, potato chip bags, and 20-ounce soda bottles. They buy the garbage and then make it into lunch bags, grocery sacks, and backpacks.

• **Serious Material** produces EcoRock, a new type of drywall made mostly from waste products. It takes 80% less energy to produce than conventional gypsum drywall, contains 85% recycled material,

What is *phytocapping*? Growing plants and trees on a layer of soil on top of a landfill.

and is recyclable. And, according to the company, it holds up better than old-fashioned drywall.

• **Mannequin Madness** buys, sells, rents, and refurbishes mannequins. They even won an EPA award for recycling 100,000 pounds of mannequins in one year. Their motto: "We work with a bunch of stiffs and dummies and love it." (Uncle John can relate.)

• **Plato's Closet** caters to fashion-minded teens with a nationwide chain of shops that sell recycled designer clothes. But what about jeans that are too ripped to resell? They're made into insulation—it's safer than the fiberglass variety and just as effective. (The Academy of Science complex in San Francisco's Golden Gate Park is insulated with denim.)

• **Interface Global,** the world's largest commercial flooring company, has created a modular carpet system where individual sections can be replaced when they're worn out, rather than having to replace the entire carpet. They also have an extensive carpet-leasing program so carpets can be reused. In addition, they've built a solar-powered factory to achieve their goal of "never taking another drop of oil from the ground." Their annual sales have grown by $200 million without an increase in natural resource use, and they plan to achieve an environmental footprint of zero by 2020.

• **FedEx** is making a push to purchase more fuel-efficient airplanes and ground vehicles.

• **Verizon** and **Cox Communications** are adding hybrid vehicles to their operations, including some that run on biodiesel.

• **Starbucks** is the largest purchaser of Fair Trade Certified coffee worldwide (for more about fair-trade coffee, see page 245). However, the Responsible Shopper Guide of Co-op America notes that fair-trade coffee makes up only a fraction of their sales. Starbucks also has ambitious "shared-planet" goals for recycling, green energy purchasing, energy and water conservation, and green construction. Because they go through billions of disposable coffee cups per year, they plan to be using 100% reusable cups by 2015.

MAKING A LOT OF GREEN

According to Joel Makower, author of *Strategies for the Green*

Economy, "There's a shift happening from being a movement to having a market"—in other words, many of these practices are simply good business tactics. And much is being accomplished with little or no fanfare: Busch beer cans now contain less aluminum, Nokia makes their shipping packages smaller and recyclable, Pampers are being made with fewer materials, and General Motors generates power from landfill gases.

These actions, reports Makower, "yield significant environmental benefits, possibly far more than some of the green-labeled trash bags, cleaning products, and recycled paper goods hyped as being better for the planet." That's because these large companies are among the world's biggest buyers of renewable energy (Intel and Pepsico), organic cotton (Wal-Mart and Nike), organic milk (Wal-Mart), sustainably harvested wood (Home Depot), and recycled products (McDonald's). While Makower is not suggesting that these corporations are truly you-know-what yet, they're improving because "there's profitability in all that efficiency." At this rate, the term "green business" may become redundant, and "green" can return to doing what it does best—just being a pretty color.

*   *   *

TINY FOOTPRINTS

Who has the smallest carbon footprint in the industrialized world? Many think it's Joan Pick of London, England, otherwise known as the "Energy Miser." She chose this lifestyle while working as a scientific adviser to energy companies in 1972. "I realized we have got the energy question totally wrong," she said. Over the last 37 years, Ms. Pick hasn't ridden on a train or airplane once, and has only been in a car twice. Instead, she runs wherever she needs to go, and estimates that she's covered more than 130,000 miles on foot. To avoid using gas for cooking and heating, she only eats raw food and wears warm (homemade) clothes in winter. Her household electricity use is limited to one lamp with an energy-efficient bulb. And at 68 years old, Ms. Pick is still living happily off the grid. "I have to experiment with the energy-efficient lifestyle," she says, "to prove it's survivable."

LIFE ON MARS?

*So what if we ignore all this stuff about saving the environment
and go ahead and trash Earth anyway? No problem—
we'll just move everybody next door.*

SPACE ODDITY

For centuries, humans have looked up at our closest planetary neighbor and wondered if we would ever live there. Today, scientists are working on making this a reality. NASA has even announced a date for the first manned mission to the Red Planet: 2031.

The bad news: It may be closer to the year 3031 before a human can take a stroll around Mars wearing nothing but a pair of shorts and a T-shirt. As it stands right now, Mars's average temperature is –81°F, its atmosphere is extremely thin, and it contains almost no oxygen. To fix all three of these problems would be, by far, the largest and boldest undertaking in human history.

The good news: Mars possesses many of the basic elements necessary for life to develop, the most crucial being water. The planet also has a promising atmospheric makeup: 95.2% carbon dioxide, 2.7% nitrogen, and 0.2% oxygen. While that's far below the 20% oxygen in our atmosphere, it's encouraging because four billion years ago, Earth's atmosphere was nearly the same as Mars's is today. So, to make Mars earthlike—or *terraformed*—it needs heat, more water, a thicker atmosphere, and lots and lots of oxygen. But how do you do it in less than four billion years? Here are two theories.

GOLDEN YEARS

One of the ways that NASA may send humans to Mars is on a ship powered by "solar sails," giant mirrors that harness the sun's energy to propel the ship forward. This same principle could be used to heat Mars by reflecting sunlight to the surface. However, the mirrors would need to be about 150 miles wide to heat enough land to make it worthwhile. Mirrors that large couldn't be assembled on Earth, so the alternative would be to assemble them in orbit out of "space junk"—floating debris from previous space missions, jettisoned fuel tanks, and old satellites (now *that's* recycling). Once installed 300,000 miles above the Martian surface, they'd be trained on the frozen polar caps and begin melting the ice. This process would release CO_2 into the atmosphere, theoretically triggering the greenhouse effect: CO_2 absorbs the sun's radiation, and having more of it would warm the planet and thicken the atmosphere.

The moving gases from the melting ice caps would also generate planet-wide dust storms, increasing the temperature even more. Eventually, Mars would be warm enough for liquid water to develop (but not freeze) at the poles. At this point, rockets filled with algae spores would be sent to this new ocean. The new algae would thrive in the water, causing photosynthesis, a by-product of which is oxygen. Humans would still need to wear air tanks for a few millennia, but the amount of oxygen would increase as the temperature slowly rose.

ZIGGY STARDUST

A quicker and more violent terraforming method was suggested by aerospace engineer Robert Zubrin in his 1996 book *The Case for Mars*. The plan: Astronauts would attach a nuclear thermal rocket engine to a 10-billion-ton asteroid (kind of like in the movie *Armageddon*). Controlled remotely from Earth, the asteroid would hit Mars with the force of 70 hydrogen bombs. The impact would raise the Martian temperature 3°F, which would melt a trillion tons of ice. This would add CO_2 to the atmosphere, triggering the greenhouse effect and melting the caps even more. One asteroid-bomb per year over 50 years could make up to 25% of the Martian surface habitable (temperature-wise, anyway). And scientists could then send their algae rockets to the planet's new seas.

Sadly, all those nukes would soak Mars in toxic radiation (so we'd better be sure there's no life there), and humans would have to wear air tanks for hundreds of years anyway. But no matter how we get there, Zubrin writes, the time to begin the journey is now. "We need a central overriding purpose to drive our space program forward. At this point in history, that focus can only be the human exploration and settlement of Mars."

SIMPLE SOLUTIONS

In Uncle John's Unstoppable Bathroom Reader *we wrote about some ingenious solutions to environmental problems, ones that make you say, "That's so obvious—I wish I'd thought of that!" Here are a few, plus some new entries that we found.*

M ONEYMAKER-PLUS
Problem: How can farmers in impoverished areas irrigate their crops without using electricity?

Simple Solution: A foot-powered irrigation pump

Explanation: Developed by Approtec, a nonprofit company in Nairobi, Kenya, the MoneyMaker-Plus has pedals just like a stair-climbing exercise machine. One person can pull water from a stream, a pond, or a well 20 feet deep, pump it to sprinklers, and irrigate up to 1½ acres per day. Approtec estimates that 24,000 MoneyMaker-Plus pumps are already in use, earning about $1,400 per year for farmers who'd previously earned less than $100 per year. The pumps help create 16,000 new jobs and generate $30 million of profits and wages annually. They're made from local materials (creating more jobs) and are easily repaired without special tools. Plus, they're lightweight (25 pounds) for easy transport, and, most importantly, they're affordable—just $38 each.

THE WINDBELT
Problem: Wind power can help communities that don't have electricity, but wind turbines are large and expensive.

Simple Solution: The Windbelt

Explanation: Shawn Frayne, a 28-year-old inventor from Mountain View, California, was visiting Haiti in 2004 when he noticed that many poor people were using kerosene lamps to light their homes. That's when he came up with the idea for a wind-power machine that doesn't require spinning turbines. Called the Windbelt, the prototype was made out of a kite: Frayne cut a piece of material a few feet long and strung it tight between two posts. Even a light breeze causes the strap to vibrate, which causes small magnets fitted near the ends of the strap to move back and forth between coils of copper wire. Result: an electrical current that can power small lights and radios. Frayne hopes that by 2010, small Windbelts will be providing power all over the world.

KENYA CERAMIC JIKO (KCJ)

Problem: In Kenya, most families use small metal charcoal-burning stoves—called *jikos*—for cooking. But they're terribly inefficient, and the price of fuel is skyrocketing.

Simple Solution: The highly efficient Kenya Ceramic Jiko stove

Explanation: The KCJ is a small, hourglass-shaped metal stove with a ceramic lining in its top half. It uses up to 50% less fuel than a coal stove—saving the average family more than $60 per year. The manufacturer, KENGO (Kenya Energy and Environment Organization), holds workshops nationwide on how KCJ stoves work, and even teaching people how to make them. The KCJ burns cleaner, reduces emissions, and costs only $3.

DIRT ENERGY

Problem: Homes not on the electrical grid can't run electric lights.

Simple Solution: Microbial fuel cells (MFCs)

Explanation: In 2007 Dr. Peter Girguis of Harvard University discovered that as microbes in soil digest organic materials, they produce a small amount of electrical energy. Girguis placed electrodes in a bucket full of soil, food scraps, and compost. He then connected the electrodes to a small circuit board and was able to power a small light. Girguis believes that once the kinks are worked out, each $15 unit could provide enough power to light a room...for a decade.

STAR FILTRATION

Problem: Arsenic contamination of groundwater in developing countries causes an estimated 200,000 deaths per year.

Simple Solution: STAR, a remarkably cheap filtration system

Explanation: In 2001 Xiaoguang Meng and George Korfiatis, scientists at the Stevens Institute of Technology, built a filter out of two buckets, some sand, and a tea-bag-sized packet of iron-based powder. This filter reduces arsenic levels in well water from 650 parts per billion (deadly) to 10ppb, the level acceptable to the World Health Organization. Cost per family: $2 per year.

Britain's government buildings emit more greenhouse gases than the entire nation of Kenya.

BLOWIN' IN THE WIND

Generating electricity is a breeze!

ANCIENT TECHNOLOGY

The Egyptians were among the first people to harness the power of wind. As early as 5000 B.C.E., they were using it to propel the world's first sailboats against the strong current of the Nile River. Much later (no one knows exactly when), the Chinese built the world's first true windmills for pumping water out of the ground. Or it could have been Persians in the Middle East who built the first windmills to grind up grain. Wherever they originated, by the 1200s, windmills had sprung up all over the European countryside. And as the New World was colonized, grain farmers brought the technology with them, making windmills ubiquitous across America for over two centuries. But by the 1930s, electricity had spread from the cities to the farms, significantly reducing the need for windmills.

No one gave them much thought after that, until the energy shortages of the 1970s gave people a taste of what would happen should fossil fuel reserves ever dry up. Suddenly, the need for alternative forms of energy became evident. And one of the most obvious was right there—just blowing, blowing, blowing.

HOW WIND POWER WORKS

Wind begins with solar power. Sunlight creates heat in the atmosphere, which creates *air turbulence*—hot air is lighter than cold air, so it needs to rise. The planet's rotational forces, combined with its mountains, valleys, and waterways, send hot and cold air scrambling all over the place, creating wind. In some places, that flow of air is continuous. And in the motion of the wind there is *kinetic energy*, meaning it can be transferred into the rotating arm of a wind turbine to generate electricity.

Turbines are comprised of three basic parts: the blades, a rotating shaft, and a generator. The blades rotate, which transfers energy to the shaft, which turns inside a generator, creating electrical voltage to generate current. (This is how most electricity is generated, except that, in most cases, coal or oil is burned to boil water into steam, and the steam pressure powers the generator.) Wind turbines come in two basic designs: horizontal-access varieties that look like propellers, and the less common vertical-axis turbines that look like huge eggbeaters.

Each of these designs relies on aerodynamics to efficiently capture kinetic energy from the wind. The blades are designed like airplane wings, with a rounded leading edge on one side and a flat edge on the other. This design takes advantage of a high lift-to-drag ratio—the blade is calibrated to take full advantage of the force of the wind, while minimizing the amount of turbulence created by its movement. (As a safety precaution, modern wind turbines also have braking systems designed to keep the blades from turning too fast and snapping off or tearing, protecting them from unexpected gusts.)

A location must have a consistent wind speed of at least three to nine miles per hour for a wind turbine to be effective. One of the best regions in the world for this is the Altamont Pass in Northern California. Home to one of the oldest U.S. "wind farms," Altamont boasts over 4,800 turbines generating 1.1 terawatt-hours of electricity per year, enough to potentially power more than 14 million homes.

ADVANTAGES

Wind power's greatest asset is that it's an infinitely renewable resource—as long as the sun shines, we'll have wind. Although it isn't currently the cheapest option (solar is pretty inexpensive as well), the costs are coming down as the technology improves. It's still cheaper than traditional electricity, costing about four cents per kilowatt-hour, versus eight cents with conventional coal-powered techniques.

One thing that makes wind power so efficient is that it builds exponentially, requiring only small increases in wind velocity to result in large increases in kinetic energy. It's also extremely clean: Just 1,000 kilowatt-hours of electricity generated by wind power—when compared to standard means—will eliminate the release of 440 pounds of solid waste, between 1,000 and 2,000 pounds of CO_2, and over 15 pounds of nitrogen oxides, sulfur, and other trace elements. It's convenient, too: Wind farms can exist alongside ranches, farms, even in the ocean—all that's needed is a stiff breeze.

DISADVANTAGES

That final advantage is also proving to be one of wind power's biggest detriments. Today's giant wind turbines are unsightly—especially when dozens or even hundreds stand side by side in wind farms, stretching along the highway for miles. (To Uncle John, they kind of look like scary sci-fi robots gathering in preparation for world domination.)

Aside from being large and imposing, wind turbines are noisy, too—which can make living close to one very trying. Plus they can be invasive, popping up like giant metal weeds that disrupt local ecosystems. The spinning blades are a menace to birds—especially where wind farms are erected along migratory routes. All of these factors have led to numerous and often messy disputes between landowners, developers, environmentalists, power companies, and the government.

On top of that, wind power only works when the wind is blowing, so there must always be a backup system in place for when the weather is calm. And then there are regions of the planet that just don't get a lot of wind. What all of this means is that wind will only supply *some* of our power needs; it will have to work in conjunction with other sources.

But where wind power has worked, it's worked very well.

THE HULL STORY

One success story is the small city of Hull, Massachusetts, a peninsula that juts out into Boston Harbor. With its sustained winds of 15 mph, Hull has long been known as "Windmill Point." In the early 1980s, the town erected its first wind turbine, which saved an estimated $70,000 in power costs until it was damaged by a windstorm in 1997. So the city's 11,000 people raised the money to build a replacement. The new turbine, installed in 2001, has saved Hull an average $185,000 in energy costs each year. A second turbine was commissioned in 2006, with four additional ones proposed for offshore installation. It's projected that these six wind turbines will one day supply all of the town's electricity needs.

It's uncertain how much power windmills will provide in the future, but in 2007, enough was generated in the U.S. to supply power to 4.5 million homes and stop 28 million tons of greenhouse gases from being released into the windy skies.

USER-GENERATED

One of the cool things about the Internet is that regular folks get the chance to speak their voice...often with hilarious results.

THE PLAN: In 2006 the United Kingdom's environment secretary, David Miliband, launched a Web site called Environmental Contract. It was in the "wiki" format, meaning that its content could be edited by readers. Miliband expected concerned Britons to contribute sound advice on how to fix the nation's eco-problems.

BACKFIRED: The site was hardly noticed in its first few weeks. But then, British political bloggers opposed to Miliband's "green slavery and forced muesli consumption" began encouraging their readers to post their "advice." Hundreds did, promoting such things as "laws against washing," "trustworthy and timely hen attacks," "Tony Blair masks," and "owl magnets." More than 170 helpful tips popped up on the page...until the site's editing function was blocked and the rude comments were removed. Miliband promised to unlock the controls, but as of 2009, he still hasn't.

THE PLAN: In 2006 Chevrolet invited visitors to their Web site to make their own TV commercials. They could choose a 30-second video that featured the Chevy Tahoe SUV driving through exotic locations, add a soundtrack, and type in written messages that would appear on the screen...just like a slickly produced commercial. All of the ads would be viewable on the site, and the best one would appear on television.

BACKFIRED: Most of the 20,000 entrants typed in favorable messages about the Tahoe...but a few thousand were much more cynical. Some examples: "Our planet's oil is almost gone. Maybe you should walk," "Here's the real weapon of mass destruction," and "How big is yours?" Each ad ended with "Tahoe—An American Revolution." When news of the spoof ads hit the Internet, more than 2.9 million people went to the site to watch them. Chevy got some press out of the fiasco, but mainly from newspapers such as the *New York Times* and the *Wall Street Journal* chastising the car company's gullibility. Chevy's marketing department kept the positive ads up, but quietly removed the negative ones.

TEDDY AND THE CONSERVATIONISTS

On page 45 we highlighted some of the green accomplishments of Theodore Roosevelt's presidency. Here are the stories of the men who worked with him…and inspired him to lay down the law to protect the land for future generations.

ROUGH RIDERS

The conservationists of a century ago were largely rough-and-tumble men who liked to hunt, fish, and take in the scenery from the back of a horse. Theodore Roosevelt counted some of these men as his friends and advisors, and was just as passionate about nature as they were. He famously camped out with John Muir in Yosemite National Park, had long discussions with naturalist and author John Burroughs in Yellowstone, formed a hunter's group for the conservation of wildlife with George Bird Grinnell, and made Gifford Pinchot, his closest friend and environmental adviser, his Chief Forester. Here are a few of their stories.

Gifford Pinchot (1865–1946). As the first head of the U.S. Forest Service, Pinchot managed millions of acres of the country's timber and water resources. Pinchot championed scientific forestry methods that ensured the long-term survival of natural resources, rather than destroying them for short-term gains. A populist like Roosevelt, Pinchot called for the "complete and orderly development of all our resources for the benefit of all the people, instead of the partial exploitation of them for the benefit of a few." He thwarted timber, mining, and electric utility companies by putting thousands of acres of timberland—and the water beneath them—off-limits to private use.

Pinchot was often a controversial figure, alienating wilderness preservationists on the "left" like John Muir (with whom he famously feuded) while battling it out with those on the "right" who sought to roll back his conservation initiatives. While continuing to head the Forest Service under President William Taft,

Theodore Roosevelt vehemently disliked the nickname "Teddy."

who was more conservative than Roosevelt, Pinchot became embroiled in a battle with Interior Secretary Richard Ballinger. Ballinger had reversed many of the Roosevelt administration's conservation rules, a tactic often employed by presidential administrations. Pinchot vehemently objected to these changes and not only denounced them, but also accused Ballinger of fiscal impropriety. Congressional hearings and a media firestorm ended with Pinchot being fired.

Pinchot went on to serve two terms as governor of Pennsylvania; helped found the Yale School of Forestry; established and served on many conservation commissions, including as honorary vice president of the Sierra Club from 1905 until '12; and wrote many books on forestry and timber.

George Bird Grinnell (1849–1938). Grinnell may be best known for his stories about the Plains Indians, including *The Story of the Indian* and *The Fighting Cheyennes*. Called by some the "Father of American Conservation," Grinnell rode along with some of the most important expeditions of the 19th century, including George Armstrong Custer's 1874 Black Hills expedition and William Ludlow's trip to Yellowstone in 1875. He also went on Edward Harriman's renowned 1899 voyage to Alaska, along with John Muir and John Burroughs. Among Grinnell's many accomplishments was the establishment of Glacier National Park in Montana, where a glacier is named after him. He also formed an early version of the Audubon Society to protect birds, and later in life was involved in the founding of the New York Zoological Association and the Bronx Zoo.

Grinnell was the editor of *Forest and Stream* magazine (later *Field & Stream*), and for decades used it to advance his belief in conservation. Grinnell, like Gifford Pinchot, was an early advocate of scientific forest and water management, which restricted the use of natural resources—a new and somewhat radical idea to most Americans in the late 1800s. Many of the environmental causes championed by the Roosevelt administration got their start as editorials by Grinnell.

Like his good friend Roosevelt, Grinnell was an avid hunter and outdoorsman and was alarmed by the loss of wildlife—especially fish, birds, and big-game animals—due to unregulated and unsportsmanlike hunting. In 1887 Grinnell, Roosevelt, Pinchot, and 20 others founded the Boone and Crockett Club, which worked to combine wildlife preservation and natural resources conservation with ethical hunting methods. Before becoming president of the United States, Roosevelt served as president of Boone and Crockett for six years, during which time he and Grinnell worked tirelessly to protect wildlife habitats in Yellowstone. Through Grinnell's efforts, unprecedented protection measures were passed by Congress in 1894.

John Muir (1838–1914). America's most influential naturalist, Muir believed that the only way to ensure the survival of the forests and waterways was to leave them completely untouched by man. This set him apart from—and occasionally at odds with—many of Roosevelt's inner circle.

But Roosevelt was a great fan of Muir and always listened to him, even if he didn't always do what Muir would have liked. Their most famous encounter was a three-day trip in 1903 to Muir's beloved Yosemite National Park, where they camped by themselves with no Secret Service agents. Muir convinced Roosevelt to incorporate more wilderness areas into the park, and the president later made Muir Woods in Marin County a national monument in honor of his friend.

Muir was a prolific writer of wilderness essays, served on many conservation commissions, and in 1891 helped organize the Sierra Club for the purpose of wilderness preservation. He served as its president until his death in 1914. Muir was also crucial to the establishment of Mt. Rainier National Park in Washington state, and a glacier is named after him in Glacier Bay, Alaska. Muir's greatest disappointment was the building of a dam that flooded the picturesque Hetch Hetchy Valley in Yosemite National Park in 1913 to create a reservoir for the city of San Francisco. Some believe that his grief over the loss of the valley may have hastened his death the following year.

John Burroughs (1837–1921). Though little remembered today, Burroughs is credited with popularizing the nature essay and establishing a "back-to-nature" movement among the growing urban and suburban middle classes that were booming in the late 1800s.

Burroughs's essays were read around the world and he became a celebrity, counting Walt Whitman, Muir, and Roosevelt among his friends. Though not a politician or activist, the 62-year-old Burroughs was invited on Edward Harriman's expedition to Alaska in 1899 along with Muir and George Bird Grinnell.

In his old age, Burroughs received prominent visitors such as Roosevelt, Muir, and Thomas Edison at his Slabsides cabin near the Hudson River in New York. Slabsides was preserved as a memorial after his death.

William L. Finley (1876–1953). This nature photographer and conservationist actively opposed the poaching of wild birds for their colorful feathers. In 1906, as president of the Audubon Society, Finley was a key witness in prosecuting Oregon milliners who were buying illegal egret plumes for use on women's hats.

Finely was also a key player in the expansion of the National Wildlife Refuge System. When President Roosevelt saw Finley's photographs of the Three Arch Rocks area on Oregon's coast, he created the first West Coast bird refuge there in 1907. The following year, the largest refuges to be established up to that time were created in Klamath Falls and Malheur, Oregon, again due in large part to Finley's photographs.

From 1911 to '30, Finley was Oregon's first State Game Warden and helped establish the State's Fish and Game Commission. Retiring in 1930, he spent the rest of his life writing, making films, and taking photos. After his death, the William L. Finley National Wildlife Refuge in Oregon's Willamette Valley was named in his honor.

*   *   *

A CONSERVATION PRESIDENT

"The days a man spends fishing or spends hunting should not be deducted from the time that he's on Earth. In other words, if I fish today, that should be added to the amount of time I get to live. That's the way I look at recreation. That's why I'll be a big conservation, environmental President, because I plan to fish and hunt as much as I possibly can."

—George H. W. Bush (1988)

NATURAL POLLUTION

Hey! It's not all our fault! Mother Nature's not so clean herself!

TOXIC SPONGES

Man-made toxic compounds can "bioaccumulate" in animals, sometimes to dangerous levels. One of these toxins is *polybrominated diphenyl ether* (PBDE), used to make flame retardants for products such as electronics, furniture, clothing, and toys. Several PBDEs have been banned because they were shown to have made their way from those products to the sea, where they're regularly found in fish and marine mammals, especially in whale blubber. But in 2008, researchers at Woods Hole Oceanographic Institution in Massachusetts studied the blubber from a contaminated whale—and found that some of the PBDEs in it *weren't* man-made: Some animals, including sea sponges, produce PBDEs naturally, perhaps to defend against predators. Further study is now underway to determine how much man-made versus natural PBDE is making its way through the animal kingdom.

OZONE WILDFIRES

Tens of millions of acres of forest, grassland, and prairie burn around the world every year in wildfires that are most often started by lightning. They release huge amounts of pollutants, including visible ones like smoke, soot, and ash, and others that aren't visible, such as carbon monoxide and hydrocarbons. Fires even contribute to the formation of dangerous ground-level ozone. A 2008 study by the National Center for Atmospheric Research in Boulder, Colorado, found that wildfires in California regularly caused ground ozone to rise to hazardous levels across much of the state, and in large portions of Nevada. Also, trees store small amounts of naturally occurring mercury in their leaves and needles, and wildfires release several tons of it into the atmosphere each year.

OILY VENTS

When an oil tanker sinks, or when an offshore rig leaks oil into the ocean, it's rightly deemed an environmental disaster. But oil also enters the oceans via seepage from natural vents in the seafloor and even cause slicks on the surface. A study carried out with the help of NASA found that in the Gulf of Mexico alone, more than 600 seep sites emit an average of 80,000 tons of oil every year. That's almost twice the amount that was spilled by the *Exxon Valdez* in Alaska in 1989. That doesn't mean that natural seeps are as harmful as human-caused spills, which are much more destructive due to the large amount of oil discharged over small areas very quickly. Most natural seeps, the report concluded, leak at a rate that is readily broken down and "digested" by the ocean.

RADIOACTIVE PONDS

Nuclear power plants receive their fair share of scorn from environmentalists. But a *natural* nuclear reaction, very similar to the the kind that generates power in a nuclear plant, once occurred at what is now a uranium mine in Oklo, Gabon, in Africa. According to geophysicists, about 1.8 billion years ago, the uranium-rich ground at Oklo was flooded with groundwater. When it became hot enough, the water boiled away—which caused the nuclear reaction to stop. Once it cooled down, water seeped in again—and the natural reactor started up again. This happened continuously...for about 150 million years, all the while spitting off radioactive waste. Scientists are studying the site today to learn what they can about the long-term effects of nuclear accidents and the storage of nuclear waste.

POISONOUS VOLCANOES

In one sense, a volcanic eruption is akin to our planet going to the bathroom—toxins are expelled from below the surface and spat into the atmosphere. These include CO_2, sulphur dioxide, nitrogen oxide, hydrogen fluoride, and "particulate matter"—tiny particles of ash and dust suspended in the gases. In areas where people live near active volcanoes, such as Kilauea on the island of Hawaii, "vog alerts" (short for volcanic smog) are issued regularly. Not only is the air harmful, but vog causes acid rain to fall. And according to the U.S. Geological Survey, volcanoes annually release 145–255 million tons of CO_2 into the atmosphere. To keep things in perspective, however, humans release about 30 *billion* tons of CO_2 annually...more than 130 times the amount emitted by volcanoes.

THE FROG IN THE MINE SHAFT

When coal mining was in its heyday, miners brought a caged canary into the shaft with them. That way, if the levels of harmful gases grew too high, the canary would drop dead...and the miners would hightail it out of there. For this article—written by BRI member and naturalist Matt Smith—think of planet Earth as the mine shaft, and amphibians as the canary.

PUDDLE OF LIFE

Early one April morning, while walking in the mist-laced cloud forest of Costa Rica, a scientist named Martha Crump rounded a bend and came upon one of the most dazzling spectacles she'd ever seen. In a shallow puddle of rainwater, no wider than a kitchen sink, a frenzied mob of Golden Toads were mating. More than 100 of the creatures—the males brilliant orange, the females blackish and spangled with red—had piled in to form a teeming, splashing, groping mass. Females who wandered into the pool were instantly set upon by a horde of desperate males, each one dead-set on mating with her. After the toads finished the ritual, they hopped off, one by one, into the undergrowth.

DISAPPEARING ACT

As an expert on reptiles and amphibians, Crump knew the importance of what she was witnessing. The Golden Toad was both an exceptional and rare species, its entire population strung along the narrow spine of a single mountain. Despite their gaudy colors, the toads had escaped all scientific notice until 1966—when they were dismissed by some as a painted hoax—and had rarely been seen since. They were thought to spend the vast majority of their time underground, emerging only briefly after spring thunderstorms to reproduce. This unusual species was literally putting all its eggs into one puddle.

But five days later, when Crump paid the puddle another visit, it was nothing but a dry dimple in the earth. Toad eggs lay in shriveled strands, some already fuzzy with mold. She returned the following spring with high hopes but could find only 10 toads.

The average American spends $100 more each year on shoes than they do on vegetables.

The next spring, there was only a solitary male, singing in vain. That was 1989—and that male was the last Golden Toad ever seen.

GLOBAL STORMING

As news of their disappearance spread, other stories emerged of disease, deformities, and sudden disappearances throughout the amphibian family tree. In California, there was the perplexing case of the Red-Legged Frog—the once-familiar species that Mark Twain featured in "The Celebrated Jumping Frog of Calaveras County"—which has now disappeared from some 70% of its former range. In Minnesota, a biology-class field trip in 1995 turned sinister when students found dozens of frogs with extra limbs, missing eyes, and other freakish mutations.

And in Australia, there was the Platypus Frog, first documented when it was found in a mountain stream in 1973. Its discoverers placed a few specimens in an aquarium and were stunned when one of the frogs calmly spat out six live tadpoles—from its mouth. The Platypus Frog turned out to be the first known vertebrate to use its stomach as an incubation chamber, a feat that had never been thought possible. The scientists rushed to plan a research program around the species—only to watch, over the next few years, as it seemingly vanished from the wild.

On the surface, the loss of a few species may not look like a disaster. After all, more than 6,000 species of frogs, toads, salamanders, newts, and caecilians make up the class Amphibia. But that number may have declined by more than 100 over the last few decades, and it's estimated that as many as 2,000 more may be threatened with the same fate. A growing band of scientists are making it their mission to find out why, and what it might mean for the rest of the planet.

A DOUBLE-EDGED SWORD

Amphibians might seem to be unlikely candidates for catastrophe. They've been around for some 400 million years, weathering asteroid strikes and ice ages, and their very name has come to suggest flexibility and adaptation. But scientists have found that some of their greatest assets have now become liabilities.

• One problem is their signature skill, the ability to move easily

---

As many as 165 modern amphibian species may already be extinct.

between land and water. Because their life cycle often hinges on success in both environments, a deterioration in either one can be fatal.

• Their permeable skin is an evolutionary adaptation that allows them to live in the depths of lakes (where the skin acts like a giant gill, absorbing oxygen) as well as in the open desert (where it acts like a sponge, sucking moisture). But a membrane that so easily absorbs the vital stuff of life can also absorb dangerous toxins and pollutants.

• Many amphibians lay their delicate eggs in shallow water, where they can now be scorched by ultraviolet radiation streaming through a weakened ozone layer. And many breed in spectacular, short-lived congregations, where diseases can spread like wildfire.

• They're able to breed and thrive in temporary habitats—but those same habitats are subject to rapid change and destruction.

Case in point: The Golden Toad—breeding in those barely-there mating pools—painted itself into a climatic corner. According to a University of Miami study published a decade after the toad's disappearance, global warming had spurred a series of exaggerated El Niño currents, which raised the cloud layer and turned the usually mild Costa Rican dry season into a struggle for existence. The toads' eggs dried out as puddles waited for refills that never came, and the toads themselves dried out without the life-giving mist soaking into their skin.

AMPHIBIOUS ASSAULT

But the trouble isn't confined to rare species. The Leopard Frog remains one of the most widespread amphibians in North America, but in parts of its range (like northern Minnesota, where that school group took its field trip), it's now difficult to find wetlands where many of the frogs are *not* grotesquely deformed. Science has yet to solve this particular mystery. Many think the culprit may be a wide array of factors, including UV radiation, hormone-mimicking pesticides, tadpole-infesting parasites, and more.

One of the most ominous of the amphibian afflictions is a mysterious fungus called the *chytrid*. Only recently discovered, it has been implicated in mass amphibian deaths in places as far-flung as Venezuela, Spain, and New Zealand, and is thought to claim its victims by clogging their skin and suffocating them. Although the chytrid's gruesome effects and sudden global emergence might suggest a sort of amphibian Ebola virus, there is evidence that frogs and toads have actually been living with it for decades, if not far longer, implying that the deadly outbreaks of recent years are a symptom of some deeper disturbance. Some believe the chytrid may have contributed to the extinctions of both the Golden Toad and the Platypus Frog and, in at least the former case, may have been accelerated by the changing climate, with subtle shifts in temperature and moisture allowing the fungus to flourish.

But the list of amphibian-killers is a long one. There's the disfiguring iridovirus that has devastated Tiger Salamanders. And there are more general threats, like deforestation and acid rain. And don't forget cars and trucks: One census of road-killed animals in Indiana found that more than 90% of the victims were frogs, toads, and salamanders. And scientists have suggested that this plague of troubles is anything but a coincidence. Instead, they may all be symptoms of the same underlying disease: an unsettling of the biosphere.

ACCIDENTAL ASSASSINS

When viewed from the historical perspective, the amphibians' current crisis looks a lot like crises they've weathered before, and they're likely to pull through it. After all, they pulled through the last such event, the asteroid strike that's believed to have killed off the dinosaurs. But the difference this time around is that the trigger may have been technology. One hypothesis for the rash of deformities in Minnesota suggests that farmers have been applying more fertilizer, which has been washing off into wetlands, which has glutted the water with nutrients, which has triggered explosions of algae, which has provided more food for snails, which have served as hosts for parasitic worms, which have then infected the frogs, with ghastly effects.

KERMIT'S DEFENDERS

Scientists and activists worldwide are working together to meet this crisis head-on. An international organization called Amphibian Ark has devised a half-billion-dollar plan to rescue the world's imperiled amphibians through captive breeding. But at this point, a huge part of their task is simply to convince people to care. The

Average fuel economy of the *Queen Elizabeth 2* ocean liner: 6 ipg (inches per gallon).

scientists' answer to that: Amphibians as a class are vital contributors to healthy ecosystems. Some forests hold more than 1,000 salamanders per acre, and one 25-acre wetland can produce more than 300,000 frogs and toads in a season. And each individual eats an enormous amount of insects and plays an integral role in cycling nutrients—functions that would be impossible to replace. Without the amphibians, the entire mix would be thrown out of balance—risking the well-being of animals *and* humans.

And then there are the possible health benefits that we're just beginning to understand. A chemical produced by the Leopard Frog has been suggested as a treatment for brain tumors; poison-dart frogs produce a painkiller 200 times as potent as morphine; and the Platypus Frog, with its uncanny ability to "turn off" its stomach acids to protect its developing young, was thought to hold promise as a model for ulcer control...until it went extinct.

Finally, amphibians may be doing us a great favor by giving us a preview of the horrors that environmental disruption could unleash. Could we soon see mutant humans with six eyes and seven limbs? The Golden Toad and its cousins may be remembered as the canary in the mine shaft, perhaps bringing enough attention to the plight of the ecosystem to make a major difference in their future. And ours, too.

* * *

GAME OVER

Do you own a video game console? On most systems, when you turn it "off," you're really flipping to a "standby" mode. If you unplug it when it's not in use, the energy and money savings are tremendous.

• If left on or in standby mode all the time, a PlayStation 3 will cost a family $134 per year in energy costs. If it's unplugged when not in use, the cost goes down to $12 per year.

• An XBox 360 cost $103 in standby versus $11 unplugged.

• A Nintendo Wii is the most energy efficient. If left on all the time, it costs $10 in annual energy costs. Unplugged: just $3.

At the University of Colorado's football stadium, over 80% of waste is recycled or composted.

HEMP MADNESS, PART I

*For thousands of years, hemp has been one of humanity's most versatile crops,
but over the last century it has also become one of the most controversial.
Here we attempt to weed out the facts from the fiction to find out why.*

THE MIRACLE PLANT

As early as 6500 B.C.E., people in what's now China utilized hemp fibers to make clothes and fishing nets. As hemp plants spread around the world, dozens of uses were found for it, from linens in Ancient Greece, to the oil in da Vinci's lamp, to the sails on Christopher Columbus's ships, to the string on Benjamin Franklin's famous kite, to the pages of the Declaration of Independence. In 1791 Thomas Jefferson stated, "Hemp is of first necessity to the wealth and protection of the country."

SO WHAT HAPPENED?

American farmers followed Jefferson's advice, and by 1850, there were more than 8,000 hemp plantations nationwide producing cloth, canvas, rope, and hemp oil for lighting and heat. But hemp production had a drawback: It needed to be processed by hand, a task performed primarily by slaves. In contrast, when Eli Whitney invented the cotton gin in 1794, it became possible to process cotton into fibers via a machine, which propelled it to the top of the cloth business. And when slavery was abolished in 1865, the work force needed to process hemp diminished. Finally, the rise of petroleum-based fuels began to replace hemp oil.

Hemp almost found new life thanks to the increased need for paper products, a side effect of bigger companies, more newspapers, committee meetings, etc. Up until the late 1800s, most of the world's paper had been made out of hemp, but not directly. It was recycled from worn-out sails, sheets, and clothes—most of which were originally made of hemp. Suddenly, the need for paper products dramatically exceeded the old-rags supply. Paper companies could either create huge hemp farms and wait for the first yields to come in—or they could harvest the nation's ample forests. The quicker, higher profit came from trees. So that's what they did.

IT'S A CONSPIRACY...OR IS IT?

That explains why U.S. hemp production fell out of favor in the U.S., but why is it illegal to grow without permission from the government? Because of hemp's association with another plant in the cannabis family: marijuana. But the exact reasons for the demonization of both plants have been somewhat muddied over the years. The most widely held theory says that marijuana, and hemp along with it—is illegal because of a conspiracy between businessmen and politicians. Most of the information for this comes from a sole source: *The Emperor Wears No Clothes*, written in 1973 by hemp activist Jack Herer.

Herer's villain: William Randolph Hearst. From the 1890s until his death in 1951, Hearst was one of the most powerful businessmen in America. At his peak, he owned 30 newspapers, several magazines, and even served in the U.S. Congress. According to Herer's theory, Hearst owned enormous amounts of timber land, and stood to lose billions of dollars if hemp replaced trees as the primary source for paper. In 1918, after a new method for the machine-processing of hemp was invented, Hearst used his clout to kill the plant.

To achieve this, Herer claims, Hearst focused his "yellow journalism" on marijuana use—the thinking being that if marijuana were outlawed, then the hemp industry would go down as well. Thousands of stories about "the killer weed" appeared over the years, with sensational headlines like "Marihuana Makes Sex Fiends of Boys in 30 Days!"

Hearst had a powerful ally in his crusade: the DuPont Company, known today as a chemical manufacturer. In the 1920s, DuPont was spending millions of dollars on research into synthetic fibers (which would eventually lead to nylon). Like Hearst, they stood to lose billions if the hemp industry wasn't eliminated.

TAXED TO DEATH

Herer's accusations go on to say that both Hearst and DuPont also exploited their long history of financial connections to the Mellon Banking family. In 1930 they convinced Andrew Mellon, then the head of the U.S. Treasury Department, to form the Federal Bureau of Narcotics (FBN). Appointed to head the department was Mellon's nephew, anti-cannabis zealot Harry J. Anslinger. Within a

year, Anslinger's anti-marijuana claims had so soured public perception of the drug that it was illegal in 29 states. But that wasn't
enough—marijuana needed to be illegal *everywhere*. So in 1937
Anslinger testified before Congress: "I believe in some cases one
cigarette might develop a homicidal mania." Result: the "Marihuana Tax Act," which levied a $100-per-ounce tax on cannabis.
Though it didn't technically outlaw it, the Act effectively prohibit-
ed the cultivation of cannabis plants of any kind, including hemp.

THE REAL STORY

While Herer's book has galvanized the pro-cannabis movement, in
recent years, a lot of holes have been found in his story. According
to critics, the hemp industry wasn't quashed because Hearst and
DuPont were threatened by it. Several of Herer's connections are
tenuous at best—in reality neither company gave a lot of thought
to hemp production. They were both making plenty of money.
And Hearst didn't create the anti-cannabis wave; he was riding it.

Today, the more widely accepted theory is that cannabis was
made illegal because of racism. In the U.S. at the turn of the 20th
century, minorities found themselves being blamed for much of
society's problems. And the popular perception was that blacks
and Hispanics were the predominate users of drugs. Prohibition
movements sprang up in churches, local city halls, and state capi-
tals. By the 1910s, the majority of U.S. states had passed laws
heavily taxing or outlawing heroin, opium, and cocaine, and in
1918 even alcohol was made illegal. This anti-drug sentiment continued through the 1920s and into the Depression years, when
marijuana became the target of choice. And Anslinger's warnings
further frightened the segregated nation.

One example of that "fright" came in 1936 when a small
church group produced a low-budget film called *Tell Your Children*,
which painted pot smokers as murderers and rapists. (The film was
rediscovered in the '70s and given a new name, *Reefer Madness*—
and is now known as an unintentionally funny cult classic.)

So basically, industrial hemp has been a victim of guilt by association. But today, it's almost common knowledge that hemp and
marijuana are not the same, so where are all the hemp farms?

Part II is on page 276.

LADY BIRD JOHNSON

*Many first ladies had a favorite crusade—for Nancy Reagan it was
the war on drugs; Laura Bush encouraged literacy. What did Lady
Bird Johnson, First Lady from 1963 to '69, do? She initiated
the largest beautification program in American history.*

PURTY LITTLE LADYBUG

P When Claudia Taylor was a toddler in Karnack, Texas, her
nanny often said she was "as purty as a lady bird." The name
stuck (even though the nanny was actually talking about ladybugs,
known as "lady birds" in Texas). In 1918, when Lady Bird was
only five years old, her world was upended when her mother died.
Swooping in to help raise the girl was her aunt, Effie Pattillo, who
encouraged her to go outside and explore. Lady Bird found solace
in the bayous of East Texas and developed a deep appreciation for
nature. "People always look back at it now and assume I was lonely," she later said. "To me, I definitely was not. I spent a lot of
time just walking and fishing and swimming."

Lady Bird also spent a lot of time studying. At a time when
women weren't expected to even go to college, she earned a
degree in history from the University of Texas in 1933, and then a
degree in journalism the following year, when she was only 22.
That's the year she met Lyndon Johnson, a congressional aide with
great ambition. He proposed on their first date; she accepted 10
weeks later. She set aside her professional ambitions to support her
husband's career, and it all came to fruition when Lyndon became
vice president in 1961. Two years later, when John F. Kennedy was
assassinated, Lyndon took over and Lady Bird became First Lady.

LBJ, LBJ, HOW MANY TREES CAN WE PLANT TODAY?

Johnson's presidency was difficult, both for the First Family and for
the country. The public was still in shock after Kennedy's death,
and Johnson's "Great Society" of social reforms became secondary
to the escalating conflict in Vietnam and the growing unrest of the
civil-rights movement. Wanting to do her part to improve morale,
Lady Bird started instituting programs to clean up the nation's
highways. "All the threads are interwoven," she wrote in her diary

An American home in 2009 contains more harmful chemicals than a chemical plant in 1909.

in 1965, "recreation and pollution and mental health, and the crime rate, and rapid transit, and highway beautification, and the war on poverty and parks. It is hard to hitch the conversation into one straight line, because everything leads to something else."

Mrs. Johnson's first act: addressing the crumbling inner city and lack of vegetation in Washington, D.C. In 1965 she sought out donors and volunteers for her organization, the Society for a More Beautiful National Capital. Some in the group wanted to plant trees, flowers, and shrubs in dilapidated areas; others thought the money would be better spent improving high-traffic tourist areas like the National Mall. Instead, Johnson used the more than $2.5 million she raised to plant thousands of daffodils, azaleas, pansies, and dogwood trees in *all* areas of the city.

HEAD OUT ON THE HIGHWAY

So successful were Johnson's efforts in Washington that the campaign went nationwide. With the help of her husband, she convinced Congress to pass the Highway Beautification Act of 1965. The idea was born during the many car trips the Johnsons had made between their Texas ranch and Washington, D.C. Every subsequent trip brought more billboards and more junkyards (both industries had grown quickly out of the "car culture" that defined postwar America). The Highway Beautification Act essentially banned these eyesores outside of "commercial and industrial" zones. In their place, the act provided for landscaping and the development of large tracts of wildflowers. "Some may wonder why I chose wildflowers when there is hunger and unemployment and the big bomb in the world," she said. "Well, I, for one, think we will survive, and I hope that along the way we can keep alive our experience with the flowering earth. For the bounty of nature is also one of the deep needs of man."

The Highway Beautification Act was just one of the more than 200 pieces of environmental legislation Johnson helped write or get passed. Others include the Wilderness Act of 1964, the Land and Water Conservation Fund, and the Wild and Scenic Rivers Program. In 1968 President Johnson gave his wife a plaque mounted with 50 pens he'd used to sign conservation laws. The inscription read, "To Lady Bird, who has inspired me and millions of Americans to try to preserve our land and beautify our nation."

"Flowers are like human beings—they thrive on a little kindness." —Fred Streeter

DRILL, BABY, DRILL?
PART II

In the first part of our debate (page 70), we covered the history of offshore drilling and the conundrum it has created. Now we head north.

ALASKA CALLING

In the 1950s and '60s, U.S. oil companies went searching for "black gold" in the largest state in the union. And in 1968 Richfield Oil hit the mother lode in Prudhoe Bay on Alaska's remote North Shore when it unleashed a 50-foot-high plume of natural gas. For production to begin, however, Richfield needed to build a pipeline to get the oil south. That took 10 years (8 to figure out exactly where and how, and 2 years and 21,000 workers to build it). In 1977 the 800-mile-long Alaska Pipeline finally reached the southern shore of the state at Valdez, where it fed ships crude oil destined for refineries in the Lower 48. Since then, the state's economy has been inextricably linked to oil.

But one inescapable fact about oil is that it's *nonrenewable*. Of the 25 billion barrels of crude that *were* in Prudhoe Bay—North America's largest oil field—only 2 billion remain. So what does an oilman do when a well runs dry? He starts looking for another.

WHERE THE BEARS AND THE CARIBOU ROAM

In the remote northeast corner of Alaska, there's a vast supply of oil located smack-dab in the middle of the Arctic National Wildlife Refuge (ANWR). But the area is federally protected, as are its populations of caribou, polar bears, musk oxen, and many other species. Just as it does with offshore drilling, the oil industry claims that the use of new technologies can minimize the environmental impact of drilling and that only a small percentage of the refuge would need to be developed.

Wildlife biologists disagree. They point to the Porcupine caribou herd (named for the Porcupine River). One of the main areas proposed for oil exploration happens to be the caribous' calving ground and nursery. When a female caribou is about to give birth, she finds a spot as far removed from human activity as she can. If

---

Worldwide, about 13 million people make their living from fishing.

drilling began there, the caribou would have to move their breeding ground, but there's nowhere else that provides the same ideal environment for their calves' survival. If ANWR is opened to drilling, the herd's ability to reproduce will be compromised. And on a larger scale, environmentalists believe that ANWR should be left untouched simply because it's one of the last truly wild places left in America.

THE PRICING PROBLEM

The oil companies have their own argument. A few animals might be disturbed, they say, and a few tiny bits of coastline might get developed, but opening up these areas will reduce America's dependence on foreign oil and keep gas prices low and stable. But the truth of that claim is also up for debate. In its "Analysis of Crude Oil Production in ANWR," the U.S. government's Energy Information Association (EIA) stated that "oil production is not projected to have a large impact on world oil prices." Another EIA study came to a similar conclusion.

According to the EIA, once offshore production starts (sometime around 2013), there will be an additional 200,000 barrels of oil per day coming from these wells. However, Americans use more than 20 *million* barrels per day, so the domestic supply will be increased by only about 1%. Similarly, the EIA estimates that recoverable oil in ANWR would supply between "0.4 and 1.2% of total world oil consumption in 2030." In short, there's not enough oil in ANWR to substantially impact prices.

PLAYING POLITICS

This battle is not limited to environmentalists and industrialists. It's a complicated political issue as well, with feuding between Democrats and Republicans, and between state and federal governments. This is especially true in Alaska, since its economy is 80% dependent upon selling oil to the rest of the country. In January 2009, shortly after Democrat Barack Obama became president, the Democratically controlled Congress drafted legislation that would forever ban drilling in ANWR. Alaska's governor, Republican Sarah Palin, said in a statement that she is "dismayed" about the bill and that ANWR is "the most promising unexplored petroleum province in North America."

But the pendulum has swung the environmentalists' way, and the arguments that Palin and the oil industry have set forth have been rendered moot—at least for now—because in the end, drilling in these sites probably won't make enough of a difference for U.S. gas-guzzlers to notice. Not in their wallets, anyway.

COMMON GROUND

So do the two sides agree on anything? Yes—that we humans need to wean ourselves from oil. It's not just about high gas prices, or about being dependent on foreign "frenemies"; many of the world's reserves are going dry. But long before that happens, they'll reach a point where they can no longer supply enough oil to sustain the global economy. When this will occur is uncertain—estimates range from 2040 to 2100, but it *will* happen.

In the meantime, oil consumption releases more and more greenhouse gases into the atmosphere. What effect that will have on the climate is also still being debated, but there's widespread agreement that the effect is considerable.

So, while the two sides agree that we must begin to shift our priorities to finding and utilizing safer forms of renewable energy, they disagree on exactly how and, more importantly, when. The oil industry says that it will take decades for alternative energies to meet global energy needs. And that until then, we'll need every drop of oil we can get our hands on.

But again the environmentalists disagree, claiming that there's no sense in risking more damage to the planet to get something that we need to stop using anyway. A wiser measure, they say, is to conserve as much oil as possible while making an immediate, worldwide investment in alternative energy technology. Whether or not we'll need the oil from increased offshore drilling and from ANWR depends on how soon this new technology becomes available…and how serious humanity is about saying good-bye to billions upon billions of internal-combustion engines.

So should we continue to cling to oil until the bitter end? Or should we plug up the drilling sites now and look to wind, solar, and even nuclear to power our lives?

The debate rages on.

Global water consumption is doubling every 20 years—twice the rate of population growth.

OF RATS AND MEN

Here's a classic tale about what can happen when humans try to alter a landscape. Even with good intentions, their best laid plans often go awry.

BACKGROUND
Macquarie Island sits in the Southern Ocean near Antarctica. It was uninhabited before British seal hunters discovered it in 1810, but the 50-square-mile island soon became a well-known hunting destination for its plentiful fur and elephant seals. And the hunters inadvertently introduced some new animals into the mix: rats and mice that had traveled with them on their ships. The rodents made themselves at home on the the the island, and started taking over. Their numbers grew so large that in 1818 the hunters brought in cats to eat the mice and rats.

BACKFIRE #1: Over the next few decades, as Macquarie Island became part of the Australian state of Tasmania, the feral cats ate more than just rats—they also decimated two of the island's bird species, driving the flightless rail and a type of parakeet to extinction. And the rats were still there.

BACKFIRE #2: In the 1870s, ships brought rabbits to the island so that if any sailors found themselves stranded there, they'd have something to eat. The rabbits did what they're known for, and by the 1960s, there were more than 130,000 of them hopping around the island...along with thousands of rats and cats. So in 1968 biologists introduced fleas infected with the *myxomatosis* virus, which is lethal to rabbits. That brought the rabbit population down to less than 10,000...and the hungry cats started eating even more birds.

BACKFIRE #3: In the 1990s, scientists started shooting the cats. They were all gone by 2000...which allowed the rabbits to make a comeback. By 2007 their numbers were again above 100,000—and they'd eaten more than 40% of the island's vegetation. So now the Australian government has announced a plan to rid the island of all of its rats, mice, and rabbits by poisoning them. It will take at least seven years and cost an estimated $24 million. (We'll tell you how it worked out in 2016.)

BOTTLED WATER BLUES

You're destroying the environment with that, uh, water. Sorry.

GUSHING FORTH

G In 1979 Americans drank about 400 million gallons of bottled water. In 2006 they drank 9 *billion*—an increase of more than 2,000%. That's 70 million bottles sold every single day...of something that's essentially free and safe to drink anywhere in the country.

Why? Bottled water is convenient, it tastes good, and it looks appetizingly crystal-clear in attractive, well-labeled bottles. And at about $1 per bottle, that refreshing treat is fairly cheap. Or is it?

DON'T JUDGE A BOTTLE BY ITS COVER

For 20 years, the bottled-water industry—the bulk of which is owned by Coca-Cola, Pepsico, and Nestlé—has been selling its product under the guise that it's premium spring water bottled at the source. But in reality, about half of the bottled water we buy is merely filtered tap water sold for hundreds of times what it costs to produce.

The upside: Tap water is tested rigorously by the EPA and municipal water departments; spring water is not. The downside: Bottled water is not well regulated or tested; there are only voluntary industry guidelines. So when you take a sip from a bottle, you do so at your own risk.

But the worst part about bottled water, by far, is the bottle itself. More than 2.5 billion tons of plastic are used each year to produce 45 billion single-use water bottles. It takes about 1.5 million barrels of oil to make them, enough to run 100,000 cars for a year. And only 15% of those containers get recycled. The rest—38 billion in total—wind up in landfills, where they may take hundreds—perhaps thousands—of years to decompose. And untold millions end up in the ocean.

THE HIGH COST OF NOTHING

One dollar per bottle may seem cheap, but if you drank the recommended daily amount of water (eight glasses) using only bottled

---

Largest oil spill ever: During the first Gulf War in 1991, Iraqi forces deliberately...

water, it would cost you about $1,500 per year. Via the tap: a grand total of 49 cents. Nevertheless, in the United States, bottled water is an $8-billion-per-year industry.

And as more and more people drink the stuff, water shortages become more common. Processing the water for bottling takes more water: two gallons for every gallon processed. Since bottling plants take whatever water they need from their local municipalities (once again, sometimes it's just tap water), this means there is less to go around, resulting in less for cities and farms.

CARRY ON

Water, bottled or otherwise, is still good for you, and bottled water is a convenient way to stay hydrated. But what do you do if you want to carry it with you but not buy it in a plastic container? There are a couple of options.

• **Reuse disposable plastic water bottles.** You can reuse the small ones once or twice, but that's it. They're made from #1 PET plastic, a thin, light plastic created for just this purpose—to be used once and then disposed of. They're difficult to clean, so there's a risk of bacterial contamination. And some of the chemicals used to make the plastic may or may not leach out, but they're far more likely to do so if they're heated, so the bottles can't go in the dishwasher.

• **Use thick plastic hiking bottles.** These quart-size containers—favored by hikers and cyclists, and manufactured by such sporting-goods companies as Coleman and Nalgene—may seem like a great option: They're endlessly refillable, and produce no waste. Unfortunately, before 2006 many were made from #7 polycarbonate, a plastic that contains a chemical called bisphenol A (BPA). Researchers discovered that BPA, a synthetic hormone, can damage human genes, a process that can lead to any number of diseases, especially cancer. The U.S. government is considering a ban on plastic bottles with BPA; in Canada, it's already been outlawed in baby bottles.

If you have an older hiking bottle, you can reuse it as a container for anything you won't eat or drink. If you really want a resealable plastic water bottle, try to find one made from #2 HDPE, #4 LDPE, or #5 polypropylene plastics. These are considered the "safe" plastics…at least for now.

STEEL AWAY

If you've given up on plastic altogether, but still want to take your water with you, the best containers are probably stainless steel or glass, provided you wash them often and refill them with water from the tap. In most U.S. cites, tap water is fine to drink. In some places—rural areas near agriculture or animal feedlots—the water might not be as safe, but all drinking water in the U.S. is protected under the Safe Drinking Water Act. If you're really curious, you can get a copy of your local water-quality report through local water utility companies or the EPA. The report lists all contaminants found in your region's water, as well as progress on water-cleanup activities.

TAPPED OUT

Depending on the contents of that report, or even if you just don't like the taste, you may want to purify your water with a home filter. They're sold in several varieties, some that attach to the tap or to your house's water line (to filter all the water that enters your home, not just the drinking stuff), and others that are embedded in pitchers that you simply fill up and keep in the refrigerator. And some fancy new fridges will dispense cold, filtered water right into your stainless-steel bottle.

And though most water filters and water pitchers are made of plastic, all of them put together don't come close to the number of cheap, plastic bottles piling up in landfills. But the message about this wasteful and unnecessary system does seem to be catching on—2007 was the first year in three decades in which sales of bottled water declined.

*   *   *

BEE RESPECTFUL

"If all mankind were to disappear, the world would regenerate back to the rich state of equilibrium that existed 10,000 years ago. If insects were to vanish, the environment would collapse into chaos."

—**Edward O. Wilson**

THE HUMAN LITTER BOX

*At the Bathroom Readers' Institute, we're proud of how integral
the flush toilet is to modern life. But alas, even that amazing piece
of ingenuity has some ecological drawbacks. Good news: There's
a new trend which uses old technology to eliminate the
"flush." What is it? The composting toilet.*

WASTE, WANT NOT

Every day, the average American flushes about 19 gallons of freshwater down the drain. That water—along with the bodily waste—then travels through a sewer. You have to pay for that water *and* for the use of the sewer system. Those costs total an average of $500 per year. Even worse, if some of that waste leaks out and infiltrates streams, lakes, and rivers, the cost to the environment comes in much more than dollars.

The composting toilet, however, requires little or no water and doesn't depend on a sewer system. It produces few if any bad smells or nasty byproducts, and actually creates something beneficial: compost. Here's the history and potential future of the composting toilet, plus a primer for building one yourself.

THE GREAT AGENT

In the 1860s, an English priest named Henry Moule was concerned that his family's cesspit was spreading disease. There was a cholera outbreak at the time, and dirty water was the culprit. So Moule built and patented the "dry earth closet." In describing his invention, he wrote, "Water neither absorbs nor effectively deodorises. The great agent is dried surface earth, both for absorption and for deodorising offensive matters."

Moule's dry earth closet was basically a wooden box with a hole on top and a bucket underneath. Located behind it was a hopper containing fine dry earth or ashes which were released in measured amounts when a lever was pulled, covering the contents and beginning the composting process. The resulting compost yielded "luxuriant growth of vegetables" in Moule's garden.

Most modern composting toilets vary little from Moule's original design, and they're fairly simple to construct:

- A metal bucket or plastic barrel located underneath a standard toilet seat captures the waste.
- A ventilation tube helps draw the smell and moisture out of the material.
- Sawdust, wood ash, or some other high-alkaline substance is added periodically to reduce moisture and kill pathogens.
- The barrel is removed when full and allowed to sit for three months to a year for the composting process to take place.

SIMPLE SCIENCE

The key ingredient to successful composting is oxygen. It encourages microorganisms, insects, and earthworms to break down the materials, in the process killing off harmful pathogens by reducing the moisture content. The less moisture, the quicker the composting. (Some toilets even have separate containers for urine, which can be an effective fertilizer by itself.) Adding holes or recesses to the bottom of the barrels can also help the drying process. Bonus: Organic materials such as eggshells, tea bags, coffee grounds, and vegetable scraps can be added to the barrels before setting them aside to compost. You can even add TP, as long as it's biodegradable.

When the transformation is complete, what was once "waste" is now useable, pathogen-free, mineral-rich agricultural compost. It can then be spread around shrubs and trees. (Some experts discourage using the compost for vegetable gardens, but studies have shown that if it's done correctly, compost is safe for agricultural uses. Study up before trying it yourself.)

THE GIFT THAT KEEPS ON GIVING

But what if you don't want to wait up to a year for your compost? Some advanced models utilize fans and heaters to give Mother Nature a nudge. You can choose among electric, battery, wind, and solar-powered models, most of which aren't much larger than a standard toilet. These advanced models are either completely contained, with the composting element and compost drawer under the toilet itself, or flushable, using a very small amount of water to send the "product" down to a remote composting unit in a basement or other location. They aren't cheap, though—costing between $1,500 to $4,000. But as it is with any new technology, the prices should drop in the years to come.

WATERLESS WORLD

In fact, the composting of human waste is proving to be so easy and inexpensive, not to mention water efficient, that these new toilets are being used in remote areas that don't have conventional plumbing, such as cabins, pool houses, state and national parks, highway rest stops, and construction sites. Unlike Porta Pottis, which need to be emptied periodically at great cost, composting toilets require very little maintenance.

Even businesses, industries, and an entire school district (Bainbridge Island, Washington) are starting to explore the composting alternative. One success story is the 30,000-square-foot C. K. Choi building at the University of British Columbia, which installed composting toilets in 1996. They're still operating...and use only about 132 gallons of water per day altogether, while standard bathrooms in comparably sized buildings use as much as 1,850 gallons.

If some forecasts about the effects of a changing climate are correct, then widespread droughts could lead to massive water shortages. But, judging by the dozens of composting awareness organizations out there, "dry earth boxes" will become more and more common over the next few years—in homes, schools, factories, and perhaps future space stations. Gardens and water supplies everywhere will reap the benefits.

*   *   *

OOPS!

For four decades, scientists have been researching ways to use old tires to make underwater reefs. One failed attempt was the Osborne Reef, constructed in 1972 off the coast of Fort Lauderdale, Florida. Inspired by smaller projects in Indonesia and Australia, the reef consisted of about two million old tires covering more than 36 acres of ocean floor. The assumption was that the mass of thick rubber would encourage natural reef formation. But unfortunately, too little attention was paid to how the tires were attached to each other. Result: The steel connectors corroded over time, allowing thousands of the tires to escape into the open sea. Some even damaged the natural reefs in the area.

WE'RE ALL GONNA DIE!!!

There's the "glass is half full" attitude, and then there are these folks.

"Give a man a fish, and he can eat for a day. But teach a man to fish, and he'll be dead of mercury poisoning inside of three years."
—**Charles Haas**

"The magnificence of mountains, the serenity of nature—nothing is safe from the idiot marks of man's passing."
—**Loudon Wainwright**

"For 200 years we've been conquering nature. Now we're beating it to death."
—**Tom McMillan**

"We're finally going to get the bill for the Industrial Age. If the projections are right, it's going to be a big one: the ecological collapse of the planet."
—**Jeremy Rifkin**

"There's so much pollution in the air now that if it weren't for our lungs there'd be no place to put it all."
—**Robert Orben**

"Man is a complex being; he makes the deserts bloom and lakes die."
—**Gil Stern**

"Human beings, who are almost unique in having the ability to learn from the experience of others, are also remarkable for their apparent disinclination to do so."
—**Douglas Adams**

"'Growth' and 'progress' are among the key words in our national vocabulary. But modern man now carries Strontium-90 in his bones....DDT in his fat, asbestos in his lungs. A little more of this 'progress' and 'growth,' and this man will be dead."
—**Mo Udall**

"We're in a giant car heading towards a brick wall and everyone's arguing over where they're going to sit."
—**David Suzuki**

"Man has lost the capacity to foresee and forestall. He will end by destroying the Earth."
—**Albert Schweitzer**

"Don't wake me for the end of the world unless it has very good special effects."
—**Roger Zelazny**

Worldwide, more bananas are consumed than potatoes and rice combined.

GREAT MOMENTS IN GREENPEACE HISTORY

*Here's a whale of a tale about how a small group of concerned
citizens grew into one of the world's most influential
environmental activist organizations.*

BACKGROUND

B In 1971 the United States government announced plans to conduct underground nuclear bomb tests on the tiny, uninhabited island of Amchitka off the coast of Alaska. Especially opposed to the idea were Canadian environmentalists, both because Amchitka is closer to Canada than to the continental U.S., and because the island was home to thousands of animal species, including the endangered peregrine falcon. According to environmentalists, the five-megaton explosion would kill most of the wildlife and trigger a tidal wave bound for mainland Canada.

The lead activists—Jim Bohlen, Patrick Moore, Irving Stowe, and Paul Cote—formed the Don't Make a Wave Committee. In 1972 they chartered a boat and traveled to Amchitka to "bear witness" to the nuclear test. According to reports, one of the members flashed a peace sign and remarked that they weren't after world peace as much as a "green peace." And with that, the organization had a new name. With support and publicity from the Sierra Club, the Amchitka protest made Greenpeace famous. But the group was unable to stop the tests, though the tidal wave never materialized. (Eventually, testing was halted and the U.S. government declared the island a bird sanctuary.)

Ever since, Greenpeace has earned the reputation as an aggressive environmental group. Though it began as strictly antinuclear, its reach now includes animal protection, anti-whaling, war protests, and reducing carbon emissions. Some highlights:

1972: In their ship the *Vega*, Greenpeace travels to the Moruroa Atoll in the Pacific, the site of French nuclear tests. The crew refuses to leave, so a French ship rams the vessel and the Greenpeace activists are arrested. The nuclear tests continue.

Good eating? By weight, most packaged cereals have more salt than potato chips.

1978: Greenpeace protests lead to the United Kingdom's banning of seal harvesting in Scotland's Orkney Islands.

1982: After years of "bearing witness" to the drastically reduced whale population, Greenpeace helps to convince the International Whaling Commission to ban whaling worldwide. However, Norway, Iceland, and Japan refuse to sign on.

1983: Greenpeace negotiates a moratorium on radioactive waste dumping in oceans with the London Dumping Convention. Ten years later, the body permanently bans the dumping of radioactive and industrial waste.

1985: Greenpeace activists take their flagship *Rainbow Warrior* (purchased from the British government in 1978) to the south Pacific for another round of protests against French nuclear testing in the Moruroa Atoll. While docked in New Zealand, a bomb explodes on board the ship, killing a photographer. The ensuing investigation concludes that the attack was authorized by the French government, prompting the minister of defense to resign.

1990: Following the grounding of the *Exxon Valdez* in Alaska, and the subsequent oil spill that killed thousands of mammals, fish, and birds, Greenpeace runs a full-page ad in the *New York Times* blaming the accident on Americans' oil consumption: "It wasn't the *Exxon Valdez* captain's driving that caused the Alaskan oil spill. It was yours."

1995: Due in part to two decades of nuclear protests led by Greenpeace, France, the United Kingdom, the United States, Russia, and China sign the Comprehensive Test Ban Treaty.

1996: After years of on-site protesting by Greenpeace, the French government permanently halts nuclear testing at Moruroa.

1997: Greenpeace funds and oversees the development of Greenfreeze, a refrigerator that doesn't utilize the ozone-depleting and carbon-emitting chemicals usually found in refrigerators. Today, there are more than 100 million Greenfreezers in use worldwide.

Only 0.2% of the water on Earth is in rivers, lakes, and wetlands.

1997: After years of lobbying world governments, Greenpeace celebrates the passage of the Kyoto Protocol, landmark legislation that sets legally-binding reductions on greenhouse gas emissions. By 2005 more than 150 countries will sign it, including China, Germany, Russia, Japan, South Korea, Israel, Canada, Spain, and the United Kingdom (but not the United States).

2003: Companies around the world that have adopted Greenfreeze technology or agreed to requests to stop using toxic chemicals in their manufacturing processes include Coca-Cola, McDonald's, Dell, Apple, Hewlett-Packard, Sony Ericsson, Samsung, Nokia, and Unilever.

2005: After one of Greenpeace's original members, Robert Hunter, dies of prostate cancer, his ashes are scattered on an iceberg in Antarctica during a Greenpeace mission to stop a Japanese whaling fleet.

2007: Six Greenpeace activists sneak into the Kingsnorth coal-fired power plant in Kent, England, scale down a smokestack, and attempt to paint British prime minister Tony Blair's name in huge letters. The six plead not guilty by way of "lawful excuse"—claiming that they wanted to shut down the station in order to defend property of a greater value (England) from danger (climate change triggered by coal-burning electricity). All six Greenpeace activists are later acquitted.

2009: At Greenpeace's prodding, Ireland becomes the first major country to ban the use of traditional incandescent light bulbs in government offices. The country switches to energy-efficient compact fluorescent bulbs.

GREENPEACE TODAY

With more than five million members and chapters in 20 nations, Greenpeace is now the world's largest environmental organization. Among the criticisms of the group are that they are too "radical" and "political" to be taken seriously by the mainstream. If their past is any indication, however, those criticisms won't slow them down at all. So look for Greenpeace to make a lot more headlines in the coming years.

In the open sea, a tsunami travels as fast as a jet.

THE ELECTRIC CAR, PART III: THE EV1

Throughout much of its history, the U.S. auto industry refused to admit that electric cars made any sense at all. Then, in the 1990s, things suddenly changed...for a while. (Part II of the story is on page 136.)

TOO MUCH OF A GOOD THING

The American passion for automobiles that blossomed in the 1910s and '20s was interrupted by the Great Depression of the 1930s and World War II. But as soon as peace returned and people had money to spend, the affair picked up right where it had left off. And more than a decade would pass before the relationship began to feel increasingly like a marriage that was going bad.

In the late '40s and into the '50s, American cars got bigger, more powerful, and a lot heavier, as automakers added tail fins and hundreds of pounds of chrome. The number of cars on the road doubled between 1945 and '56, but road-building more than kept pace as individual states built thousands of miles of new roads and the federal government launched the 46,000-mile Interstate Highway System.

BREATH TAKING

Road construction kept traffic congestion at bay for a time, but by the late 1950s, automobiles jammed the streets in many urban areas. And smog, which in many places had been only an occasional problem, grew worse each year. Laws regulating auto emissions helped improve air quality in the 1960s, but the number of cars on the road kept growing.

Cars of the late 1960s and early '70s used a lot more gas than they do today, and that made for even more pollution. In 1973 the *average* American car got 12 miles to the gallon. Such low mileage may have seemed fine when gas cost 38¢ a gallon, but the Arab oil embargo of 1973, followed by a second energy crisis in 1979, pushed the price of gas to nearly $1.50 a gallon by 1980.

Suddenly, the idea of owning a car powered by something other than gasoline didn't seem like such a bad idea after all.

In 1973 Shell Oil engineers designed a prototype car that got 370 miles per gallon.

BETTER LUCK NEXT TIME

Even before the oil embargo sent gas prices soaring, GM had been toying with electric cars—over the years, they'd built electric prototypes of the Chevy Corvair (1966) and Corvette (1976), and produced some tiny vehicles called Urban Electric Cars (1973) from scratch. Other automakers experimented with electric cars too, but they all ran into the same problem: Battery technology had not improved much since the days of Thomas Edison, 70 years earlier. Lead-acid batteries were still the only ones that were cheap and powerful enough to be practical, but the cars they powered still couldn't go very far, or very fast. And the batteries added 1,000 lb. or more to a car—they contained *lead*, after all—which meant that much of the energy they produced was cancelled out by the heavier mass they had to move.

GM built a few electric cars that were about the size of cars that consumers were used to driving, but they were too heavy for the batteries to get them very far. If GM made the cars small enough and light enough to give them a decent range, they were too silly-looking to win over the public. The Urban Electric Car, for example, was a tiny two-seater that looked like a gumdrop on go-kart wheels; it was barely half the size of a Volkswagen Beetle. Other automakers who made stabs at designing electric cars fared no better.

BACK TO EARTH

All the problems that remained to be worked out with electric cars in the early 1980s might have been solved if gasoline prices had remained high. But they didn't—the energy crisis was followed by an oil glut that sent gasoline prices into a long downward slide. By the time the price dropped below 90¢ a gallon in 1987, gasoline was cheaper, adjusted for inflation, than it had been in 1973. And the improved fuel economy of newer cars made the savings even greater. When the prices fell at the pump, much of the public's demand for alternative vehicles disappeared with it, and automakers happily went back to business as usual.

PUBLICITY VEHICLE

Gas was still very cheap in 1990, so it came as a bit of a surprise when GM president Roger Smith unveiled a new electric car at

Fake fir: In 2007 more than a third of all Christmas trees purchased were artificial.

the Los Angeles Auto Show in January of that year. Dubbed the GM Impact, the car accelerated quickly, had a top speed of more than 70 mph, and could run for 55–75 miles on a single charge. And it actually *looked* like a car that people might want to drive. Improved technology, which made the car much lighter than an ordinary one and maximized the power of the lead-acid batteries, had made the difference.

When Smith introduced the Impact, he proclaimed that in the relatively near future, GM would add electric cars to its lineup. But it's anyone's guess as to whether he really meant it. For years, auto executives had been generating publicity by touting "cars of the future"—atomic cars, jet-powered cars, Corvettes with gull-wing doors—that never actually made it into production.

YES, YOU CAN

Nine months later, the California Air Resources Board (CARB), accepting at face value Smith's claim that electric cars were just around the corner, issued a new regulation: By 1998, 2% of all new cars sold in California by GM, Ford, Chrysler, and the largest foreign manufacturers would have to be Zero Emission Vehicles, or ZEVs. And by 2003, 10% of *all* vehicles would have to be ZEVs. Electrics were the only kind of cars that produced no emissions, so GM and the other automakers would have to make them whether they liked it or not. Or would they?

NO, WE CAN'T

If you've seen the 2006 documentary film *Who Killed the Electric Car?*, you know that GM's Impact, later renamed the EV1, never made it past the consumer-testing phase. More than 800 EV1s were leased to customers in California and Arizona beginning in 1997, but that was as far as the program got. GM stopped making new EV1s in 2000 and killed the rest of the program in 2003, withdrawing the existing EV1s from the marketplace when their leases were up. All but a few of the vehicles were crushed and sent to the scrap heap.

Other auto companies followed suit. Ford, Chrysler, Toyota, and Honda had also launched their own electric-vehicle test programs in response to the CARB mandate, most involving conversions of existing models that ran on gasoline. (Ford's vehicle was a

Ranger pickup truck; Toyota's was a converted RAV4.) But none of these programs resulted in an all-electric vehicle coming to market, and nearly all of the test cars were destroyed.

In the end, all of the big automakers gave up on their electric-car programs and instead decided to pressure the California Air Resources Board into modifying its Zero Emissions Vehicle mandate. In 2001 CARB relented, altering the mandate to allow manufacturers to claim partial credit for hybrid vehicles like the Toyota Prius and the Saturn Vue.

J'ACCUSE

What happened to all those promising electric-car programs? Fans of electric cars are still arguing with the auto companies about it. And GM—perhaps because it launched its program with the most fanfare, or perhaps because it's made a fortune over the years selling gas-guzzling SUVs like the Chevy Suburban and the Hummer H1—has taken the most heat.

The few people who leased EV1s loved them. And many, along with other electric-car aficionados, accuse GM of deliberately killing a potentially successful vehicle to protect its core business of gasoline-powered cars. For its part, GM claims that while the cars were popular with a small and dedicated fanbase, most drivers rejected them because of their limited range of 55–150 miles per charge. The vehicles also had problems operating in very hot and very cold climates, which GM feared would limit the market to states that had moderate weather year-round.

Though GM leased the EV1s at a relatively reasonable price, the cost to actually buy one would have been around $80,000. Producing them in large quantities would have brought down costs, but GM feared they'd never be able to sell the car at a price that would attract customers and earn a profit at the same time. The other automakers must have had similar fears, because they scrapped their programs, too.

Will the electric car ever have its day? Read on— the final chapter is on page 263.

The North Pole is warmer than the South Pole.

GREEN BULLETS

Is there anything that doesn't come in "green" these days?

G REEN 3D GLASSES. If you're worried sick about the environmental degradation caused by 3D glasses, then worry no more. In 2008 Disney and Dolby 3D Cinema released the digitally animated film *Bolt*. People attending the film were given a set of 3D glasses that, Dolby claimed, were "reusable, environmentally friendly glasses that can be used hundreds of times." (Whew!)

GREEN BILLBOARDS. In 2008 printer and copier giant Ricoh Americas Corporation erected a huge, flashy billboard in Times Square that they call the "eco-board." Like most electric bill-boards, it uses a huge amount of energy—but unlike the others, this one creates its own. How? Attached to the eco-board are wind turbines and solar panels. A company spokesman said the eco-board will produce the equivalent of 18 tons of carbon-based fuel every year to operate itself.

GREEN BULLETS. Bullets are normally made with lead, and for decades hundreds of millions of them have been sprayed into the ground at military practice ranges. Not good: The lead dissolves into the soil and contaminates groundwater. So in 2000, the U.S. Army started using "green bullets"—they're made of tungsten, which doesn't dissolve in water. But not every green idea works out, which the army learned in 2006 when dissolved tungsten was found in the soil at Camp Edwards in Massachusetts. The base switched to plastic bullets for a while, but in 2008 the Army scrapped both the plastic and the tungsten bullets...and went back to lead.

GREEN MONEY. After failing in the 1980s to get people interested in the Susan B. Anthony $1 coin (it looked too much like a quarter), in 2000 the U.S. Mint tried again with the Sacagawea "Golden Dollar." Though it looked nothing like a quarter, it didn't catch on, either. In 2008 the government made yet another attempt at a new gold coin, this time with a green theme. Here's the pitch: "With the $1 Presidential Coin, every man, woman, and child will make a personal statement about the money they spend. The coin is 100% recyclable and lasts for decades, offering consumers—and Mother Earth—tangible benefits that are especially relevant today." One question: Who'd want to recycle a dollar?

GREEN SOCKS. Fox River Mills in Osage, Iowa, is a knitting factory that's been making socks since 1900. Since the 1970s, they've been on a mission to make them in the most environmentally friendly way possible. Aside from reducing their energy use by 30% and their garbage production by 50%, they also make socks with "Ingeo," a fiber made entirely from renewable resources... such as corn. (Hopefully the socks don't *cause* corns.)

GREEN BOMBS. Biochemists in Munich, Germany, announced in 2008 that they had developed a new type of explosive that is much less harmful to the environment than TNT. The new explosive is safer to handle, creates much less toxic gas, and isn't toxic, as TNT is. (It'll still blow things to holy heck, but in an environmentally friendly way.)

GREEN FONTS. In 2008 Dutch media firm Spranq started working on a eco-friendly font design. "After lots of late hours (and coffee)," their Web site says, "this resulted in a font that uses up to 20% less ink." They call it "Ecofont," and it has tiny holes in it—"like Dutch holey cheese," thereby using less ink than normal fonts. An example of Ecofont: I'm everything you always wanted in a font...AND LESS!

*　　*　　*

TANKED

In 1995 Sweden was experiencing an ethanol shortage, which all of their buses ran on. Since ethanol is basically a form of alcohol, transportation officials came up with an alternative: The buses were fueled with cheap red wine.

ECO-NUTS

How far is too far when it comes to making a difference?

NOT NEUTRAL
Switzerland's government has passed what may be the farthest-reaching animal-rights legislation in history. Among the new laws: Fishermen must take a "humane treatment of fish" class, animals listed as "social" (sheep, goats, yaks, etc.) must always be kept with members of their own species so they don't get lonely, goldfish must be kept in opaque fish tanks so they're not disturbed, and pigs are secured the right to take showers. Some Swiss animal-rights activists are still unhappy, though, because the government still allows cat-fur trading (some claim that, when ingested, cat fur may relieve the symptoms of arthritis).

STICKY SITUATION
In 2008 environmental activist Dan Glass, 24, was invited to London to receive an award from British prime minister Gordon Brown. But Glass had other ideas. He hid five pouches of quick-setting glue in his underwear, slathered it onto his left hand...and then glued himself to the sleeve of Brown's suit, demanding to know why the government wouldn't meet with residents opposed to an expansion of London's Heathrow Airport. Brown laughed and tore the young man's hand off his suit. Glass later said to reporters, "It really hurt." (The award he was there to receive was for his work as an activist.)

BEAUTY IS ONLY SKIN DEEP
PETA (People for the Ethical Treatment of Animals) often targets celebrities, but they saved their most creative scorn for Mary-Kate and Ashley Olsen, former child stars of TV's *Full House*. Because the twins refuse to stop wearing fur, PETA has an online game that lets players "Dress Up the Trollsens" with bloody animal carcasses such as "butchered beaver boots," "baby bearskin bloomers," and a "strangled skunk sweater." The game features dripping blood and gruesome sound effects. Most creepy: "Hairy Kate" and "Trashley's" bloodshot eyes follow your cursor around the screen.

ZERO WASTE

*How cool would it be if the next time your weekly trash pickup
came, you didn't have a single piece of garbage to put out on
the curb? How much cooler would it be if no one did?*

THE CAN-DON'T ATTITUDE

Ever since the first Earth Day in 1970, the "3Rs" have been an eco-mantra: By reducing, reusing, and recycling, optimistic Americans were going to save the world from getting buried under a layer of garbage. But nearly four decades later, there's more trash than ever—about 400 million tons of municipal waste are produced each year. The national recycling rate of 32%—meaning that Americans dutifully recycle about a third of the material that can be recycled—can't keep up with all that trash. Besides, only 20% of U.S. waste comes from homes; the rest comes mainly from manufacturing, construction, agriculture, and oil, gas, and mining extraction. Is there anything that can stop it? According to some innovative thinkers in industry and ecology, the answer may be what's called Zero Waste. And the concept is already being implemented in cities all over the world.

This lofty goal not only attempts to deal with the trash we have, but to systematically change the entire manufacturing system by designing products that don't ever need to be thrown away. This means taking the environment into account through every step of a product's life—the source materials, manufacturing and production, packaging and distribution, and, finally, the way we consume and dispose of it. All that's required is an entirely new mindset on the part of industry...and the consumer.

AN UNWELCOME BARGAIN

When you purchase a pair of scissors, a set of headphones, or anything similar, you get a lot more than you paid for. You also get a tightly packaged, sealed plastic bubble that's often twice as big as the product itself. In the case of a one-inch memory card for a digital camera, the packaging is big enough to hold a dozen of them. And once you pry the plastic open, there's a sheet of cardboard or

Styrofoam inside, and maybe some paper instructions, twist ties, staples, or more bits of plastic holding individual parts in place. Just take a stroll through any Wal-Mart and you'll notice there's more packaging on the shelves than product.

Why is everything packaged this way? For one thing, it makes items easy to display in the aisles of giant stores. It also means they won't break while traveling thousands of miles by ship from (usually) Asia, and then hundreds more miles by truck. Plus, the plastic bubbles are easy to make in automated molds in overseas factories with low labor costs and lower environmental standards. And compared to a lot of other packaging material, plastic is fairly cheap. It's an efficient process…as long as you don't think about the trash. If you do, then you learn that packaging alone accounts for about 30% of total municipal waste.

Then there's the product you're buying, which only lasts so long. The scissors are made of plastic with a cheap metal blade that will be dull in a couple of years (from cutting up all that packaging). It would cost more to have the blades sharpened than to buy another pair of scissors in another plastic bubble. Small electronics, such as headphones, are notorious for breaking easily and are quickly made obsolete by newer technology. All of these products have to be thrown away, just like the plastic bubble and other packaging, because none of it can be recycled, at least not without a lot of effort. In truth, only a small percentage of materials we use on a regular basis can be recycled. All the rest is garbage.

UPSTREAM, DOWNSTREAM

There's little we can do by ourselves to eliminate all this waste (though there are several tips in this book for reducing it). In fact, the manufacturing process in most factories produces waste long before the product even gets to us. And this system of production has been in place since the beginning of the Industrial Revolution. "Waste is the result of bad design," says Eric Lombardi of EcoCycle in Boulder, Colorado, the largest nonprofit recycler in the U.S. "The concept of Zero Waste leads upstream to the designer's desk, where waste needs to be designed out."

Supporters of Zero Waste argue that products shouldn't be valued for their low retail price or the fact that they're a "new and improved" version of something that was introduced two years earlier. Instead, they should be valued for their conservation of nonrenewable resources such as energy and water; by their minimal packaging, long product life, and nontoxic components; by their ability to be reused or refurbished; and by their recyclability if they can't be reused. The last resort should be throwing something away in a landfill.

EPR AND EPP

There are two key points to Zero Waste. The first is called *extended product responsibility* (EPR), commonly known as "producer takeback" programs. In an EPR system, the manufacturer takes back its product at the end of its life cycle and refurbishes or recycles it. Also, governments set environmentally sustainable standards for products so they're designed to produce less waste in the first place. Though the burden is on the manufacturer, the consumer plays an active role, too, by refusing to purchase products that aren't made to last.

The second part of Zero Waste is *environmentally preferable purchasing* (EPP). This component is aimed at businesses and governments that purchase vast amounts of products, ranging from copy machines and copy paper to cars, trucks, and light bulbs. Federal, state, and local governments alone buy about $750 billion worth of goods and services per year, and that doesn't even include the military. Colleges, universities, hospitals, corporations, and small businesses also wield hundreds of billions of dollars in purchasing power. What if they all insisted that the things they buy be environmentally friendly? Or what if they were required by law to use green products?

Institutional EPP programs—the few that exist—buy products that are made with the fewest nonrenewable resources, are the least harmful to the environment, and produce the least waste. The government standardizes the criteria for EPP, and the purchasing volume of large and small institutions reduces the overall cost of greener products. And once green products are used in institutions, they often find their way into retail stores. EPP programs are largely responsible for the recent popularity of such things as nontoxic cleaning products, recycled paper, and energy-efficient light bulbs.

All natural: A cathedral in the Czech Republic has a chandelier made of human bones.

A WOK IN THE PARK

Another component of Zero Waste is the Eco Park, a variation on those sprawling industrial parks that exist in virtually every town and city. What if, instead, they were open-air markets entirely dedicated to recycled stuff? An ideal Eco Park would have a central recycling center for cans, glass, plastic, and paper, and even food and yard waste, which would be turned into compost and sold to local parks and recreation departments as fertilizer.

Then there'd be another "shop" where you could drop off construction debris like concrete and wood, which could be sold to local construction companies or furniture makers. You'd find repair and resale shops for clothes, housewares, books, and music, plus a fix-it shop for bicycles, lamps, electronics, furniture, etc. They might incorporate "lending libraries" for seldom-used items—just imagine going to the Tool Library to borrow a power drill, or to the Kitchen Library for a wok. Or how about a Creative Reuse Center that collects yarn, paper clips, fabrics, or CD discs for use by artists, schools, or community crafts groups?

Urban Ore in Berkeley, California, is a living model for the Zero Waste Eco Park. Known as the ultimate salvage store, Urban Ore collects and resells old wood and construction materials, appliances, sporting goods, and anything else people want to get rid of—even the kitchen sink. Occupying three acres in an old steel mill, Urban Ore carries a dizzying array of home-improvement items, with 28 different types of doors alone. Less than 5% of the 5,000 tons of materials they process each year goes to the landfill.

DIVIDING BY ZERO

So is Zero Waste just a pipe dream? Not at all—it's become an official goal in the cities of San Francisco, Seattle, Austin, Toronto, Vancouver, Buenos Aires, and Canberra, Australia, as well as the entire nations of Scotland and New Zealand. Organizations like Sierra Club, major car companies, and even Wal-Mart have jumped on the bandwagon. San Francisco's goal is to reach Zero Waste by the year 2020. It now keeps 70% of its garbage (more than 1,367,000 tons annually) out of landfills. The city has also banned plastic grocery bags and the sale of bottled water. And as part of its successful "Fantastic 3" recycling program, food scraps from more than 1,800 restaurants are collected and made into

"Four-Course Compost," a rich fertilizer that's sold to northern California vineyards. Wines from these grapes are then sold in local restaurants. So the compost not only enriches the local soil, but the local economy, too.

MINIMALISTS

• Wal-Mart and Rocky Mountain Recycling teamed up to create a recycling project that's not only used at Wal-Marts, but soon may be in lots of other stores as well. Machines in Wal-Mart stores crush together plastics like shrink-wrap, apparel bags, and plastic hangers and flatten them into a square layer. Then they crush paper and cardboard into two more layers, placing one under and one on top of the plastic layer. The result: what's known as a Plastic Sandwich Bale. The bales are shipped to recyclers (it's easier to ship waste plastic when it's crushed between two sturdier layers), who separate the layers and sell the sorted material—at a profit—to companies that use it instead of virgin materials at much less cost and environmental impact.

• Garbage companies are also getting the message. Waste Management, one of the biggest trash-hauling companies in the country and once an opponent of Zero Waste, is now becoming one of the U.S.'s biggest recycling companies. Their new division, Upstream, designs Zero Waste and other waste-reduction plans for businesses. And Casella Waste Systems now has five power plants in the Northeast that generate electricity from recycled landfill gas.

• Kraft Foods is turning used whey, a by-product of the manufacture of Philadelphia Cream Cheese, into biogas, hoping to replace a third of the natural gas they use for energy—equivalent to what it takes to power 2,600 homes.

• Dell Computers, though initially reluctant to "take back" any of their computers for recycling, now has "the best policy of any global electronics company, period," says Robin Schneider of the Texas Campaign for the Environment. The service is free, whether you buy another computer from them or not.

• And finally, a company called Dreamscapes has a recycling program for used or broken sex toys. Anyone can mail in items, and Dreamscapes disassembles them into base materials—including rubber, silicone, plastic, metal, and batteries—and sells them to companies that recycle or reuse them. Eeew-la-la!

UN-ENDANGERED

The ultimate goal of putting animals on the Endangered Species List is to one day get them off of there. Here are some success stories.

SPECIES: The Key deer. Found only on a few islands in the Florida Keys, it's a subspecies of the much larger white-tailed deer that became isolated on the small marine islands about 10,000 years ago. Over the millennia, it adapted into a unique species: Whereas white-tails can weigh 400 pounds, Key deer top out at 80, and they stand just 30 inches high at the shoulder. They even developed the ability to survive on saltwater for short periods of time when freshwater is unavailable—something biologists still don't understand.

THREAT: Because of their small habitat size, there were probably only a couple thousand Key deer on the islands at the best of times. In the late 1800s, colonizing Europeans started hunting them. By the 1940s, there were fewer than 50 remaining.

PLAN: Like so many other recovery stories, the Key deer's was long and slow. It began in 1939, when hunting them became illegal. Then, in 1957, the National Key Deer Refuge was established, and in 1967, the species received federal protection, saving areas of their island habitat from development.

THE RETURN: By 1974 Key deer numbers had risen from 50 to more than 400. Today there are more than 800, and the population continues to grow slowly. They're still on the Endangered Species List, but considering how close they were to extinction, this is a remarkable success story for conservationists.

SPECIES: The whooping crane, North America's tallest bird, reaching five feet in height

THREAT: In the early 1800s, there were about 20,000 whooping cranes migrating all the way from the Arctic down to Mexico. After settlers destroyed much of the birds' habitat, by 1870 there were just 1,400 whooping cranes left. By 1941 only 15 remained.

THE PLAN: In 1922 the Canadian government established Wood Buffalo National Park in far northern Alberta to protect the endangered Wood buffalo. Fortunately, it was also the summer

---

nesting ground of the last whooping crane flock. In 1937 the U.S. Congress established the Aransas National Wildlife Refuge in Texas to protect that flock's wintering ground. In 1967 the U.S. Fish and Wildlife Service started a recovery program, raising birds in captivity and reintroducing them to the wild, and in 1973, the whooping crane was protected under the Endangered Species Act.

THE RETURN: Whooping cranes are by no means safe, nor is their recovery close to finished—but the fact that they've rebounded from a total of 15 left is amazing. Today there are around 380 whooping cranes in the wild, with another 140 in captivity.

SPECIES: The Big Bend gambusia, a tiny freshwater fish discovered in West Texas in 1929 living in just two spring-fed ponds

THREAT: Although Big Bend National Park was established in the area in 1944, by 1956 development of the park and the introduction of nonnative fishes, along with natural events such as flooding and unusually cold winters, had reduced gambusia numbers to a few dozen in just one pond. By 1960 they were gone completely.

THE PLAN: Luckily, in 1956 wildlife officials had captured 29 gambusia, but only three survived—two males and one female.

THE RETURN: Those three fish successfully mated in captivity, and their young were reintroduced into three artificially fed ponds. Today, there are more than 50,000 gambusias in the park.

SPECIES: The bald eagle, the U.S. national symbol

THREAT: Prior to the arrival of Europeans, there were more than 250,000 bald eagles in North America. When the bird was named the U.S. national symbol in 1782, there were more than 75,000 mating pairs in the Lower 48 states. Habitat destruction, hunting, and the pesticide DDT steadily dropped the bald eagle's numbers. By the 1960s, there were fewer than 500 pairs.

THE PLAN: In 1940 Congress passed the Bald Eagle Protection Act, making it illegal to capture, sell, or kill eagles; in 1967 Congress passed legislation that protected their habitat; in 1972 DDT was banned; and in 1973 the bald eagle became the first species protected under the Endangered Species Act. In the 1990s, U.S. Fish and Wildlife agents began trying a more direct approach: They removed eggs from eagle nests, prompting the mother eagle to mate again and lay another batch which she would raise while the biologists raised the batch they took. When old enough, the captive-raised eagles were released into the wild to join their brothers and sisters.

RECOVERY: By the 1990s, there were more than 5,000 nesting pairs of bald eagles in the Lower 48, and the bird's federal status was reduced from "endangered" to "threatened." And in June 2007, they were taken off the list altogether. Delisting species is often a controversial move, but in the case of bald eagles, it was celebrated as a major conservation success. As of today, bald eagle numbers have grown to more than 10,000 mating pairs. (Uncle John's note: While this entry was being written, a bald eagle landed in a tree across the street from the BRI!) ·

SPECIES: The aptly named Virginia big-eared bat (its ears really are quite big), found mainly in the Appalachian Mountains, in the region's numerous limestone caves

THREAT: Once numbering in the hundreds of thousands, they sharply declined in the 20th century due mostly to pesticide contamination, but also because more and more people were entering their caves. Disturbance by humans during hibernation months causes bats to lose the fat they've built up to survive the winter, and often leads to starvation. And disturbing the females with young during breeding months can cause entire colonies to abandon their caves—leaving their young behind to die. By 1979 there were only about 3,500 left in just a handful of caves.

THE PLAN: Since the 1980s, the Virginia Cave Board has educated people to stay away from the caves, and even closed some to the public during hibernation and breeding months.

THE RETURN: The big-eared bat is still on the endangered list, but today there are an estimated 19,000 living in hundreds of caves in the region, and protection of the species continues.

EXTRA: In 2005 the Virginia big-eared bat was named the official state bat. Along with his signature on the legislation, Governor Mark Warner added a little poem he had written:

> We have a state dog and a fish and a bird.
> And of the fossil I'm sure you have heard.
> So why not a bat?
> What's wrong with that?
> The state beverage is no more absurd.

LESSONS OF ANIMALS

We can learn a lot from those with claws, paws, beaks, fins, and antennae.

"Animals are such agreeable friends; they ask no questions, they pass no criticisms."

—George Eliot

"There is nothing in which the birds differ more from man than the way in which they can build and yet leave a landscape as it was before."

Robert Lynd

"An ant on the move does more than a dozing ox."

—Lao Tzu

"If we treated everyone we meet with the same affection we bestow upon our favorite cat, they, too, would purr."

—Martin Delany

"Horse sense is the thing a horse has which keeps it from betting on people."

—W. C. Fields

"The frog does not drink up the pond in which he lives."

—American Indian proverb

"By gnawing through a dike, even a rat may drown a nation."

—Edmund Burke

"You can't be suspicious of a tree, or accuse a bird or a squirrel of subversion, or challenge the ideology of a violet."

—Hal Borland

"All of the animals except for man know that the principle business of life is to enjoy it."

—Samuel Butler

"Mosquitoes remind us that we are not as high up on the food chain as we think."

—Tom Wilson

"From the oyster to the eagle, from the swine to the tiger, all animals are to be found in men and each of them exists in some man, sometimes several at the time. Animals are nothing but the portrayal of our virtues and vices made manifest to our eyes, the visible reflections of our souls."

—Victor Hugo

"The best thing about animals is that they don't talk much."

—Thornton Wilder

"Birds sing after a storm; so why shouldn't we?"

—Rose F. Kennedy

As you're reading this, there are about 1,800 thunderstorms taking place on Earth.

ICE, ICE MAYBE

Here's an adventure that will take you from the top (and bottom) of the world to the slide of a microscope.

R AIDERS OF THE LOST ICE
By day, Lonnie Thompson is a quiet, ordinary-looking college professor with big glasses from Columbus, Ohio. But for a few months out of the year, Thompson becomes the "Indiana Jones of scientists." Only, Thompson doesn't go after artifacts; he studies glaciers, and is considered the world's leading glaciologist. Since the 1970s, he's led more than 50 expeditions to Earth's most remote places, including some where no human footprints have ever been before. When Thompson heads out on a trip, he packs ice axes, snowsuits, crampons, a giant solar-powered drill, and about six tons' worth of other equipment. He then assembles a dedicated team of humans, mules, yaks, or whatever else is available...and climbs to the limits of human endurance.

One typical adventure: During an expedition in Peru, on which Thompson set a world record for a high-altitude stay—53 days at 20,000 feet—a sudden blast of wind sent Thompson's tent, with him inside, skidding toward a 10,000-foot precipice. He saved himself by grabbing an ax and driving it through the tent floor into the ice. This was nothing new: He regularly evades avalanches, crawls across the edge of deep crevasses, and weathers hurricane-like conditions while dealing with frostbite, altitude sickness, and scathing sunburns. And he suffers from asthma. And he has a heart defect.

But Thompson is just one of dozens of intrepid researchers who study long, narrow cores of ice, each containing a climate record spanning tens of thousands of years, that are extracted delicately, at tremendous expense and effort, from the world's dwindling glaciers. And with Earth's present climate lurching into uncharted territory, its past climate has never been more relevant.

THE ICE CORE SAMPLE'S STORY
Just as tree wood contains rings marking seasonal changes in its growth, ice sheets form faint but visible layers as the seasons pass.

Summer snow has a subtly different texture from winter snow, and as they're compacted by subsequent snowfalls, the two types of snow settle into alternating bands that can be counted for a rough estimate of age. Observing the width of each layer can reveal, in general terms, how much snow fell that season. But the secrets of the ice don't end there. "Ice will archive anything that gets trapped by it," says Thompson.

Each snowfall, like each snowflake, is unique and forms a distinctive molecular signature. Each layer accumulates traces of dust and chemicals and, as it falls and settles, traps tiny pockets of air. All of these things are buried by the next season's snow and pressed into ice. Traces of dust may indicate ancient desert storms blown in from halfway around the world; grains of pollen preserve the identity of long-lost plants; methane levels reveal the range of global wetlands; ash bears witness to great volcanic eruptions; and traces of metal iridium serve as the calling cards of meteor strikes. In more recent times, an unsettling record of pollution from human industry has built up, layer upon layer, as have radioactive signals from bomb tests and Chernobyl. An experienced ice reader (with a lab full of equipment) can read a core like a history book.

And there are still more secrets that, if fully unlocked, might give us a vital leg up on one of the most critical challenges of our time. To find the most reliable, most detailed, and longest record of the planet's past climate, you have to travel to the most forbidding study site of them all: Antarctica.

THE BOTTOM OF THE WORLD

Antarctica is a land of paradox—it's the largest, most barren desert on Earth and holds more than two-thirds of the planet's freshwater in its ice sheet. Miles thick in places, the ice sheet preserves an unparalleled record of hundreds of thousands of years of global change. Buried within that record are countless historical lessons with modern-day relevance—including, perhaps, an answer to the biggest question of all: What happens to the climate when the atmosphere is choked with greenhouse gases?

If you really want to get away from it all, you couldn't do much better than the Vostok Station. In the middle of Antarctica's blank interior, hundreds of miles from the nearest evidence of civilization, Vostok consists of a handful of homely, mismatched

---

If you want a plastic bag at a store in Ireland, it costs 15 cents extra (19¢ U.S.).

buildings—some abandoned and covered by snow—and has an international population of scientists that fluctuates seasonally between about a dozen and two dozen. It's officially the coldest place on Earth, with a record low of –130°F, and among the driest: Precipitation averages about a fifth of an inch per year. Situated on a vast, towering plateau, across which the wind regularly howls at up to 50 mph, Vostok sits in air so thin that its altitude of 11,000 feet feels more like 16,000. But, despite these challenges, the station's tenacious residents have managed to produce one of the most eagerly anticipated—and universally renowned—scientific findings in recent history.

INCONVENIENT EVIDENCE

Anyone who has seen the 2006 global-warming documentary *An Inconvenient Truth* will remember a jagged graph showing temperatures and carbon dioxide levels over the last several hundred thousand years, with the two marching in virtual lockstep across the screen. Especially alarming are the sudden peaks and chasms in the temperature graph, which fit snugly into the corresponding fluctuations in greenhouse gases; these represent global swings of 10 or even 20°F sweeping across the planet every 100,000 years or so and plunging it into or out of ice ages. CO_2 concentrations over these periods never climbed above the threshold of 300 parts per million. But they're well over that level now—humans shattered the record in the course of a few decades.

It's a stunning graphic with sweeping ramifications. And how did scientists arrive at all the data for this graph? By studying the ice in a Vostok core sample that dates back more than 400,000 years. The CO_2 readings were relatively straightforward, if mindbendingly difficult to measure: The scientists had to extract the air from the microscopic bubbles trapped in each razor-thin layer and count the gas molecules in each with the help of some highly sophisticated equipment.

The temperature readings required even fancier footwork. Although a major infusion of math is required, decoding oxygen ratios in those same ice samples has allowed climatologists to reconstruct temperatures over astounding stretches of history. But even the 400,000-year time machine at Vostok was about to be eclipsed.

CONFIRMATION

At a similar Antarctic site, named Dome C, a European team embarked on a drilling project of their own. The result, the EPICA core (the "European Project for Ice Coring in Antarctica"), studied the temperature and CO_2 records even farther back—an additional 320,000 years. The good news? During the stretch in which they overlap, the EPICA and Vostok data line up nicely, lending credibility to the ice corers' methods and models. The bad news? Nowhere in either graph can a precedent be found for today's predicament.

Although the EPICA core can't serve as a magic mirror in which we can read our future, it may help to narrow down our predictions. One unsettling feature of the Vostok temperature graph is the narrowness of the spikes; the balmy periods between ice ages have always been fleeting and fragile. Pop-culture interpretations like the movie The Day After Tomorrow have milked this grim notion for all it's worth, conjuring a near future in which we reach a tipping point and teeter off into a global winter. Yet further back in the EPICA data, scientists claim to have found a better analogy for today's situation, a period when warm stretches were milder and longer, suggesting that we may have more interglacial time left than we'd thought. But, as the EPICA team points out, that's assuming the climate is simply left to run its natural course. If it's not—and so far, it's not—this is far from a safe bet.

Despite the efforts of ice hunters around the world, many uncertainties remain in the climate record and its interpretation. The most notorious involves the chicken-and-egg question about greenhouse gases and temperature: They seem to be locked into parallel tracks, but which is controlling the other? Do infusions of CO_2 (along with methane and other gases) trigger hot spells, or does a rising thermometer somehow tip the scales in favor of a greenhouse atmosphere? There are few more crucial questions with regard to predicting our modern climate's next move, but the EPICA and Vostok cores aren't enough to sort it out. Part of the problem is that they were collected in bone-dry environments, where each year's snowfall is a mere dusting that leaves very little actual material to test.

FINAL EXAM

That's why a new project, funded by the National Science Foundation, has set up shop on the West Antarctic Ice Sheet Divide, an oasis compared to Vostok and situated close enough to the coast that clouds from the Southern Ocean roll in to deliver a respectable amount of rain each year. The ice there is rich with detail, and although the core won't be as long as others—it goes back perhaps only 100,000 years—it will allow a closer look than ever before at the fine-scale variations of past climate. The crew also has an ambitious plan to stack their core sample up against those from yet another ice sheet, from clear around the world in Greenland. The new project promises to unlock valuable secrets about global circulation patterns and atmospheric mechanisms. If the plan succeeds, its reward may be a dazzling and authoritative biography of Earth over the entire history of modern humans. And it just might give us a vital advantage in our fight to save the world as we know it.

But for Thompson and other climate studiers, there is a growing urgency to their work. If current trends continue, by the end of the 21st century much of the world's ice—including glaciers and the Antarctic ice sheet that hold the evidence of the planet's past—will have melted. "The ice will be gone," says Thompson, "and history will be gone." And our chances for understanding what the future holds in store for us will disappear with it.

* * *

MUTING THE RINGTONES

As cell phones have become more common, they've also become a growing source of noise pollution. And some people haven't gotten the message that there are places where the phone should be turned off (movies, restaurants, operating rooms, etc.). But a Japanese engineer named Hideo Oka has figured out a way to jam a cellular signal without using electricity. His system consists of a layer of magnetic material sandwiched between two thin layers of wood paneling. The material interferes with the electromagnetic waves that cell phones rely on. That means that any home or business could use it to create a "cell-free" zone. Not surprisingly, the cell-phone industry isn't pleased with Oka's invention, and a legal battle may be looming.

Trash rotting in landfills produces a third of all harmful methane emissions worldwide.

REUSING AT HOME

There are many creative (and odd) ways to reuse household items that might otherwise end up in the garbage.

TOILET PAPER ROLLS

• Paper-towel rolls make good extension cord holders (the cords won't get tangled). You can also use the tubes to store pantyhose, grocery bags, or Christmas lights.

• TP rolls make great craft items and even greater toys. (Uncle John often uses one as a megaphone to announce staff meetings.)

• The paper towels themselves can often be reused. If you used a few towels to wipe up some water, just let them dry. (In many cases, a cloth will do the job better and won't waste paper.) Another tip: Buy rolls with half-sheets—they'll last longer.

BOTTLES, JARS, AND STORAGE CONTAINERS

• Use spaghetti sauce jars to store broth and soup.

• Baby food jars make great storage containers for small things such as hair ties and paper clips.

• Plastic food containers, such as tubs used for butter spread and yogurt, work great for storing leftovers.

BRUSHES

• Use old makeup brushes to clean camera lenses or to dust the nooks and crannies of knickknacks.

• Old toothbrushes make great tools for cleaning bicycle chains, power tools, and other dirty items with lots of tiny spaces.

• Keep a box of old hairbrushes in a box in your shed and use them to clean off muddy shoes.

LOW-WASTE FOOD PREPARATION

• Cooking grease makes great suet for birds. Pour the cooled grease into a plastic container, then place a string in it and put it in the fridge. Each time you add more grease, add some food crumbs—the more, the tastier. When the tub is full and the grease has hardened, pop it out and you'll have a bird treat ready to hang from a tree.

Woo hoo! A group of blue jays is called a *party*.

• Here's a stock tip: Instead of tossing food scraps or leftovers in the trash, use them to make soup stock. Good candidates are leftover veggies, peelings, and chicken bones. Boil them together, season to taste (there are many good recipes), and presto, you have a chicken-broth base for soups, stews, and other dishes.

• When a recipe calls for a greased pan, just use the wrapper from a stick of butter.

• Save your old coffee grounds and lightly sprinkle them into your garden to add nitrogen to the soil.

WRAPPING PAPER

• Many cities don't offer wrapping-paper recycling because of its high metal content. Instead of stuffing them into the trash, do what Uncle John's mom always told him: "Open that present carefully so we can reuse the paper." (His family still has some wrapping paper that, judging from its garish colors, dates back to the 1970s.)

• If you do want to buy new wrapping paper for a fancy gift, consider using hemp paper. A typical hemp brand is recyclable, chlorine free, made with vegetable-based inks, and completely biodegradable.

• Alternatives to conventional paper: reusable gift bags, Sunday comic strips, scraps of fabric, calendar pages, outdated maps, or a picture that your kid drew.

MORE REUSABLES

• **Aluminum foil** and **Ziploc bags** can be washed and reused several times.

• **Cereal bags** make great freezer bags and some can even be substituted for waxed paper. Use empty **cereal boxes** to store documents and other odd items.

• An old **tissue box** can be turned a plastic bag dispenser.

• Among the hundreds of uses for **newspapers**: Stuff them into wet shoes to dry them, or into hats to help keep their shape.

• If you're not ready to let that old yellow **Tonka dump truck** go, use it as a planter in your garden. (Lots of old things—not just toys—can be turned into planters.)

• **Junk mail** is such a big subject that we've given it its own article on page 25.

IT'S FERAL CAT DAY!

Here are the stories behind some fun animal-themed holidays.

SQUIRREL APPRECIATION DAY

Date: January 21

Origin: This holiday was created in 2001 by Christy Hargrove, a wildlife rehabilitator from Asheville, North Carolina. At first, the holiday was just a fun way to get local kids interested in the region's many squirrel species, some of which are endangered. But over the last few years, Squirrel Appreciation Day has grown more and more popular at schools throughout the United States. Why is it in January? That's when food for squirrels is the most scarce, so celebrants are encouraged to put out some seeds, nuts, or suet for the furry little creatures. The holiday is also a great way to pass on some great squirrel facts, like this one: The word goes back to the Greek *skiouros*, a combination of "shade" and "tail," which meant "creature who sits in the shadow of his tail."

NATIONAL PIG DAY

Date: March 1

Origin: Ellen Stanley didn't think that people gave pigs enough credit as intelligent animals that make great pets. So in 1972 the art teacher from Lubbock, Texas, founded National Pig Day. Today it's celebrated by pig owners and just plain old pig lovers all over the country. Now you can, too. A recommended present for your favorite pig: apples. Pigs just love apples!

INTERNATIONAL MIGRATORY BIRD DAY

Date: The second Saturday of May

Origin: This holiday was started in 1993 by ornithologists at the Smithsonian Migratory Bird Center and the Cornell Laboratory of Ornithology. Their goal: to increase awareness of the many migratory bird species in the Western Hemisphere. Government-sponsored events take place on the big day from Canada down to Latin America. Want to take part? Go to *birdday.org* and download a bird-count form. Then print it out, go for a birdwatching walk, and submit your data back to the Web site.

Save the date: November 15th is "America Recycles Day."

NATIONAL COBRA DAY

Date: The fifth day of the moonlit fortnight in the Hindu month of Shravan (translation: sometime in July or August)

Origin: This Hindu holy day, known locally as "Nag Panchami," has been celebrated all over India for centuries. Different regions have their own ways of revering the sacred serpent. In the state of Punjab in the northwest, huge "dough snakes" are made from flour and butter and carried in noisy, colorful processions through the streets, after which the "snake" is blessed and buried. In the state of Maharashtra on India's west coast, snake charmers carry baskets with live cobras inside them through crowds of celebrants. The charmers play their flutes and cry out, "*Nagoba-la dudh de Mayi!*" ("Give milk to the Cobra oh mother!") Women come running out from their houses dressed in their finest saris. The deadly snakes are released and the women sprinkle spices and flowers on their heads and feed them sweetened milk.

NATIONAL FERAL CAT DAY

Date: October 16

Origin: This holiday is celebrated all over the world by feral cats who get together for mice-and-beer parties. Okay, not really. It was actually started by humans at Alley Cat Allies, a national cat-protection organization founded in Bethesda, Maryland, in 1990. Their goal is a serious one: ending the mistreatment and killing of feral cats in the United States. (An estimated 70% of the cats that go to U.S. shelters are killed.) One fun activity you can do on National Feral Cat Day: Get some live traps, trap some feral cats, and organize a "Spay and Neuter Feral Cats" event with your friends. (Do not attempt this without first consulting a veterinarian or animal shelter.)

LEARN ABOUT BUTTERFLIES DAY

Date: March 14

Origin: This holiday is so unofficial that we couldn't even find out who created it. But we're guessing it was a teacher, because every March 14, schoolkids all over North America learn about butterflies. They watch butterfly videos, read butterfly books, and draw pictures of not just butterflies, but caterpillars and cocoons, too! (We're not sure why a holiday about a summertime insect takes place in the winter, but it does give the kids something to look forward to.)

NATIONAL OWL DAY

Date: November 3

Origin: Created in 1986 by one of the world's premier owl experts, Johan de Jong, founder of the Dutch Barn Owl Working Group, the holiday helps raise money and awareness for the endangered European barn owl. The group's efforts have paid off, and the barn owl's numbers are steadily rising. This success has prompted de Jong to get the day recognized around the world, as there are many more endangered owl species. You can do your own part by holding a National Owl Day celebration in your community this November. They're a real hoot!

PENGUIN AWARENESS DAY

Date: January 20

Origin: This began in the 1980s as a lark by biologists studying penguins in the Antarctic. Few people (in the Northern Hemisphere, anyway) gave the holiday much thought until 2006, when two penguin-themed movies took the world by storm—the French documentary *March of the Penguins* and the animated musical *Happy Feet*. Thrilled with the sudden interest, penguin advocates publicized the holiday as a means to educate people about the world's endangered penguin species. Suggested activities for Penguin Day:

• Organize a field trip to the nearest zoo that has penguins.

• Rent a tux (or just wear black and white) and waddle around handing out literature about penguins.

• Rent one or all of these lesser-known penguin films: *The Adventures of Scamper the Penguin* (a 1988 animated movie about a young Adélie penguin), *Little Kings* (a 1999 documentary about penguin expert Mike Bingham), or our all-time favorite, a 1950 animated short called *8 Ball Bunny* in which Bugs Bunny must help a lost "pen-gu-in" find his way home to the South Pole. (Every time the little guy cries an ice cube, it just breaks Uncle John's heart.)

RIVER OF GRASS

We bring you two stories: one about a woman who wrote a book, and the other about the subject of that book, the Florida Everglades. If it weren't for the woman, they might have become the "Neverglades."

HIGH SOCIETY IN THE LOWLANDS

Though Marjory Stoneman Douglas barely topped five feet and weighed only 100 pounds, her sharp tongue and quick wit made her an imposing figure. Born in 1890, this well-to-do daughter of a newspaper publisher began her journalism career covering tea parties and social events for the *Miami Herald* back when Miami had a population of only about 5,000. Over the years, the town grew into a large city, and Douglas got tired of writing about how wonderful all the new development was. This "high society," she knew, was having major repercussions on the landscape...and few people seemed to care. So Douglas laid it all out in the pages of her book, *The Everglades: River of Grass.* Published in 1947, it painted a vivid picture of the Everglades, with "their vast glittering openness, wider than the enormous visible round of the horizon, the racing free saltness and sweetness of their massive winds." The book, which sold half a million copies, turned the Everglades from a local attraction into a world-famous destination.

But the task that Douglas championed—preserving the Everglades—has proven difficult. In the 60 years since *River of Grass* was published, the number of wading birds in the region has diminished by 90%, the amount of water by almost 60%, and 68 animal and plant species have become threatened or endangered.

A SOGGY HISTORY

One of the reasons that Douglas's work was so groundbreaking was that no one had previously given much thought to the Everglades. They were "discovered" in 1773 by British surveyor John Gerard de Brahm, who mapped the coast of Florida and called the interior southern swamp region the "River Glades." At some point (exactly when is unknown), the word "Ever" came to replace "River."

What no one knew then is that the Everglades had survived

Worth the wait: It takes up to five years for an oyster to make a pearl.

there for more than 17,000 years. They were created when sea levels rose and runoff water from Lake Okeechobee, the second largest freshwater lake wholly within the United States, overflowed, creating a vast marshland. The area encompasses 18,000 square miles from central Florida down through the Keys, and contains one of the most unique collections of fauna and flora in the world.

"THE ONLY EVERGLADES IN THE WORLD"

That's the opening line of Douglas's book, and an apt description. The region lies in the middle of the only subtropical climate in the continental U.S, giving it hot, humid summers and dry, mild winters. The Everglades' unique geology of porous layers of lime-stone helps sustain a marshland of nine dynamic habitats and millions of plant and animal species.

What makes the Everglades such a special habitat is its water, which flows from numerous rivers in Florida into Lake Okeechobee, through the wetlands and southward, and then out to the Gulf of Mexico, Biscayne Bay in Miami, and Florida Bay on the southern tip of the state. The water is home to more than 360 species of birds, 300 different types of fish, 40 kinds of mammals, and countless rare reptiles and amphibians. It's the only habitat on Earth that hosts both alligators and crocodiles. A complex system of plant life including cypress trees, pines, mangroves, ferns, and palms, supported by the continuous flow of water, turned the Everglades into a stable ecosystem, which it was for millennia. And then came the developers.

DOWN THE DRAIN

In the 1800s, the Everglades were regarded as little more than a worthless swamp in need of reclamation. As settlers moved farther south, water was drained into canals to create more dry land for the burgeoning population. Still more land was drained in the early 20th century for the state's growing agricultural needs, such as sugar cane production. Then came the expansion of railroads and the need for attractive tourist destinations. Young towns like Fort Lauderdale and Miami transformed their coastlines by remov-ing mangroves and replacing them with palm trees for better ocean views. Result: The wetlands dried up, failing to provide storage for excess wet-season waters, and debilitating droughts

Florida's Okeechobee Lake is as big as Rhode Island...and only nine feet deep.

began. Throw in a few strong hurricanes—one in 1928 and two in 1947—and more of the Everglades was washed away.

Making matters even worse, in order to get rid of the native vegetation, farmers burned much of the Everglades. From *River of Grass*:

> Cattlemen's grass fires roared uncontrolled. Cane-field fires spread crackling and hissing in the saw grass in vast waves and pillars and billowing mountains of heavy, cream-colored, purple-shadowed smoke. Training planes flying over the Glades dropped bombs or cigarette butts, and the fires exploded in the hearts of the drying hammocks and raced on before every wind, leaving only blackness.

A CALL TO ARMS

The book's grim descriptions brought the plight of the Everglades into the public eye. Though a conservation movement had sprung up in the 1920s, culminating with a small section of the region being turned into a national park in 1947, it wasn't until *River of Grass* was released that Congress took serious preservation measures by enacting the world's most comprehensive water management system, the Central and Southern Florida Project. Led by a joint effort between the U.S. Army Corps of Engineers and the South Florida Water Management District, a new network of canals, levees, and water conservation areas were installed, preserving water for the dry season while blocking its runoff to urban areas.

As noble as the intentions may have been, the project unintentionally damaged the natural ecosystem even more. Estuaries, bays, rivers, and other wetland areas were often blindly redirected for the benefit of urban and agricultural interests. Now, more than half of the wetlands that acted as organic filters and water-retention areas have vanished. Over 1.5 million acres are infested with invasive nonnative plants and animals. The rising demand by businesses and a rapidly increasing need for a dependable and economical supply of water will likely surpass the available amount, resulting in shortages. One million acres are under health advisories for mercury contamination. And the defoliation of sea grasses has significantly reduced fish populations, which are crucial to the local economy.

LET'S TRY THAT AGAIN

Now the task is to *sustainably* improve the quantity, quality, tim-

---

Gasp! 90% of Californians live in an area where air pollution exceeds legal limits.

ing, and distribution of freshwater in the park. Those are the goals of the Comprehensive Everglades Restoration Plan (CERP), authorized by Congress in 2000. With 68 components and a price tag of roughly $7.8 billion, CERP's ultimate goal is to protect both nature *and* water rights.

But as of late, projects are way behind schedule and federal enthusiasm has waned after CERP's most powerful proponents in Congress left office. And the government's priorities were diverted, first by the Iraq War in 2003, then by hurricanes Katrina and Rita two years later. The financial crisis that began in 2008 drained still more funding from the project.

Good news: In 2007 the Everglades National Park was removed from the United Nations' list of endangered World Heritage sites, sending the message that the region has been healed. Bad news: That's not quite the case. At best, the restoration progress has been slow and inconsistent. Currently, the most vocal proponents are citizens and environmentalists following in Douglas's footsteps. They're raising public awareness and urging Americans to write Congress and demand that more efficient conservation efforts be taken. And in Florida, the word is out to everyone to curb their use of water, which the Everglades still need badly.

GRANDMOTHER OF THE GLADES

Marjory Douglas lived long enough to witness the many trials and tribulations that reshaped the region in the 20th century. She was 103 years old in 1993 when President Bill Clinton awarded her the highest honor that can be bestowed upon a citizen, the Presidential Medal of Freedom. "Marjory Stoneman Douglas personifies passionate commitment," the inscription reads. "Her crusade...has enhanced our nation's respect for our precious environment, reminding all of us of nature's delicate balance. Grateful Americans honor the 'Grandmother of the Glades.'" Douglas lived another five years and received many more honors. After she died—at 108 years old—her ashes were scattered throughout the Marjory Stoneman Douglas Wilderness Area in Everglades National Park.

Final irony: Though she fought to save the Everglades, Douglas wasn't that keen on actually spending time there: "It's too buggy, too wet, too generally inhospitable."

Weather fact: What do you call the ice that forms when fog freezes on outdoor objects? *Rime.*

FIELD OF GREENS

Let's see: Thirty major-league baseball teams multiplied by 81 home games multiplied by about 20,000 fans at each game multiplied by, say, two beer cups for each fan equals…lots of waste. But change is coming.

WASHINGTON NATIONALS

The Montreal Expos moved to Washington, D.C., in 2005 and became the Washington Nationals. They needed a new stadium, and the D.C. city council approved it, on the condition that it be as environmentally friendly as possible… and be the first stadium certified by the United States Green Building Council.

The Nationals hired stadium architectural firm HOK Sport, who pulled out all of the stops in order to create a green ballpark. Among the measures:

• 95% of the steel was recycled.

• More than 5,000 tons of the waste generated during construction was recycled.

• It was built on a site that was formerly contaminated with toxic waste, also known as a "brownfield" (it was thoroughly cleaned).

• The lights that illuminate night games use energy-efficient LED bulbs requiring 20% less electricity than traditional lights.

• All toilets in the stadium are low-flow water savers.

• Concession-stand refrigerators are cooled by air instead of water, saving six million gallons of water annually.

• The park is close to public transportation, which encourages fans to leave their cars at home.

• There's even a grove of cherry trees in the outfield stands.

PITTSBURGH PIRATES

In 2007 Bob Nutting bought the team and immediately began making pro-environmental changes to the organization. Prior to 2008, none of the 800,000 cups and bottles used at games were recycled; now they all are. Stadium bathrooms now stock 100% recycled toilet paper, team publications are printed with soy-based ink, and Pirates scouts drive hybrid vehicles.

Due to underwater volcanic activity, some parts of the ocean are as hot as 194°F.

PHILADELPHIA PHILLIES

In 2008 the Phillies purchased 20 million hours' worth of carbon-emission credits to offset the utilities usage at Citizens Bank Park, the equivalent of planting 100,000 trees. The team has also urged food vendors to participate in a program to recycle frying oil into biodiesel fuel, use condiment pumps instead of packets, and use locally grown produce whenever possible.

OAKLAND A'S

The A's banned all non-biodegradable utensils, cups, napkins, and food containers from the Coliseum. Instead, fans use products made out of corn, which are then recycled, broken down into mulch, and sold to northern California farms and wineries.

SEATTLE MARINERS

At Safeco Field, the Mariners operate a compost facility that can handle 25% of game-generated garbage. In 2008 the stadium composted 350 tons of organic materials (and recycled all of its glass and plastic garbage).

NEW YORK METS

The Mets moved into a brand-new stadium called Citi Field in 2009. The stadium's designers worked with the Environmental Protection Agency to make sure it was environmentally sound. The park is constructed from 95% recycled steel and has a unique stormwater runoff system: Because concrete deflects rainwater and deposits it into the streets and sewers, essentially wasting it, Citi Field is equipped with 70,000 square feet of porous ground and drainage beds, which filter rain and return it to the groundwater. Citi Field also has waterless urinals, which save more than four million gallons of water per year.

Here comes the sun: The San Francisco Giants, Colorado Rockies, Cleveland Indians, and Baltimore Orioles have all installed solar panels at their respective ballparks. It's all part of MLB's league-wide "Team Greening Program." Said commissioner Bud Selig: "Baseball is a social institution with social responsibilities and caring for the environment is inextricably linked to all aspects of our game."

A million plant and animal species depend on coral reefs for their survival.

GRAYWATER

Never head of this word? You probably will as water supplies start to dwindle.

MURKY TREASURE

MURKY TREASURE
Graywater is the technical term for water that drains from showers, bathroom sinks, and clothes washers. Making up nearly 85% of all residential wastewater, graywater is usually allowed to drain into sewers along with what gets flushed down the toilet (technically known as *blackwater*). But by way of some not-so-advanced technology, graywater can be diverted before it gets to the sewer, filtered, and then used again—not for drinking, but to irrigate your yard or even flush your toilet. This "personal sewage system" isn't legal everywhere, and where it is, it requires an installation permit from the local health department. A system can cost anywhere from $200 for to $5,000, depending on the how much water you want to reuse. A professionally installed system that works alongside a rainwater catch system can dramatically reduce your water bills. A system usually pays for itself within a year or two.

FLUSHED WITH SUCCESS

According to Oasis Design, a California company that's been selling home graywater systems since 1980, there are many benefits to reclaiming home wastewater: lower freshwater use; less strain on septic tanks and municipal water-treatment plants, which can also result in less energy and chemical use; increased nutrients for the topsoil in your yard; and improved groundwater replenishment, allowing previously barren landscapes to flourish without the use of traditional irrigation.

Graywater's already a popular water source, and not just in off-the-grid cabins. It irrigates golf courses in Hawaii, provides cooling at a nuclear-power facility in southern California, and waters grapes in some Napa Valley vineyards. Two multistory apartment buildings in Canada are using treated bathwater for flushing toilets. And as more homes and businesses are refitted to reduce their environmental impact, we'll be seeing more and more of these systems that don't throw the money out with the bathwater.

The Atlantic Ocean grows an inch wider each year. The Pacific shrinks an inch.

SMART WOOD

*Here's the tale of how a man who wanted to get away from it all began
a grassroots movement that first grew locally, then regionally—
and eventually transformed an entire industry.*

GO NORTH, YOUNG MAN

As the Vietnam War slowly came to a close in the mid-1970s, many young Americans felt lost. Veterans had
returned home to resentment, and it was hard for "hippies" to
keep up their optimism in the face of violence in the streets and
the burgeoning conservative movement. Even former hot spots
such as Haight-Ashbury in San Francisco had lost their luster.
That's where a man named Jan (pronounced "Yon") Iris was living
at the time. A product of both worlds—a former logger and Vietnam vet with hippie leanings—Iris wanted out of the city. So he
and his wife Peggy packed up and went to the woods, settling in a
town called Briceland on the remote North Coast of California.

The counties of Humboldt and Mendocino are known for their
towering redwoods and mighty Douglas firs, as well as for their
wild rivers, salmon runs, and rugged coastline. But when the Irises
landed in southern Humboldt County, they found a landscape that
was nearly dead. The industrial "cut-and-run" logging companies
had taken nearly all of the biggest trees for the housing boom following World War II, leaving barren hillsides with no protection
against erosion except a few "undesirable" hardwood trees like tan
oaks and madrones. The Irises bought a plot of land and got to
work building their life. From the outset, though, they and other
new residents were ostracized by the local logging community,
most of whom were out of work due to automation, government
restrictions, and overharvesting. Times had been tough for loggers.

GREEN THUMB

Still, Jan Iris loved the area and was so fascinated with forestry
that he taught himself as much as he could and studied up on
biology and ecology. His goal was lofty: to heal the dying landscape. To rehabilitate the damaged watersheds, Iris secured a few
grants, gathered some friends with strong backs, and started plant-

---

How much of California's old-growth redwoods were logged from 1850 to 2000? Over 96%.

ing trees. They repaired the logging roads that had washed away and returned soil back to the local streams, which helped renew fish-spawning habitats. Then they selectively thinned overplanted new-growth forests that posed a severe fire hazard. "Holistic forestry," explained Peggy Iris, "is all-age, all-species management, very gentle forestry, not ever letting any heavy equipment leave the roadways."

This type of "forest gardening" was difficult work, and the couple still needed to pay their bills. So in 1985, they started a business, Wild Iris Forestry, that sold dried hardwoods—from the same oaks and madrones that the logging companies had deemed "undesirable." The Irises practiced the sustainable forestry they'd been preaching for years, adding flooring and cabinetry to their line. And though business wasn't great, they were able to put some money back into the local economy, helping the North Coast with its revitalization process. Slowly but surely, new homes began popping up, as did community centers and an alternative school built from the Irises' lumber. But it was all happening on a small scale, and the resentment among disgruntled loggers still ran high.

SEEING THE TREES FOR THE FOREST

Just like logging, the fishing industry was teetering on the brink of collapse. Populations of the once-abundant Pacific salmon were dangerously low after their spawning habitats had been polluted and washed away, and the ocean had been overfished. For both industries to rebound, major changes needed to be made. The Irises took this on as their mission and began working with local fishermen and loggers to help them continue doing what they loved, but using more sustainable methods. "It doesn't always have to be cut, cut, cut, chop, chop, chop," Jan told them. "You may cut trees in the morning and do stream rehab in the afternoon. A lot of things need to be done." Due in no small part to the Irises, these disparate groups began working together in the late 1980s.

The most significant shift in thinking was in the approach: The new philosophy was to not look for the best trees to take, but to determine which ones need to be pruned or removed for the benefit of the forest. Often it was only 1 out of every 10 trees, and rarely would they take an old-growth redwood or Douglas fir, and then only if they needed to create a fire break. While the yields weren't as high as they'd been during the cut-and-run days, these methods ensured that the forest would be there the next year and the year after that. And because Wild Iris Forestry used the wood to make furniture locally, jobs would be there as well.

Over the next few years, this new type of forestry had proven so effective that other interested "eco-loggers" hounded the Irises to train them. Jan and Peggy did their best to oblige, but touring the lecture circuit was cutting into their business. Knowing that this project was larger than their small-scale efforts, in 1991 the Irises formed the Institute for Sustainable Forestry (ISF), a non-profit organization consisting of loggers, organic farmers, biologists, and ecologists. Its goal: to inform the public of the benefits of eco-forestry, to pressure government into keeping forests healthy, and to set up the nation's first ecological forestry certification program—SmartWood Certification. The idea behind a certification program was that if consumers could recognize and buy responsibly made wood and paper products, then the forestry industry would be forced to cater to those consumers to survive.

Sadly, just a few months after the ISF was formed, Jan Iris died of cancer that may have been linked to his exposure to Agent Orange in Vietnam. But ISF continued without him, and was soon eclipsed by an even larger eco-organization.

CONSUMER-DRIVEN

Changing an entire industry wasn't easy. For decades, forest industry giants such as Weyerhaeuser and Louisiana Pacific—along with federal forest agencies—had talked about "sustained yield." But their practices were anything but sustainable, both for animals that depend upon the forest—salmon, spotted owls, and many others near extinction—and for the people whose livelihoods were made there. The problem was that no one was watching the watchers; the government was looking the other way and not enforcing what regulations it had.

In 1993 a new certification board—the Forest Stewardship Council (FSC)—was born. The FSC followed in the footsteps of Iris's ISF, but had much larger feet—with headquarters in Bonn, Germany, the FSC now has chapters in 57 countries, all working toward the goal of sustainable forestry. From their mission statement:

> In many forests around the world, logging still contributes to habitat destruction, water pollution, displacement of indigenous peoples, and violence against people who work in the forest and the wildlife that dwells there.... The link between logging and these negative impacts can be broken, and forests can be managed and protected at the same time.

STAMP OF APPROVAL

The FSC now works as an accredited "third-party" certifier with no economic stake in the wood or paper business. While touring forests and mills, their inspectors talk to employees and local residents, asking them whether they—and the community—are being treated fairly. Only after a set of stringent qualifications are met can the FSC "SmartWood" label be stamped onto a product. "Certifying wood is a way to help assure people that the wood products they buy come from well-managed forests," explains Doug Stewart of the National Wildlife Federation. "The whole idea is market-based, not regulatory, which is why profit-hunting corporate executives and environmentalists are able to share an interest in it."

In the late 1990s, this "market-based" approach helped convince national wood distributors such as Home Depot, Lowe's, and IKEA to carry FSC-certified products. The impact was immediate: Consumers began buying the eco-certified furniture even though it was a bit more expensive than the chemical-filled particleboard products that were the standard of the day. In the years since, this increased consumer demand has led to more than 2,500 certified companies that trade in FSC-labeled wood and paper products.

ACCEPT NO SUBSTITUTE

Proving that old habits die hard, some of the larger wood and paper companies are fighting against the FSC certification program, claiming that it makes it too difficult to keep their costs down and results in lower pay for their workers. In a countermove that many environmentalists believe is designed to confuse consumers, the American Forest and Paper Association has created the Sustainable Forestry Initiative (SFI), a certification program similar to FSC but with much weaker standards. One conservation group,

Credible Forest Certification, warns that "the SFI does not protect forests or deliver credible assurances, but condones environmentally harmful practices including large-scale clear-cutting and chemical use, logging of old growth and endangered forests, and replacement of forests by ecologically degraded tree plantations."

FILLING IN THE GAP

Meanwhile, back on California's North Coast, the Irises are long gone (Peggy moved to the East Coast), and the road to sustainable logging hasn't always been smooth. But there has been progress. After a series of bitter corporate takeovers, lawsuits, and tree-sitters, today the region is reaping the rewards of certified wood products…even though, ironically, the business is now dominated by one large corporation.

After the Pacific Lumber Company filed for bankruptcy in 2007, it was taken over by the Fisher family, billionaire owners of the Gap clothing company. The Fishers had previously bought out the ailing Louisiana Pacific lumber company in 1998 with the goal of "restoring industrial forestlands as part of a viable business plan." Within two years, the company was FSC certified, and in 2008, the Fishers opened another company, Humboldt Redwood, which is in the process of becoming certified.

If all goes as planned, California's redwood and Douglas fir forests will one day return to their former glory, as will the fish, rivers, and towns. Though it seems as if the timber wars may be coming to an end, many of the scars still show. But what's been achieved there over the last few decades may serve as a model to other communities around the world—proof that making a profit and being environmentally responsible can both be parts of the same plan.

*　　*　　*

PAGING DR. GREEN

More than 120 therapists now specialize in the emerging field of "ecopsychology"—the treatment of patients who are convinced that their own carbon emissions are directly the cause of global warming.

TREE HUGGERS

I think that I shall never see / a page as lovely as a page about trees.

"The creation of a thousand forests is in one acorn."
—**Ralph Waldo Emerson**

"Birth, life, and death—each took place on the hidden side of a leaf."
—**Toni Morrison**

"Someone sits in the shade today because someone planted a tree a long time ago."
—**Warren Buffett**

"I like trees because they seem more resigned to the way they have to live than other things do."
—**Willa Cather**

"Every green tree is far more glorious than if it were made of gold and silver."
—**Martin Luther**

"Evolution did not intend trees to grow singly. Far more than ourselves they are social creatures."
—**John Fowles**

"You can gauge a country's real wealth by its tree cover."
—**Richard St. Barbe Baker**

"As an instrument of planetary repair, it is hard to imagine anything as safe as a tree."
—**Jonathan Weiner**

"Except during the nine months before he draws first breath, no man manages his affairs as well as a tree does."
—**George Bernard Shaw**

"Never say there is nothing beautiful in the world anymore. There is always something to make you wonder in the trembling of a leaf."
—**Albert Schweitzer**

"Whoever knows how to talk to them, whoever knows how to listen to them, can learn the truth."
—**Herman Hesse**

"Trees go wandering forth in all directions with every wind, traveling with us around the sun two million miles a day, and through space heaven knows how fast and far!"
—**John Muir**

"Like the trees, we are visitors, guests of the earth."
—**Kim Stafford**

Half of all North American bat species are endangered.

COW FARTS

Settle into your seat, relax, and prepare yourself for an amazing journey through the digestive tracts of hoofed mammals.

MOO-THANE

Scientists now know that the farts and burps of farm animals, primarily cattle and sheep, are significant contributors of greenhouse gases. Why them, and not other animals? For a couple of reasons. First, they're *ruminants*: hoofed herbivores that utilize "foregut fermentation" to derive nutrients from the plants they eat—which are very difficult to digest. That process creates *methane*, one of the most potent of the greenhouse gases. This wouldn't be such a big problem if there weren't more than *two billion* domesticated cattle and sheep all over the world, grazing, burping, and farting...all day, every day. And on many farms they're overfed, resulting in even higher methane production.

BLEATER'S DIGEST

Before the cows and sheep can fart, their food goes on a wild ride. You've probably heard that cows (and other ruminants) have "four stomachs." That's useful descriptively, but not really true. As biology teachers like to say, cows have *fore*stomachs: three specially adapted chambers through which food passes and is largely broken down before getting to the last one, the "true" stomach. Here's how the four chambers—the *rumen*, the *reticulum*, the *omasum*, and the *abomasum*—process food:

• When a cow eats, food is masticated and mixed with saliva, swallowed, and passes into the rumen, which sits on the left side of the cow's abdomen. It's enormous, able to hold more than 200 pounds of food. The hardest-to-digest plant particles may stay in this chamber for as long as 48 hours.

• The food, now called "cud," then passes into the reticulum, which sits at the end of the throat and is much smaller. If the food hasn't been broken down enough, the reticulum sends the cud back up the esophagus to the mouth to be chewed again—that's what "chewing the cud" means.

- After some more chewing, the cud is swallowed again and goes back through the process.
- When it's broken down enough, the reticulum passes the food to the omasum, behind the reticulum. There it's further broken down, then finally sent to the abomasum—the true stomach—at the bottom of the abdomen, where strong acids break the food down even more. From there it's sent to the intestines and eventually emitted as urine or feces. All along the way, nutrients from the food are absorbed into the bloodstream, and...

FLBBLLBLLLBBTT!

Back to the rumen. As we said before, it's there that foregut fermentation takes place, sometimes lasting as long as two days. That's what produces the infamous greenhouse gases. Millions of microbes—mostly bacteria—live in the rumen, where they extract nutrients from the plant matter through the process of fermentation, not unlike the process used to make wine or beer.

Bacteria "eat" the cellulose in the plants and convert them into by-products: sugars and starches, which go into the animal's bloodstream to provide it with nutrients, and methane gas. The methane is released by the animal...from both ends...as cow burps (mostly) and cow farts (which is more fun to say). That's how ruminants make greenhouse gases.

ROO-MINANTS

But not all animals with hooves do this. Kangaroos and wallabies eat hard-to-digest grasses and ferment them in their foreguts in a way that is similar to ruminants. They're not classified as ruminants, though, and don't produce nearly the amount of methane that cattle and sheep do. Why? In 2008 a team of researchers in Queensland, Australia, isolated a bacterium that lives on the stomach linings of kangaroos that stops the production of methane. The scientists hope that the discovery could lead to the introduction of the bacteria into cattle and sheep digestive systems so that they produce more environmentally friendly farts.

*　　*　　*

"There is no sadder sight than a young pessimist."
—**Mark Twain**

Bright idea: Regular incandescent light bulbs are illegal in Australia.

READ THE LABEL

Uncle John loves to complain about how complicated food shopping has become in recent years. So we went out and tried to decipher the labels for him. He's right—it is complicated.

STICKER SHOCK

Food packaging is some of the most complex reading material published today. There's a lot to look at: seals, stamps, trademarks, lists of ingredients, and charts of nutritional values. Some of the claims made on food labels are regulated by one or more government agencies, but others that are categorized as "marketing" or "advertising" can be almost completely untrue. A lot of label language falls somewhere in between—there may be some truth to a given claim, but it doesn't mean that the food is actually good for you, or that its production was good for the environment.

The only way to really know what you're getting is to take the time to read the labels while you're in the grocery store, and to try to learn what all the different claims mean. Even then, it can be a leap of faith. Here are some of more common labeling claims and what they mean.

100% Organic/USDA–Certified Organic: This label has a green-and-white seal issued by the U.S. Department of Agriculture (USDA). To earn this label, the food and all its ingredients must meet the following conditions:

• Crops must be grown without the use of synthetic fertilizers, synthetic chemicals, or sewage sludge.

• Crops cannot be genetically modified or irradiated (subjected to a low dose of radiation to kill harmful microorganisms).

• Animals must be fed only organically grown feed (containing no animal by-products) and cannot be treated with synthetic hormones or antibiotics.

• Animals must have access to the outdoors, and ruminants (hoofed animals) must have access to pasture.

• Animals cannot be cloned.

Warning: Even with the label, there's no guarantee that all of these measures were met. (See why on page 140.)

Natural or All Natural: Only meat and poultry products have official USDA guidelines for Natural or All Natural claims. Such meat can only undergo "minimal processing" and cannot contain "artificial colors, artificial flavors, preservatives, or other artificial ingredients." But this doesn't mean that "Natural" meats are organic. It also doesn't require that animals be free of added hormones or antibiotics.

For all other types of food, from potato chips to soups, the Natural or All Natural label is only a marketing term, and can mean pretty much whatever the manufacturer wants it to.

Cage Free: There's no official government standard for this label, which claims that egg-producing poultry are not raised in cages. But Cage Free eggs can still come from birds raised entirely indoors in what amount to crowded warehouses. Cage Free also doesn't guarantee anything concerning the chickens' diet.

Free Range: This label is regulated by the USDA, but only for meat-producing poultry—not for pigs, cattle, or egg-producing poultry. It promises that the chickens are "not confined," meaning they get to go outside at least once a day. But the USDA requires only five minutes of outside time to qualify for the Free Range label, and there's no requirement about exactly where outside the chickens go. So a Free Range chicken could have spent 23 hours and 55 minutes in a cage, and 5 minutes on a concrete slab outside. The best way to ensure that the chickens you eat were not raised in overcrowded cells is to buy locally and, if possible, visit the farm you're buying from. Another option: Look for eggs with the "Certified Humane Raised and Handled" label. These farms operate under strict guidelines for humane care and feeding.

Antibiotic Free: Though it sounds like a straightforward term, the USDA considers its official term of "antibiotic free" to be unapprovable. Just why is under debate: Some sources say that political or bureaucratic obstacles have blocked the verification system, or that the USDA just hasn't developed one yet. It's common for some large-scale animal feedlots to give cattle, pigs, and poultry low-dose antibiotics "to promote growth and prevent disease," and consumer-advocacy groups worry that this could result in the spread of antibiotic-resistant bacteria from the animals into the environment at large, even to humans. Other food producers only use antibiotics to treat sick animals, but even these medications may be passed along through the food chain. Producers have the option of using the labels "Raised Without Antibiotics" or "No Antibiotics Administered" to indicate that over an animal's lifetime, it received no antibiotics. If an animal receives antibiotics for any reason, none of its meat, milk, or eggs can be certified Organic or labeled as Raised Without Antibiotics.

Grass Fed: Pasture feeding is the traditional way to raise many large animals. But in recent years, meat producers have been feeding animals corn and other grains instead of grass because it's relatively cheap and fattens the animals more quickly. But some studies have shown that grass-fed meat may have health and safety benefits over corn-fed meat. And grass-fed animals are usually bred on smaller farms that cause less harm to the environment than the giant feedlot operations known as Confined Animal Feeding Operations, which do just that—confine animals in indoor pens or cages.

As of 2007, the USDA approved a "Grass Fed" label for meat from ruminant (hoofed) animals, including cows and lambs. Grass-fed animals must be allowed to roam freely in outdoor pastures during most of the growing season, and be fed 100% grass and forage, with no grain or grain products (such as corn). The label does not exclude the use of antibiotics or hormones, and does not apply to dairy animals.

Here's the confusing part. To qualify for a "USDA Grass Fed" label, meat producers must volunteer to have their farms inspected by the USDA. But a producer can use the term "Grass Fed" without "USDA" with no inspection or oversight whatsoever.

Fresh: "Fresh" means different things for different food products. When it's applied to meat, the USDA term "Fresh" is a general claim that implies a meat product has not been frozen, processed, or preserved. But the rules allow chicken to be stored at temperatures as low as 24°F, which is 8° below freezing. This can mislead a consumer who might assume that "fresh" means not frozen.

For fruits and vegetables, the Food and Drug Administration (FDA) definition of "fresh" is a "food that is raw, has never been frozen or heated, and contains no preservatives." However, the rules allow for waxes or coatings, some pesticides, a mild chlorine acid wash, and "treatment" with irradiation.

Neither the USDA nor the FDA regulates the use of the "fresh" label on any other type of food product, so claims of "fresh milk" or "freshly baked bread" are essentially advertising and may mean just about anything.

GMO-free or No GMOs: A Genetically Modified Organism is a plant or animal that has been genetically engineered (GE) by the process of transferring genes from one organism into another. GMOs are highly controversial, with many industries supporting their use, while consumer groups argue that more testing is needed to determine their effects on health and the environment. Worldwide, there are about 200 million acres of farmland—most of them in the U.S.—that now grow GE crops, including cotton, corn, and the most common, soybeans. Most of these crops are engineered to be pest- and weed-resistant; some GMOs even have pesticides engineered directly into them. Some foods labeled GMO-free or USDA-Organic may contain some GMOs, since pollen from crops that literally blow in the wind can contaminate other crops nearby.

rbGH-free Milk: Recombinant Bovine Growth Hormone (rbGH) is a genetically engineered synthetic hormone designed to increase milk production in dairy cows. And, like many additives fed to farm animals, it's become controversial. USDA Organic milk is required to be rbGH free, and as a result of widespread consumer demand, more and more nonorganic dairies are now producing rbGH-free milk as well. Various political battles have caused some states to actually prohibit the use of the rbGH-free label, and then reverse the ban under pressure from the public. And milk products that bear the rbGH-free label must also bear the disclaimer that the "FDA acknowledges no difference between milk produced with or without the hormone." This hasn't stopped consumers from actively seeking to ban rbGH.

Treated with Irradiation or Treated with Radiation: The FDA requires that "irradiated" foods are labeled with one of these two phrases and a round, green flower symbol called a *radura*. Irradiation is most commonly used to kill bacteria and other microorganisms in meat and raw foods. But consumer and environmental groups believe that there hasn't been enough testing to know whether irradiated food is safe to eat, and also argue that radiation may deplete the nutritional value of foods. Industry groups and many in government claim that this low-dose type of radiation is not harmful, but there are many ongoing legal, regulatory, and public relations battles concerning this practice.

Fair Trade Certified™: This label ensures that farmers in developing countries who produced the food receive a fair price for their product, access to credit, and a living wage. It also means that it was produced using no forced child labor. The label is often seen on shade-grown coffee, which is grown using sustainable farming methods and without harmful pesticides. These farmers belong to cooperatives or unions, and buyers help the local community by contributing to development projects that improve healthcare and education, among other things. Common Fair Trade Certified products also include tea, rice, and (our favorite) chocolate.

Healthy: Finally, to fully appreciate just how confusing food labels can be, we present, word for word, the FDA's guidelines for "healthy" foods. (And these are merely the guidelines, not the regulations, which are even more complex.)

A "healthy" food must be low in fat and saturated fat and contain limited amounts of cholesterol and sodium. In addition, if it's a single-item food, it must provide at least 10 percent of one or more of vitamins A or C, iron, calcium, protein, or fiber. Exempt from this "10-percent" rule are certain raw, canned, and frozen fruits and vegetables and certain cereal-grain products. These foods can be labeled "healthy" if they do not contain ingredients that change the nutritional profile, and, in the case of enriched grain products, conform to standards of identity, which call for certain required ingredients. If it's a meal-type product, such as frozen entrees and multi-course frozen dinners, it must provide 10 percent of two or three of these vitamins or minerals or of protein or fiber, in addition to meeting the other criteria. The sodium content cannot exceed 360 mg per serving for individual foods and 480 mg per serving for meal-type products.

In conclusion, we'd just like to say to Uncle John: Good luck the next time you go food shopping. And happy reading.

HERE FISHY, FISHY...

Salmon is low in fat, high in protein, and full of other nutrients like omega-3s. And look: here's some on sale for $5 a pound! Not so fast.

GO FISH

In 2006 marine biologists at Dalhousie University in Halifax, Nova Scotia, released a study regarding the state of fish populations in the oceans. The shocking result: 29% of commercial fishing stocks had collapsed and, if current trends continue, by 2048 there will be essentially no more wild seafood. That's a threat to both the natural world and humanity's food supply. The culprit: commercial overfishing.

Even if the fish run out in 30 years, we'll still have fish to eat: farmed fish. Have you ever bought "Atlantic salmon" at the grocery store? It's the bestselling fish variety in the world today. But this is not a fish caught by a fisherman, but raised inside an offshore (not necessarily off the Atlantic coast) underwater network of net-cages. Called "aquaculture facilities" by the industry, they're commonly referred to as "fish farms."

MRS. PAUL'S CANTHAXANTHIN STICKS

Here's how salmon are farmed. Each net-cage is crowded with fish. Each fish basically has enough room to float; the restricted movement ensures a plumper fish. It takes about 30 months to raise a salmon for sale (8 to 10 pounds), and over that time the fish is fed a diet of steadily larger food balls made up of processed fish meat, grains, minerals, vitamins, and fish oil. To encourage even faster growth, many fish farms feed the fish special antibiotics, which also fend off disease. Still, an average fish farm can lose up to 40% of its stock to disease.

Unlike wild salmon, which have naturally pink flesh, farmed salmon have an unappetizing brownish-gray color because of their anemia-inducing environment and homogenized diet. The solution: Farmed salmon are fed pigments, such as *astaxanthin* and *canthaxanthin*, which turn their flesh as pink as a natural salmon's. Today, canthaxanthin is used in smaller quantities than it was when salmon farming began in the 1980s, especially in Europe,

On average, organic crop yields are 20% lower than yields for conventional crops...

where the European Commission limited the dye's use after studies revealed that overconsumption causes eye damage in humans.

The end result is a fish that looks like a wild-caught salmon. But it isn't one. Farmed salmon are full of saturated fat and a chemical called *polychlorinated biphenyls* not found in wild salmon. Studies show that people who eat farmed salmon once a week are subject to PCB poisoning, which has been linked to immune suppression in adults and slowed development in children.

And because they can be made in large, predictable quantities—unlike wild salmon—farmed salmon can be sold cheaply in most areas for about half of the cost of wild salmon.

POOP ZONES

Not only are farmed salmon of questionable health value, they're not doing much for the environment, either. Most salmon farms are adjacent to the oceans, so that's where their waste goes. A salmon farm breeding 200,000 fish at a time—the industry average—reportedly releases salmon poop equivalent to the feces of 60,000 people each year. This can lead to a marine phenomenon known as *dead zones*—sections of ocean where the water is so low in oxygen that it suffocates fish and crustaceans. This leads to more and more dead, unusable wild fish in commercial catches. In fact, as much as 25% of all catches are now thrown back, dead on arrival.

Ironically, fish farms are also hastening the depletion of natural fish stocks in other ways. A third of the world's wild fish are annually processed into those fish pellets to be fed to the farmed fish. Even worse, the fish meal is an inefficient food source for the farmed salmon: Every three pounds of fish meal fed to salmon yields just one pound of farmed salmon. And in addition to salmon, most of the shrimp you buy and eat at restaurants was bred in similar farms.

BORN FREE

Several environmental groups, such as Fish and Water Watch, are lobbying governments to put an end to these fish farms, but they're swimming against the current of industry and market demand. In the meantime, it's up to consumers to make the choice between farmed or wild-caught fish in grocery stores all over the world.

GLOBAL WARMING, PART II

On page 130 we learned that climate change really is occurring. Now the questions become: How will it affect us? And what can we do to stop it?

R EAL-WORLD EVIDENCE

As we mentioned in Part I, a June snowstorm in Topeka doesn't mean that global warming is a hoax. To look at climate change, scientists have to study a region over an extended period of time. And in 2008, a group of biologists from the University of California, Berkeley, did just that—inadvertently. They traveled to Yosemite National Park to conduct a survey of small animals. In a follow-up to a detailed survey performed in the park 90 years earlier, their assignment was to see how animal populations had shifted over the past century. According to head researcher Craig Moritz: "The most dramatic finding was the upward elevational shift of species. When we asked ourselves, 'What changed?' it hit us between the eyes: the climate."

Nearly every species, from shrews to mice to ground squirrels, had moved to higher elevations—1,600 to 2,000 feet higher. Because the climate had warmed, they'd had to move higher to stay in their preferred temperature ranges.

But this kind of climate change isn't confined to wilderness areas—you can see it in your own backyard. Many birds are arriving earlier, as are bees, wasps, and mosquitoes. Why? Because flowers are blooming earlier. Spring itself is arriving several days earlier than it did just a generation ago.

STEPPING INTO THE TWILIGHT ZONE

The Department of Agriculture maps out U.S. climate zones for planting and gardening, which tell you what types of plants will thrive in your area. The zones are based on a number of factors, including the lowest temperatures in the winter and the average date of the last frost.

When the USDA updated their climate zones in 2003, they

More than two-thirds of Central America has been clear-cut for cattle pastures.

had to change them significantly from the 1990 version. Every region of the country was now milder, with moderate climate zones moving hundreds of miles farther north and hot southern climate zones shifting north as well. This is great news if you're a gardener in Massachusetts—you can plant earlier and you can grow a greater variety of veggies. But the effects are wider-ranging. For one thing, pest species are moving north, too.

Take pine bark beetles—they love eating pine trees, so much so that they kill them. The pines adapted by growing only in areas that got very cold in the winter—cold enough to kill off most of the pine beetles. But unlike shrews and ground squirrels, pine trees can't move upslope when the winters get milder. Result: Pine beetles have moved into millions of acres of forests in the Rocky Mountains, destroying vast areas of woodlands, leaving them little more than dead, dry tinderbox. The forestry and tourism industries have lost millions of dollars as a result, and the cost of deadly fires that sweep through these devastated regions is astronomical.

The pine beetle kills only pine trees, but the anopheles mosquito kills people. This malaria carrier used to be confined to the warmest tropics. But it's estimated that within a few years, it will be able to survive in the southern U.S. At one time, only tourists and those living near the equator needed malaria shots; soon we may all need them. And in the native languages of Alaska, there's no word for "wasp" because wasps have never been seen there…until now. Suddenly, wasp stings are becoming a problem for Alaskans. And that's just one of many challenges they face.

THE ICE IS MELTING!

In the Arctic, changes are coming much faster than anyone had expected. While the world as a whole has warmed up by about 1.5°F, the Arctic has warmed up by at least twice as much. And in a land long dominated by ice, that warming is changing everything.

After declining steadily over the last few decades, Arctic sea ice shrank dramatically during the summer of 2007 to the lowest level ever recorded, less than half the size it was in the 1950s. For the first time, the Northwest Passage is ice-free in the summer, allowing ships to cut around the top of North America through the Arctic. Good for shipping, bad for everything else.

Why? Ice is white and reflects sunlight, which keeps the Arctic cool. But open water is dark and absorbs sunlight, which warms the water. Just a few years ago, scientists predicted an ice-free Arctic by 2100. It now appears that it will happen much sooner—but exactly how soon is uncertain. And how will an ice-free Arctic affect the weather for the rest of us? No one knows yet. It could mean milder winters for Minneapolis and Chicago...or it could mean more intense storms, blizzards, and tornadoes for everyone.

Another problem with the melting Arctic: methane. Millions of tons of this greenhouse gas are trapped in the Arctic, in the permafrost on land and in the ice that floats on the sea. As temperatures rise, that methane is released, causing an even greater greenhouse effect. And because this exact scenario has never occurred before, scientists don't know what might happen.

EVEN MORE ICE IS MELTING!

During the Ice Age, massive glaciers covered much of Europe, Asia, and North America. Some glaciers remain today in mountain ranges around the world. But lately, these glaciers have been melting away, and many of them are a fraction of the size they were just a few years ago. Montana's Glacier National Park now has only 27 glaciers, down from 150 in 1910. The experts now say that this melt-off is conclusively tied to climate change.

How do melting glaciers affect everyday life? For starters, receding Sierra Nevada glaciers mean that less water feeds into the rivers that provide drinking water and irrigation for millions of Californians; it's also played a part in devastating the fishing industry. Meltwater from glaciers feeds the rivers that, in turn, feed people all over the world. Billions of people are affected, from Peru to India to China.

The ice is also melting rapidly in Greenland and Antarctica. Greenland holds 8% of the world's freshwater in an ice sheet 1.5 miles thick and 1,540 miles long. And it's melting fast. If it melts completely, sea levels will rise 23 feet. Antarctica holds 70% of the world's freshwater; if that all melted, sea levels would rise as much as 180 feet. Will all of it melt? No one knows yet, but it's losing about 36 cubic miles of ice each year.

World's largest man-made "structure": the Fresh Kills Landfill in New York City.

ANYONE FOR A SWIM?

No place will be affected by rising sea levels more than the world's coastal cities. The U.S would have to say good-bye to New York, Boston, Charleston, Miami, Los Angeles, San Francisco, and New Orleans. And in the rest of the world, tens of millions of people who live in low-lying delta lands in Bangladesh, Egypt, and China would all be displaced.

And it won't happen in a nice, smooth curve, but in lots of little jumps and dips. On a local scale, it may mean occasional massive storm surges, like the one that nearly wiped out New Orleans during Hurricane Katrina. We're already seeing surges just like that in coastal areas all over the world, particularly on Pacific islands, thanks to rising ocean temperatures over the past few years. Since water expands as it warms, a warmer Pacific means higher sea levels. And although 2008 saw cooler seawater temperatures, the overall trend is up, up, up.

CAN WE FIX A BROKEN CLIMATE?

A lot of doomsayers are claiming that the only way to solve this problem is either to spend so much money on it that we'll permanently cripple the world's economy, or to change our lifestyle to the point where we're all riding horses or living in caves. Both of these scenarios are unlikely.

The good news is that people have already begun the shift. For example, California has recently managed to keep its energy use from growing, even with a swelling technology-using population, simply by increasing efficiency. The same model could be applied to the U.S. as a whole: Some estimates place the efficiency of the nationwide energy sector at less than 30%—which means that Americans waste 70% of the energy the system creates. That gives us a lot of room to cut CO_2 output from power plants while still maintaining the same lifestyle.

That's great...for the United States. But what about the rest of the world, especially developing countries and massive energy consumers such as India and China? In the end, it has to be a global effort. Hopefully the global-warming "debate" is coming to an end as people begin to accept the climatologists' evidence. And once we've all agreed about that, perhaps we can collectively find a way to fix it.

Australia has enough untapped geothermal energy to power the nation for 2.6 million years.

MORE SIMPLE SOLUTIONS

A few more clever inventions that are changing the world.

O N A ROLL
Problem: In South Africa, more than 15 million people have to carry water from wells or rivers to their homes—sometimes miles away. It's traditionally done by balancing five-gallon buckets on top of the head, requiring many trips and often leading to neck and back injuries.

Simple Solution: A rollable plastic water barrel

Explanation: The Hippo Water Roller looks and works just like a lawn roller. Fill the large, barrel-shaped drum with water, screw on the lid, lay it on its side, attach the handles, and then just push or pull it home—the barrel becomes the wheel. It holds 20 gallons of water and weighs 200 pounds. But the clever design makes it feel like just 22 pounds, so even kids and the elderly can handle it. And it's made of UV-stabilized polyethylene, so it's durable enough to ride over roots, rocks, and even broken glass. Cost: about $60. The manufacturer, Imvubu Projects of Johannesburg, has donated thousands of the rollers to water-needy communities all over southern Africa, and to date more than 27,000 of them are in use.

SAUSAGE POWER

Problem: Dairy farmers in rural Costa Rica are forced to travel to faraway towns to buy propane for their cooking and heating. The process is expensive and time-consuming, and the propane frequently runs out.

Simple Solution: A biodigester

Explanation: In 2006 the Santa Fe Women's Group of Santa Fe, Costa Rica, a small dairy-farming community, installed *biodigesters*, simple devices that create *biogas*, a natural product of the breakdown of organic material that can be used much like propane or natural gas. As we told you on page 55, the most widely used form of biogas is cow manure. Here's how the biodigester in Santa Fe works: Cow poo from the farms is mixed with water in a rectangular, cement-lined pit. Bacteria in the mix digest the manure and create gas, mostly methane. The pit is topped with plastic fabric,

---

eGuilt: Every Google search emits about 0.2 grams of carbon emissions.

which expands like a balloon as the amount of gas increases. The women call the contraption a *sachicha*. Translation: a "sausage" biodigester. (When inflated, it looks like a giant sausage.) PVC piping transports the methane from the pit to the community kitchen, where it's used in conventional gas stoves. The women have built 16 biodigesters so far, bringing them close to complete independence from propane. Bonus: The biodigesters help alleviate the community's manure problem.

RADIO-FREE EARTH

Problem: Many Africans can't get vital information about news and health care because they lack televisions and radios. In many areas there's also no electricity, and the cost of a set of batteries could top an entire month's salary.

Simple Solution: A windup radio

Explanation: Englishman Trevor Baylis learned about the problem in 1993 while watching a documentary on the spread of AIDS in Africa. In 1995 Baylis unveiled the BayGen Freeplay, a spring-driven radio. Wind the crank, and a specially designed coil spring powers a small generator, which in turn powers the receiver. Turn the crank for just 30 seconds and you can listen to AM, FM, or shortwave stations for more than 30 minutes—and the spring can take 10,000 windups before it wears out. So far, tens of thousands of the radios have been distributed in developing nations around the world.

Update: In 2004 the Freeplay Radio was updated to include a powerful, detachable LED light, digital station scanning, and a battery pack—powered by a small solar panel. Set the radio in the sun, and it charges the battery even while the radio plays.

COOKING ON SUNSHINE

Problem: In many developing countries it's increasingly difficult to obtain propane, wood, or coal for cooking.

Simple Solution: A solar-powered oven

Explanation: Since the 1970s, Sherry Cole and Barbara Kerr of Solar Cookers International have held hundreds of workshops in impoverished villages, providing the materials and know-how to make solar ovens. All that's needed: some cardboard, aluminum foil, glue, and a plastic bag (an oven cooking bag works best). Even on partly sunny days, the oven will reach 300°F. Meat, beans, rice, vegetables, breads, and other foods can be cooked without using any fuel. It often takes longer than conventional ovens, but the benefits far outweigh this drawback. Another plus: Put the food in the solar oven, go about your day, and come back later—the solar cooker won't burn the food; it will just keep it hot.

A VISIONARY PLAN

Problem: In 2002 the World Health Organization estimated that one billion people around the world who needed eyeglasses could not get them. In the African nation of Ghana alone, there were only 50 opticians for a population of 20 million. This makes it difficult for kids to read, for bus drivers to judge distances, for fishermen to fish, etc.

Simple Solution: Universal, adjustable eyeglasses

Explanation: In 1996 Oxford University professor Dr. Joshua Silver started Adaptive Eyecare. After years of research, he invented glasses with lenses that are filled with a clear silicon oil. A small pump on the frame changes the amount of oil in the lenses, thus altering their curvature. (The pump is removed after the adjustment.) That means that as a person's sight deteriorates over time, they don't have to find an optician—they simply turn a knob until their vision is in focus, and *voilà*! A new pair of glasses! And each lens can be adjusted separately. The glasses are universal, keeping manufacturing costs down. (One solution that's still needed: The glasses work only for near- and far-sightedness, not for people with astigmatism.)

Silver was approached by a few of the eye-care industry giants who wanted to buy the technology. But he refused, afraid they wouldn't make the glasses economically viable for the developing world. Under Silver's watch, the glasses are available for less than $20 per pair (and he's working to lower the price even further). Nonprofit groups and governments are the biggest buyers. Even the U.S. Army put in an order for 20,000 pairs to hand out. "There are guys walking down the street in Angola with a smile on their face because for the first time since they were kids they can see their town," boasted Marine Maj. Kevin White. Silver's ultimate goal: one billion glasses served.

EPA: THEN AND NOW

*This story bounces from idealism to corruption and back
to idealism so many times, it'll make your head spin.*

THERE'S SOMETHING HAPPENING HERE

The 1960s were a time of environmental awakening in the United States. People across the nation began to question the unchecked industrial progress of postwar America: Oily rivers were burning, cities were covered in smog, and factories spewed their waste into towns, lakes, rivers, and oceans.

One catalyst for this awakening was Rachel Carson's seminal 1962 book *Silent Spring*. An immediate bestseller, it warned of the dangers of pollution and pesticides, particularly DDT, which was killing off numerous plant and bird species. Words such as "environmentalism" and "ecology," used almost exclusively by scientists until then, were now becoming a part of the national lexicon. The modern green movement was born.

TRICKY DICK

Even politicians started paying attention. Just days after taking office in January 1969, President Richard Nixon established the National Industrial Pollution Control Council (NIPCC). On the surface, it seemed that Nixon was genuinely concerned about the environment. But in reality, the committee was just for show—it was made up entirely of corporate executives, usually not the most ardent environmentalists. The public was skeptical.

Attempting to prove that he was indeed concerned about the planet, Nixon asked NIPCC member Roy L. Ash (founder of defense contractor Litton Industries) to chair the President's Council on Executive Organization in May 1969. Ash soon determined that the best way for the government to enact environmental change would be to combine all of the government's "green" offices, committees, and activities under the guidance of a single agency.

In late 1969, the U.S. Senate passed Sen. Gaylord Nelson's (D-WI) National Environmental Policy Act (NEPA). And the NEPA wasn't just for show—it called for all federal agencies from then on to clear any projects that might impact the environment.

Leonardo da Vinci was a vegetarian—he'd buy live birds from poultry sellers and free them.

Each and every project would have to file an "Environmental Impact Statement" and await review.

The president signed the NEPA into law on January 1, 1970. A few weeks later, at his State of the Union address, he told the nation that the 1970s would be a "historic period when, by conscious choice, we transform our land into what we want it to become."

THE LOUD MINORITY

Still, many Americans didn't believe Nixon, who hadn't lived up to his campaign promise of ending major combat operations in Vietnam. Senator Nelson, after touring the U.S. to speak to college students about conservation, came up with a plan for what he later called a "huge grassroots protest over what was happening to our environment. I was satisfied that if we could tap into the environmental concerns of the general public and infuse the student anti-war energy into the environmental cause, we could generate a demonstration that would force this issue onto the political agenda. It was a big gamble, but worth a try." Nelson's gamble paid off and, on April 22, 1970—dubbed "Earth Day"—more than twenty million people across the nation gathered to demand that the government provide more than lip service when it came to clean air and water.

The success of the first Earth Day put Nixon's plans for a new agency into high gear. Under Reorganization Plan 3, issued by Nixon in July 1970, the Environmental Protection Agency would be created. Its mission: "The establishment and enforcement of environmental protection standards consistent with national environmental goals."

E PLURIBUS UNUM

Specifically, the EPA would be charged with researching the adverse effects of pollution and how to reduce them. Then it would change public policy to reflect its findings. It would also, through grants and research assistance, help private organizations curb and prevent pollution. Some of the preexisting offices that were moved into the EPA's jurisdiction included the Federal Water Quality Administration (formerly an Interior Department office); the National Air Pollution Control Administration and the FDA's pesticide research division (both from Health, Education, and

Welfare); and the Bureau of Radiological Health. In all, 15 programs were transferred to the EPA from other departments. President Nixon wanted the EPA to consider "air pollution, water pollution, and solid wastes as different forms of a single problem" and to develop a systematic approach to solving that problem. Congress approved Reorganization Plan 3, and on December 2, 1970, the Environmental Protection Agency officially opened.

EARLY SUCCESS

The EPA's first administrator, former Assistant Attorney General William Ruckelshaus, was determined to keep any conflicts of interest out of the new department. Called "Mr. Clean" by both friends and foes, he plainly stated that the EPA had "no obligation to promote commerce or agriculture."

Almost immediately, Ruckelshaus set out to fix three particularly polluted cities: Cleveland, Detroit, and Atlanta. Their mayors were given six months to comply with pollution regulations or they would face legal repercussions. Cleveland and Detroit were accused of polluting the Lake Erie basin, while Atlanta was cited for polluting the Chattahoochee River. In the end, compliance took far longer than six months, but all three cities are much cleaner today than they were in 1970.

Also on the hit list was DDT, the pesticide that helped spark the environmental movement. After seven months of hearings, the EPA banned most uses of DDT in 1972. The pesticide's manufacturers protested and filed suit, but the ban held up in court.

It seemed to many at the time that America's environmental problems could—and would—be solved in that decade. On television, Woodsy Owl, Smokey Bear, and a crying Indian urged people to be more responsible. And in Washington, D.C., the EPA, it seemed, was holding corporate offenders accountable. According to Ruckelshaus, "We thought we had technologies that could control pollutants, keeping them below threshold levels at a reasonable cost, and that the only things missing in the equation were national standards and a strong enforcement effort." But it wasn't going to be that simple.

THE INDUSTRY PROTECTION AGENCY

As the 1980s began, there was less reason for optimism. The

Reagan administration put environmental concerns on the back burner, and corporate interests began to take precedence over everything else. The government agency once hailed as the "good guys" had abandoned the movement that helped create it.

"In my 25 years with EPA," said whistleblower William Sanjour in 1998,

> I have heard countless remarks and witnessed many heartless actions denigrating environmental concerns and, most particularly, community environmental activists. While for the outside world, EPA puts on a face of concern and caring for the unfortunate victims of environmental pollution, the agency is permeated with contempt for these same people.

One of the most alarming claims made by Sanjour: In the 1980s, the EPA knew that Westinghouse Corporation was dumping its toxic waste in Bloomington, Indiana. Although concentrations of toxins in the area were more than 15 times higher than recommended levels, the public was told there was no danger (even though EPA staffers wore protective respiratory equipment at the sites). Why so hush-hush? According to the EPA, alerting the public would have "upset the negotiations" with Westinghouse. And that's just one of many similar stories that have leaked out.

RECENT VIOLATIONS

• One week after the September 11th attacks in New York City, the EPA stated that the air around Ground Zero was safe to breathe, even though it contained harmful levels of asbestos, lead, concrete, and glass fibers. Two years later, the Office of Inspector General of the EPA issued a report that stated they "did not have sufficient data and analyses to make such a blanket statement," but the White House Council on Environmental Quality "convinced the EPA to add reassuring statements and delete cautionary ones."

• In the 2000s, the EPA was criticized for overestimating gas mileage on some car models by up to 50%. This angered auto manufacturers who believed their rivals received unjustly high ratings. In 2006 the EPA altered the way it calculated gas mileage, resulting in lower and more accurate estimates. This angered car owners, including Toyota Prius owners who discovered that the car's 60 mpg rating had been downgraded to 45 mpg.

• In 2006 *Scientific American* claimed the EPA had dragged its feet in regulating pesticides, many of which the scientific community had already deemed dangerous. Even EPA staffers have questioned whether the agency is "too closely allied with the chemical companies and the makers and users of these pesticides."

• Two years later, the EPA dismissed neurotoxin specialist Deborah Rice from a committee that was evaluating the effects of fire-retardant chemicals. Rice had previously run afoul of the American Chemistry Council—a trade association for the chemical industry—when she claimed that a certain chemical was toxic. Now the ACC wanted to have her removed from the committee, claiming she was biased and that her inclusion "called into question the overall integrity" of the panel. The EPA caved to the pressure.

SO CAN WE TRUST THE EPA?

Many widely read magazines and studies quote statistics from EPA reports. But, given the agency's tumultuous history, how accurate are they? For the most part, figures on municipal waste and the like are probably on the mark. As former employee Sanjour attests, most EPA staffers just want to do their jobs. And, obviously, they work best when there's no conflict of interest. But a confidential survey of 1,600 EPA scientists revealed that more than 50% worry about political pressure affecting their work. Since the EPA is now heavily influenced by policy makers with little scientific knowledge, balancing the political and scientific aspects of its work has become one of the agency's biggest challenges.

But, as has been the case from the beginning, the EPA is only as effective as the current presidential administration allows it to be.

CHANGE

At the time of this writing, just weeks after a new president has taken office, there is cause for optimism. One indicator is that Rep. Henry Waxman (D-CA), a longtime environmental champion, was named Chairman of the House Committee on Energy and Commerce. An outspoken critic of the EPA's conflict of interest, Waxman has been hailed by the environmentalist community as the first high-level politician in a long time who has given them reason to hope.

A November 2008 *Time* magazine article covering President-elect Obama's new energy policy stated that, "It's not yet clear how he'll act, but his renewable energy advisor Jason Grumet has said that Obama would be willing to use the EPA to directly regulate CO_2—something President George W. Bush refused to do." For his part, Obama said, "I think the slow chipping away against clean air and clean water has been deeply disturbing. Much of it hasn't gone through Congress. That is something that can be changed by an administration, in part by reinvigorating the EPA, which has been demoralized."

So will the Environmental Protection Agency once again be able to protect the environment without the the meddling of industry? Only time will tell.

*   *   *

SOME OF THE EPA'S ACCOMPLISHMENTS

1971: Banned the use of lead-based paint in toys.

1972: Banned the dumping of toxic chemicals in the ocean.

1972: In cooperation with the Canadian government, spearheaded the cleanup of the heavily polluted Great Lakes, which supplied drinking water to 25 million Americans.

1973: Began the phaseout of heavily polluting leaded gasoline.

1974: Congress passed the Safe Water Act, which allowed the EPA to regulate the quality of public drinking water.

1978: Began the phaseout of chlorofluorocarbons (CFCs), the propellant in aerosol cans that damage the ozone layer.

1980: Congress passed the EPA's Superfund initiative, which cleans up toxic waste sites. To date, the EPA has helped clean more than 1,000 formerly uninhabitable locations.

1991: Helped popularize recycling with the passage of the Federal Recycling Order, which required government offices to implement waste-reduction and recycling programs.

1996: The bald eagle, once threatened due to exposure to DDT, was removed from the endangered species list, owing in part to the EPA's ban of the pesticide in 1972.

IT'S A WEIRD, WEIRD WORLD

Proof that truth is stranger than fiction.

A BIG DAM PROBLEM

In 2008 environmental demonstrators inspecting a nature reserve in northern Poland were shocked to find evidence of illegal logging. They reported that at least 20 trees had been removed, and more were marked for later felling. The investigators followed a trail through the woods where it was evident that trees had been dragged away. The trail led them all the way out of the reserve…right to a beaver dam in a nearby river

IT ISN'T AL GORE

See if you can guess who used to live in this house: It's heated and cooled at 25% of the normal cost thanks to geothermal heat pumps that circulate water through underground pipes. A tank collects rainwater as well as the water from sinks, which is then purified to irrigate the home's landscaping of mostly native plants and flowers. Many environmentalists have hailed it as one of the greenest houses in the United States. Located in Crawford, Texas, it was where George W. Bush lived while he was president.

OIL AND HAIR AND MUSHROOMS, OH MY!

When Lisa Gautier heard about an oil spill near San Francisco's Bay Bridge in 2007, she knew right away that she could clean it up. How? Gautier runs a charity called Matter of Trust, which matches donated goods to the right recipients—and it just so happened that she had 1,000 "hair mats" on hand: She collected hair from San Francisco salons, wove it into scouring pads the size of doormats, and intended to donate them to the city to clean up motor oil on roads. But the 58,000 gallons of oil washing up on the shore took precedence, so Gautier distributed the hair mats to cleanup volunteers. The mats worked great, both at absorbing the oil in the water and at sponging up what had landed onshore. But then what? What do you do with 1,000 oily hair mats? Enter mushroom expert Paul Stamets. He donated $10,000 worth of oyster mushrooms (they're fungi, not sea animals) to the relief effort. The mushrooms were placed on top of the hair mats, and in three months they'd absorbed all of the oil. The mats can be used again, and the mushrooms went into compost.

ALIENS ARE JERKS

One night in November 2008, residents of Lincolnshire, England, reported seeing several glowing balls of light in the sky. A few moments later, they heard a loud crashing sound. The balls of light were gone, but the town's wind turbine farm had been badly damaged: One whole turbine had stopped working, and a 65-foot blade had been torn off of another. There was no foreign debris in the vicinity, and officials have no idea what caused the freak accident, leading the residents of Lincolnshire to assume that the wind farm was ripped apart by a UFO.

THAT'S GARBAGE!

What reward did 53-year-old Eddie House receive for reducing his garbage output to zero? A lawsuit. It was served in January 2008 by the city of San Carlos, California, after House cancelled his trash pickup service. He didn't need it anymore—he recycles his paper, metal, and plastics, feeds food scraps to his dog or his garbage disposal, and sells or gives away larger items. City officials cited the municipal code, which requires all residences to contract for weekly garbage pickup—but said they were only drawn into the matter after House's neighbors claimed he was burning his garbage in his fireplace (House claims he was burning wood). "I don't understand a city ordinance that requires you to fill up a can," he said. "That's downright foolishness."

GAS-TEROID

Indiana University geochemist Simon Brassell published a study in 2008 alleging that the climate of Earth circa 70 million years ago had been much warmer than previously thought. Brassell suggests that dinosaurs, like modern cows, digested food through fermentation. As cows "release" methane gas, the study concludes, so did dinosaurs. And maybe a lot more of it, leading some to ponder: Did the dinosaurs burp and fart their way out of existence?

THE ELECTRIC CAR, PART IV: A NEW HOPE

*See the U–S–A in your e–lec–tric Chev–ro–let! Would
you believe that the company that "killed" the electric
car may be on the verge of bringing it back to life?*

(Part III of the story is on page 200.)

HERE WE GO AGAIN
Killing their own electric car in the late 1990s may have
seemed like a good idea to General Motors at the time,
when gas was still cheap and it looked like it would stay that way.
But timing is everything, and at about the same time that the last
EV1s were being taken off the streets and GM was launching its
10-mpg Hummer H2, the price of gasoline began its long, steady
climb from about $1.50 a gallon in the summer of 2003 to $3.00
by July '06 and well past $4.00 in the summer of '08. GM was
caught flat-footed as customers abandoned the large pickups and
SUVs that had become the company's bread and butter in recent
years in favor of subcompact imports and gas-sipping hybrids like
the Toyota Prius.

SHOCKING

The conventional wisdom within GM as late as 2005 was that
electric cars were too impractical to succeed in the marketplace.
The following year, however, a Silicon Valley automobile startup
company called Tesla Motors unveiled a prototype $100,000 two-
seater sports car powered by lithium-ion batteries, the same type
used in cell phones and laptop computers.

The market for $100,000 sports cars is small, and the technolo-
gy behind the Tesla Roadster was brand new and largely unproven.
But senior GM officials were stunned by the fact that a company
with no automotive experience was about to produce an electric
car with Porsche-like performance and a battery that could run for
244 miles on a single charge—almost twice the range of the best
electric cars of the previous generation.

GM was still reeling from a series of bad business decisions that

---

had hobbled the company in recent years. Killing the EV1 program had generated a storm of negative publicity for the company, and the hundreds of millions of dollars that GM spent building the Hummer brand and developing large trucks and SUVs had gone up in smoke when gasoline prices soared to record highs. Neglecting small cars and surrendering the hybrid market to competitors like Honda and Toyota proved to be just as disastrous. In 2005 GM lost more than $8.6 billion, and there was a growing consensus on Wall Street that the company was headed for bankruptcy. Now GM seemed on the verge of losing out on the electric car market as well, after having spent more than any other automaker trying to bring a practical electric car to market.

TIME FOR A CHANGE

Company executives decided that GM needed a "game-changing" product that would restore the company's image and repair its finances in the same way that the iPod had restored Apple to health after years of declining sales of its Macintosh computers. What they needed was an *iCar*, as the executives called it. And they didn't have to look far to find one: Years earlier, when engineers working with EV1 test cars had gotten tired of waiting several hours for the car's batteries to recharge, they rigged a small gasoline engine up to a generator and installed it in the car so that the generator would recharge the batteries *while* the car was being driven. The setup had extended the EV1's range dramatically, but at the time the company was so focused on developing a car that would comply with the Zero Emissions Vehicle mandate that they never tried to incorporate the engine (which produced emissions) and generator into the production EV1s that were leased to the public. The idea never made it past a single demonstration vehicle before it, and like the EV1 program itself, it was scrapped.

BACK IN THE GAME

It was this discarded, one-off demonstration car that became the focus of GM's strategy to resurrect itself. The car became the basis for the Chevy Volt, a plug-in hybrid car (GM prefers to think of it as an "Extended Range Electric Vehicle") that will run on lithium-ion batteries alone for up to 40 miles before a small gasoline engine kicks in. Unlike with the Toyota Prius, the Volt's gasoline engine does not power the vehicle directly. Instead, it powers the generator that feeds electricity into the electric motor.

Since 75% of Americans commute less than 40 miles round-trip to their jobs, this means that most people would be able to drive to work and back on batteries alone, without using a drop of gasoline. And unlike purely electric cars, this hybrid car won't strand them for several hours after the battery is drained, because the small gasoline engine will extend the vehicle's range to 360 miles for each tank of gas. And when the gas runs out, the driver can just fill up at a gas station as with any other car. When the driver gets home, he can plug the car into a standard electrical outlet and recharge the batteries overnight. The Volt will be a four-door family car that GM hopes to price at $40,000 or less, which, while pricey, will put it within range of many American families. And it will get the equivalent of 100 miles to the gallon on a tank of gas. GM has announced plans to bring the Volt to market in 2010.

TOO LITTLE, TOO LATE?

GM hopes that the Volt will allow it to leapfrog ahead of Toyota to become the industry leader in hybrid technology. But that will only happen if 1) the Volt lives up to its advertising, and 2) the company doesn't go out of business before it can bring the car to market. It's anyone's guess at this point whether GM will be able to pull it off. And even if they do succeed, the record-high gas prices in the summer of 2008 prompted nearly every major automaker to announce an electric or hybrid car program of their own. Even if the Volt turns out to be everything it's promised to be and more, it could have plenty of competition.

PROMISES, PROMISES

A lot has changed since the first electric cars came to the market more than a century ago, but one thing that hasn't changed is the battery conundrum: The technology that will finally make electric cars competitive with gasoline-powered cars has yet to materialize. Lithium-ion batteries show promise—they weigh less than other types of batteries and offer more power—but when used in laptop computers, they overheat and sometimes even burst into flames. Even if these problems can be worked out, it remains to be seen whether they'll be rugged enough to to take 10 years' and 150,000 miles' worth of abuse. Another question is whether they can be manufactured cheaply enough to be used in mid-priced vehicles that ordinary people can afford.

The battery for the Chevy Volt is still in development. But because there's no time to lose, GM has taken the risky and unusual step of developing the rest of the car first, *before* the company is even sure that the batteries it's testing will work.

And what happened to Tesla Motors and their electric sports car? The first lithium-ion powered Roadsters began rolling off the assembly line in 2008, but the cars are still too new and too few in number to determine whether their batteries will last. And it remains to be seen whether Tesla itself will survive: As of the fall of 2008, the company was down to its last several million dollars and the global economic downturn was making it hard for the company to raise fresh capital to stay afloat.

THE WAITING IS THE HARDEST PART

Would-be electric-car manufacturers find themselves in pretty much the same spot they were in back in 1901, when Thomas Edison jumped into the electric-car business and promised that better batteries were just around the corner. Edison's better batteries never really materialized, and though it seems possible that lithium-ion batteries will finally make electric cars competitive with gasoline-powered cars—a huge step in reducing the emissions that contribute to global warming—we're still several years away from knowing for sure.

In the meantime, if you don't have $100,000 to spend on a Tesla Roadster and can't wait for a Chevy Volt, you may want to look into several smaller electric-car manufacturers with catchy names like Zenn, GEM, Dynasty, and Th!nk. These companies' small "Neighborhood Electric Vehicles" are available now and are legal to drive on roads with posted speed limits of 35 mph or lower. A typical NEV has a top speed of 25 mph, a range of 30–40 miles per charge, and costs between $10,000 and $20,000. They're not perfect, but they'll give you something to drive while you wait for an electric car that can be driven at highway speeds for hundreds of miles at a stretch.

Let's hope we don't have to wait much longer.

SHOOT THE SMOGLING!

*Here are some real (and strange) video games that not only tell you how to
save the environment, but let you blow things up while you're learning.*

Chibi-Robo: Park Patrol (2007). You control a tiny robot
that's programmed to restore an ecologically ravaged park.
Chibi-Robo earns points by spraying water on evil balls of
pollution called "smoglings." Points are traded for beautification
items such as shrubs, water fountains, and hills.

Eco Fighters (1993). On a "planet of water and green," the evil
Goyork Company is plundering the natural resources. A benevo-
lent scientist named Dr. Mory sends in his grandchildren (you) to
pilot fighter jets and blow up all of Goyork's bases (which is probably not that great for the environment).

Ship Shop (2006). You fly a fighter jet and shoot at people on
the ground who are polluting rivers and streams. During the game,
tips on how to help the environment pop up on screen.

Adventure Ecology (2007). Two teenagers named Dash and Bay
fight physical manifestations of environmental problems and
social ills, including Agent Waste, Professor Ignore, Miss Lies,
and the biggest bad guy of all, Global Warming (who has really
sharp claws).

Save the Whales (1984). Commercial fishing boats and rogue
whalers shoot harpoons and nets into the water. You must pilot a
submarine and shoot torpedoes at the harpoons and nets to deflect
them away from all of the whales swimming around.

Steer Madness (2004). Bryce the Steer has escaped from a
slaughterhouse and must not only free his cow friends, but warn
humans about ecologically harmful methods of raising livestock.

Eco-Creatures: Save the Forest (2007). The Mana Woods are
under assault by the Mecha—evil, polluting giant robots. A kid
named Dorian leads an army of magical wood nymphs to defeat
the Mecha. While they fight, the good guys also plant trees, clean
up garbage, and properly dispose of toxic waste.

Disney World mowers travel 450,000 miles a year cutting the park's 2,000 acres of lawn.

BUTT LOG

This glossary of forestry terms was originally two and a half pages, but we had to selectively thin it to get it down to two.

Seedling: A young tree, from germination to sapling.

Sapling: A tree between seedling and pole, at least 4 ½ feet tall and 2 to 4 inches in diameter.

Pole timber: Trees past the sapling stage, with a diameter of about 4 to 10 inches.

Bole: The trunk of a tree.

Canopy: The generally continuous cover of a forest consisting of the branches and foliage that make up the tops of the tallest trees.

Crown: The uppermost branches and foliage of a tree.

Dominant: A tree whose crown extends above surrounding trees and gets direct sunlight on the top and sides.

Codominant tree: A tree whose crown extends above the canopy, receiving direct sunlight from above, but limited sunlight from the sides.

Felling: Also "tree-felling," the proper name for the cutting of standing trees.

Stand: A group of trees of generally the same species and age that can be managed as a single unit.

Old-growth: A forest that has never been harvested by humans, typically containing large trees more than 200 years of age. (Also referred to as *primary, ancient,* and *virgin.*)

Clear-cut: Harvesting method in which all trees in a given area are felled. The logic given for this oft-maligned practice is that some species of tree need a lot of sunlight to germinate and begin growth, so clear-cutting, when done correctly, can actually result in forest recovery in a way that thinning a forest can't.

Thinning: The selective felling of trees in an immature, dense stand to improve the health of the forest.

Salvage cut: Felling dead, injured, and diseased trees.

Butt log: A log cut from the bole just above the stump.

Crook: A defect, usually a sharp bend in the main stem.

Mast: The flowers, fruits, nuts, and seeds of trees that serve as food for wildlife.

Aspect: The compass direction a slope faces. For example, "Saplings on the south-facing aspect grew faster than those on the north."

Diameter at breast height: Standard measurement of tree diameter, usually taken at 4½ feet above the ground.

Frilling: A method of killing unwanted trees that aren't meant to be removed from the forest. (Also called "girdling.")

Blaze: A paint mark or cut in the bark of a tree to delineate property lines in forests.

Lumber: Generally, wood that has been cut into boards.

Sawlog or sawtimber: A tree or log at least 11 inches in diameter (some foresters say as little as 8 inches) and deemed suitable for lumber.

Buck: To cut a felled tree into shorter lengths.

Skidder: A large vehicle with a winch and a cable used to drag logs out of the forest.

Stump height: The distance from the ground to the top of the stump of a cut tree—12 inches or less is preferred.

Wolf tree: An old tree with a large crown of great value to wildlife and a forest in general, but not for lumber.

Den tree: A tree with cavities that can be used as nesting sites by birds or mammals.

Snag: A dead, still-standing tree. (They also provide nesting sites for wildlife.)

Windthrow: Also "blowdown," a tree felled by wind.

Epicormic branches: Branches that grow out of the main stem, usually in response to injury or environmental strain. They grow so quickly that they can fall off and damage the tree, resulting in less valuable lumber.

Board foot: A 144-cubic-inch unit for measuring wood volume in trees, logs, or boards, equal to 1 foot by 1 foot by 1 inch.

Silviculture: The art and science of growing and maintaining forests.

Forester: A professional forest manager with at least a bachelor's degree in forestry.

Timber: Standing trees, but also used to describe felled trees or even boards. (And if you ever hear someone yell this word in the woods, run!)

Gives 'em a head start: Human hair makes a good fertilizer for plants such as sage and basil.

WHY NOT NUCLEAR?

*The history of nuclear power (page 107) is fairly straightforward.
But its future is much more complicated.*

UNCLEAR POWER

The debate over how to manage our energy resources plays out in the headlines every day: Should we continue to damage the land, sea, and atmosphere to extract the coal, oil, and natural gas we need to keep up with our ever-growing demand for electricity? Or should we pour billions of dollars into developing alternative energy sources such as solar, wind, and geothermal? Or why not just use what some have called the "perfect" energy source: nuclear power?

No matter what benefits it may have as a power source, for many people, the word "nuclear" brings to mind a mushroom cloud, or the nuclear accidents that happened at Three Mile Island in Pennsylvania and Chernobyl, Ukraine. But supporters of nuclear energy insist that the public is misinformed about this powerful power source, especially its latest technology. And according to them, it's now or never—fossil fuels are killing us. To get you up to speed on the debate, here's a look at a few of the most commonly cited pros and cons concerning nuclear energy.

ADVANTAGES

• Nuclear power plants emit almost no greenhouse gases, while fossil-fuel plants emit hundreds of millions of tons' worth every year.

• We don't have to spend more money researching how to generate energy form nuclear power—the technology is ready *now*.

• Wind and solar power are not equipped to meet the growing demand on the power grid. Nuclear is.

• Current nuclear technology is far more advanced than it was a few years ago, and the safety record of new plants is much better than that of old ones. There hasn't been a major accident in more than 20 years.

• Some U.S. nuclear power plants use fuel from dismantled nuclear weapons. Ever since the program began in 1993, the fuel

---

Rock band Cake's 2009 album was the first recorded entirely with solar power.

from more than 13,000 weapons has been converted into fuel for power plants.

• Nuclear energy can generate *a lot* of power. Currently, the Palo Verde nuclear plant in Arizona produces 3.2 gigawatts of power, the second-highest electricity producer in the U.S. (after the hydroelectric Grand Coulee Dam in Washington state). As new technology further improves output, fewer plants will be necessary.

DISADVANTAGES

• Nuclear facilities are potential targets for terrorism. Though supporters maintain that the thick, lead-reinforced structural walls would prevent a leak of radioactive waste after an impact by a missile or airplane, if the attackers made it *inside* the plant, they could cause a catastrophic incident. (In 2003, 19 Greenpeace activists snuck inside a nuclear plant in Suffolk, England, and went undetected for five minutes.)

• The technology to run plants may be here now, but the technology to store the radioactive waste is not. The worst kind—spent fuel rods—have been sitting in pools at power plants for years.

• Because electric power stations only produce about 21% of greenhouse gases (industry, transportation, agriculture, and other sources make up the rest), switching to nuclear would only make a small dent in the climate-change problem.

• If the go-ahead is given for new nuclear power plants, it could potentially divert most of the funds that would have been used for solar, wind, and geothermal research and development.

• Nuclear energy is very expensive when all of the factors are added up: construction and operation of the plant; mining, milling, fabricating, and enriching the uranium; and the costs of waste storage. According to estimates, it could take 25 years to make back the $3–$6 billion investment in building a new plant.

CONCLUSION?

There really isn't one yet, so the debate continues among scientists, citizens, pundits, politicians, and industry insiders. One thing is certain, though: As the fossil fuels continue to burn, all options remain on the table. "As president," said Barack Obama in 2008, "I will find ways to safely harness nuclear power."

Were they nuts? Early diesel engines were formulated to run on peanut oil.

AFTER THE BIG ONE

Modern society got you down? Want to get back to nature and live off the land like our ancestors did? Good news: You may get your chance sooner than you think. Here's a mostly fun (but partly serious) article with tips on how to prepare.

POCALYPSE SOON?

A Although most forecasts still say we have a few years before the polar ice caps melt and the seas rise and the hurricanes intensify and the crops all die, recent events show that our financial and industrial systems may fail well before then. Or civilization could be destroyed by a good, old-fashioned natural disaster like an asteroid passing too close to our atmosphere. Or it might be a nuclear terrorist attack so skillfully implemented that it destroys much of the world's infrastructure, causing governments to collapse and all hell to break loose. But what happens after that?

Should you survive the initial crumbling, then you'll face the next challenge: Grocery and hardware stores will be emptied almost immediately, gasoline will be so valuable that you'll have to defend it with your life, cell phones and landlines will be useless, and your television will transmit nothing but static (provided you have a generator...and it still works).

If you want to survive, you should probably start your preparations soon, even today. And don't worry—you don't have to become that creepy survivalist who lives at the end of the street and scares children. Having an escape plan doesn't mean that you have to be paranoid. As Aesop wrote, "The ants will have a storehouse and the grasshoppers will be begging for a place to stay." So your first order of business is...think like an ant.

ANTICIPATE THE WORST

As bleak as it sounds, you can't count on anything being provided for you if chaos occurs. You don't want to be standing in the bottled-water line with everyone else; ideally, you want to be in your gassed-up, well-stocked vehicle headed out of town to your secret survival post (more on that later). And you should be ready to go on a moment's notice. Here are a few things to plan ahead of time:

- **Stockpile food and water.** Access to clean water is often the first priority after a disaster. Keep a three-day supply on hand: two to three gallons per person per day for both drinking and washing. The same goes for food—three days' worth. Even if your secret survival post is only a few hours away, it may take much longer to get there than you anticipate.

- **Gas up.** Try to keep your car's gas tank full at all times. (That's also why it's important to choose a survival destination that's less than one tank of gas away.)

- **Make a "bug out" kit.** FEMA's Web site has a good list of what your kit should contain, including first aid, a 30-day supply of medications, toiletries, and warm clothing. In a waterproof bag, store photocopies of your critical documents such as passports, birth certificates, and prescriptions. Also keep some cash in your kit in case ATMs and credit cards can't be used.

- **Lose the Chihuahua.** In the beginning, you'll be fending for yourself and your family, so you may want to consider only having animals that can feed themselves, provide protection, or assist in hunting. Difficult choices may come down to how many mouths you'll have to feed.

PLAYING HOUSE

After the disaster, crowded cities may not be safe and the suburbs might not fare much better. Your best bet is probably to go to the woods, someplace off the beaten path that has a steady supply of clean water. Choose a spot on high ground, upstream of any settlements, and always have more than one way out. Look for an area with an abundant, easily harvested fuel supply. A plot of land in the sticks is relatively inexpensive—you can purchase a prime spot and hire someone to build a yurt or a cabin—or, if you're up for it, build it yourself. And if the apocalypse doesn't come, you've got yourself a nice vacation home.

Store enough food at your destination to sustain your family for at least a year. What kind of food? According to survivalist Jim Rawles, his California safe house contains "quite a bit of wheat, rice, beans, honey, rolled oats, sugar, you name it. We've got large quantities salted away. Most of it is stored in five-gallon plastic food-grade buckets." The important point is to choose wisely and implement storage techniques that will keep your food fresh.

If a cabin in the woods is a bit beyond your means, then at least purchase a really good tent—not one of those cheap pop-up rigs. Army/navy surplus stores have a great collection of canvas tents (along with scarier supplies to stock up on, like gas masks). Another option: Buy a recreational vehicle. Remember, though, that if the gas supply runs out, you'll be stuck inside a highly visible, not-mobile tin can on wheels. All in all, a stocked shelter away from the cities is your best chance.

HUNKER DOWN

The first few weeks will probably be difficult, and you'll know immediately what it was that you didn't plan for. Here are two important things that you can't let slip through the cracks.

Power. Generators are a mixed blessing—they provide convenience and comfort, but they also use an immense amount of gasoline and can make it difficult to wean yourself off the comforts of the past. They're also loud, which could draw unwanted attention. For the long haul, consider solar panels and wind turbines. If there's a creek nearby, you can construct a waterwheel to generate power. For people who live off the grid in remote areas, these skills are fairly commonplace.

Communication. An AM/FM/shortwave radio is essential. Smaller models, used judiciously, have a long battery life, and crank-powered radios are readily available. But for transmitting, you'll need a ham radio. Police scanners may come in handy to find out what's going on near you without making your presence known. Otherwise you won't know who's out there…or what their intentions may be.

GETTING TOUGH

Even if the apocalypse goes more smoothly than anticipated—e.g., even if most people are nice—there will still be those few Mad Max wannabes who may attempt to raid other people's storehouses. And in the days just after Armageddon, many otherwise "normal" people will be in a state of shock and may not be themselves. If you decide to get a weapon, learn how to safely use, clean, and securely store it.

If you keep your wits about you, you may not have to brandish a weapon all. One clever trick is a "decoy box" that you can give up if you're robbed. Include some "fancy" jewelry, batteries, a little cash, and if you're so bold, some fake documents that have your fake personal information. Keep your real valuables well hidden.

Once you've arrived at your fortified destination, raiding humans won't be your only problem; wild animals have to be protected against as well. Research your area to find out what predators or scavengers live nearby and how to keep them away from your goodies.

BACK TO SCHOOL

A few generations ago, most people knew how to plant a garden and harvest the food, shear a sheep, card the wool, and knit a sweater. Can you? Mere hobbies today could keep you and your children fed and warm tomorrow. Your first step: Buy some survival books, starting with the Boy Scout Manual. It's chock-full of useful information written in a simple, straightforward manner. Among other things, you'll learn how to tie a slipknot and build a simple shelter. Then stock up on books on farming, trapping, basic mechanical skills, etc. Then get out and start doing them—plant a garden, build a lean-to shelter, go on "roughing-it" vacations to test your new skills in the field, and start looking for your hideaway.

IT TAKES A VILLAGE

Because it's impossible to educate yourself on every necessary survival skill, it may be wise to choose a select few compatriots who will be privy to your plans. Examine your own skills, and then look for others whose talents fill in your deficits. Some people who don't have sharp survival skills may have other things (such as a big piece of land near the lake) that make them a good fit. In addition to the hands-on skills that people may have (carpentry, cooking, hunting), there are the intangible skills such as negotiating, bartering, or even making people laugh—all of these talents make up a community. And an especially lucky find would be a friend who's a doctor or a nurse.

Once you've assembled your list of potential survival buddies, invite them over for an (admittedly awkward) dinner party. If you can convince them to join you in a disaster preparedness plan without making them think you're crazy, then you will be among the few who know what to do when the you-know-what hits the fan.

Thanks to recycling programs, aluminum cans now make up less than 1% of American trash.

HEMP MADNESS, PART II

On page 181 we learned why hemp production fell out of favor in the United States. Here's the story of the struggle to get it growing again.

WAR HERO

In the 1930s, manufacturing hemp was still technically legal in the U.S. But few farms remained—hemp was highly taxed; the cotton, paper, and petroleum industries had taken its place; and hemp's association with marijuana hurt it even further. Besides, even cheaper plants were being imported from overseas, including "manila hemp" from the Philippines, which isn't technically hemp—it comes from the abaca plant (used to make manila envelopes).

Hemp appeared to make a comeback in 1942, when a 16-minute movie called *Hemp for Victory* was shown to U.S. farmers, urging them to grow hemp for the war effort. Who made it? The U.S. government. Were they high? No—the Japanese had captured the Philippines, cutting off the supplies of manila hemp, which was used to make cloth for parachutes and uniforms. But when the war ended, the imports resumed and hemp was dropped again, still a victim of its relation to marijuana.

PUBLIC ENEMY NUMBER ONE

Remember Harry Anslinger? He remained head of the Federal Bureau of Narcotics for 32 years, and never let up on the evils of marijuana and the degenerates who smoked it—even in the face of evidence that said it wasn't really that harmful.

• In 1945 Anslinger denounced the "LaGuardia Marijuana Report" from the New York Academy of Medicine, which stated that marijuana had minimal detrimental effects and numerous beneficial ones. At Anslinger's urging, the American Medical Association described the report's findings as "gutter science."

• In 1948, at the onset of the Cold War, Anslinger changed his tune and said that pot caused people to become "pacifists"—and it would help the Communists defeat the U.S. if it was made legal.

• In 1961 President Kennedy fired Anslinger, but wasn't in office long enough to push for any laws to change. And later in the

1960s, illegal marijuana use increased immensely and came to be associated with the youth counterculture movement.

In 1970 the Marihuana Tax Act was finally repealed, but that year's "Controlled Substances Act" kept marijuana use illegal and made it even more difficult to attain permission to grow industrial hemp. President Nixon had picked up where Anslinger left off—he wanted to eliminate the plant in all of its forms from U.S. soil. And then the government's "War on Drugs" efforts of the 1980s kept the campaign against pot alive. By then, few people outside of farming even knew what hemp was.

But then, in the 1990s, public perception began to change, thanks to both the pro-hemp and pro-marijuana activists. Study after study said that marijuana is much less harmful than cocaine, heroin, and methamphetamine (though opponents warn that pot use can lead to the harder drugs). And medical marijuana is increasingly being used to ease the pain of chronic-disease sufferers.

That's promising news for the marijuana advocates, but the pro-hemp people are still trying to educate the public about the useful properties of their plant, and why it could play an important role in the 21st century. But first, there is one widely-held myth about the cannabis plant that still persists.

MARIJUANA VS. INDUSTRIAL HEMP

Technically, it's not illegal to grow hemp, but you must first attain permission from the U.S. Drug Enforcement Agency, which currently is extremely difficult. Why? The DEA is concerned that hemp farmers will secretly grow pot in their fields, making it nearly impossible for DEA helicopters to spot marijuana from the air. This isn't possible, though, as marijuana and industrial hemp are planted, tended, and harvested in different ways. And neither can be grown in the same field; the plants will cross-pollinate, making them both useless for their intended purpose.

But that's not even their biggest difference. The psychosomatic agent in marijuana is the compound *delta-9 tetrahydrocannabinol* (THC). In order for the plant to be potent enough to get someone "high," it must have a THC content of 3% or higher. Hemp, by contrast, only has 0.5% or less of THC. In other words, smoking hemp to get high would be a meaningless effort. Besides, there's so much else that it *can* do.

Windy city: Rock Port, Missouri, (pop. 1,395) gets all of its energy from wind power.

MULTI-TASKER

As the drawbacks of harvesting trees and burning fossil fuels become more apparent, the better hemp production starts looking. It can be used to make paper, rope, netting, baskets, and clothing. Hemp is a good food source, as well—hemp seeds have a nutty flavor, and like nuts they're very nutritious, containing protein, omega fatty acids, and vitamins. (Hemp oil can even be made into beer.) In addition, hemp can be manufactured into plastics and construction materials. The best news: hemp production has a low environmental impact.

• Unlike trees, hemp grows rapidly—from seed to mature plant in 120 days—allowing for two harvests per year in some climates. It requires few, if any, pesticides, and the plants can be grown very close together, resulting in a high fiber yield per acre.

• Up to three times more paper can be produced from hemp than from trees. And tree pulp must be bleached using environmentally destructive chemicals such as chlorine. Hemp pulp can be bleached with relatively harmless hydrogen peroxide.

• Growing hemp for textiles requires much less water and fewer pesticides than cotton does. And while hemp cloth has a reputation for being rough, recent technological developments have made it much softer.

• Hemp seed oil can be used to make biofuels, similar to corn-based ethanol, but hemp, again, is a more environmentally friendly crop than corn, requiring less water and fewer pesticides.

THE GREEN MOVEMENT

Currently, hemp is legally grown in more than 30 countries, including Australia, Canada, China, Russia, the U.K., France, and Italy. The European Union even subsidizes the plant's production. In the U.S., several states have begun issuing permits allowing for the farming of industrial hemp. Not all have received the necessary permission from the DEA, but supporters are hopeful that those numbers will increase—and the restrictions will decrease—under the Obama administration.

So in the not too distant future, hemp may be let loose on American farms—and may once again regain its stature as one of the world's most useful crops.

UNSUNG HEROES

On page 97, we told you the stories of pioneers who made big contributions to environmental causes, but whom most people have never heard of. Here are a few more.

MURRAY BOOKCHIN (1921–2006)

Claim to Fame: Author, green-movement pioneer

Life Story: Born in New York to Russian immigrants, Bookchin spent a few years in the American Communist Youth Movement before becoming disillusioned with the authoritarian policies of Stalin in the 1930s. After that, he bounced around from libertarianism to anarchism to socialism, but he made his greatest impact as a conservationist. Writing 27 books under several pseudonyms, Bookchin was among the first to speak out against chemical food additives and toxic pesticides, and to advocate for the use of alternative energy sources. One of his most important works, *Our Synthetic Environment* (written under the pen name Lewis Herber), was released in 1962, six months before Rachel Carson's *Silent Spring*. Were it not for his need to keep a low profile (his political leanings made him unpopular in some circles), Bookchin would most likely be as famous as Carson.

In 1974 Bookchin founded Vermont's Institute for Social Ecology. He later played a significant role in organizing the Green Party. In 1992 London's *Independent* named Bookchin "the foremost Green philosopher of the age."

Environmental Statement: "The great project of our time must be to open the other eye: to see all-sidedly and wholly, to heal and transcend the cleavage between humanity and nature that came with early wisdom."

NORMAN E. BORLAUG (b. 1914)

Claim to Fame: Saved a billion people from starving

Life Story: In the early 1960s, after earning his doctorate in plant pathology, Borlaug was invited to work with the International Maize and Wheat Improvement Center in Mexico to increase wheat yields. Because there wasn't much space left for expanding agricultural acreage, Borlaug needed to enhance yields in the land

In one year, an acre of mature trees absorbs the CO_2 produced by 26,000 miles of driving.

already available. He crossbred several different types of wheat until he developed a strain that was tall, strong, and disease resistant. His methods increased Mexico's wheat yields by an astounding 600%. Before long, Mexico, which had once had to import much of its wheat, was now an exporter.

Borlaug then took his Mexican wheat to India and Pakistan. During a dangerous time of famine and war, he was able to help both nations create new disease-resistant crop varieties of wheat and rice and introduce new fertilizers. It's estimated that he saved a billion lives—nearly single-handedly.

Now in his mid-90s, Borlaug is still at it, experimenting with a new kind of grain that is not only easy to grow, but also highly nutritious. He is one of only five people who have earned the Nobel Peace Prize, the Presidential Medal of Freedom, and the Congressional Gold Medal (the other four: Martin Luther King Jr., Mother Teresa, Nelson Mandela, and Holocaust survivor Elie Wiesel).

Environmental Statement: "You can't build a peaceful world on empty stomachs and human misery."

EDWARD PAUL ABBEY (1927–89)

Claim to Fame: Author, rabble-rouser

Life Story: Walt Whitman once said, "Resist much, obey little," and those words became Edward Abbey's life motto. Called the "Desert Anarchist," Abbey wrote tirelessly about saving the American West from unchecked development—and he didn't mind upsetting people along the way.

Abbey's most famous novel, *The Monkey Wrench Gang* (1975), told the story of a ragtag crew of meat-eating, gun-toting environmentalists who destroy bulldozers and plot to destroy dams in the Southwest.

Over four decades, Abbey wrote 21 books as well as essays, letters, and speeches. With eyes that squinted like Clint Eastwood's and a Grizzly Adams salt-and-pepper beard, Abbey was an intimidating figure. But his eloquent words lasted well beyond his death.

Environmental Impact Statement: "May your trails be crooked, winding, lonesome, dangerous, leading to the most amazing view. May your mountains rise into and above the clouds." (From *Desert Solitaire*, 1968)

WHEN YOU GOTTA GO...

*Now that you know how to recycle all of your stuff,
how do you recycle yourself when the time comes?*

KICKING MORE THAN THE BUCKET

In this day and age, dying costs a lot—both to the family of the dearly departed and to the environment. Monetarily, a traditional funeral will set you back $6,195, according to the National Funeral Directors Association. That doesn't even include the cemetery costs, which can add another $1,128. The casket alone costs an average of $3,930. And what are you purchasing for all of this money? Some extremely unfriendly environmental practices.

YOU CAN RUN, BUT YOU CAN'T FORMALDEHYDE

The first and perhaps worst step in the process is embalming the body. The primary ingredient in embalming fluid is formaldehyde, a suspected carcinogen. The risk is substantial enough that OSHA regulates the use of embalming fluid for funeral home personnel, who must be specially trained to even be around the stuff. It's considered hazardous waste and has to be disposed of properly. (An estimated 827,000 gallons of embalming fluid are buried underground each year.)

Proponents of embalming—who include the companies that manufacture the fluid—claim that it helps to control the spread of bacteria and disease by keeping microbes inside the body. However, the U.S. Centers for Disease Control stated in 2006 that embalming is *not* prescribed as a method of protecting public health.

Are you required by law to get embalmed? Not in most states, although the funeral home will most likely require it if the family chooses to have a public viewing.

DEAD PEOPLE INSIDE DEAD TREES

Choosing a traditional coffin is like buying a fine piece of furniture—exotic hardwoods, satin-lined interiors, and elegant finishes. And not only are forests depleted to build them, but considerable

One billion of the world's 6.8 billion people don't have access to clean drinking water.

energy is used to transport them to funeral homes and cemeteries. Metal caskets are another option, but they're often more expensive than wood and can be just as harmful due to the processes used to manufacture and transport them. That's a lot of fuss over a box that will be seen by a few people for a few hours before it gets buried for eternity.

And it's not just the box that goes underground. In most locales, vaults are required to prevent the soil above the casket from collapsing. Typically constructed of concrete or metal off-site, the heavy vaults eat up still more resources to manufacture and install.

Added up, throughout the United States, some 30 million board feet of hardwood, 90,000 tons of steel, 2,700 tons of copper and bronze, and 1.6 million tons of concrete are buried in cemeteries each year. And to keep their "pastoral" look, most cemeteries maintain their grounds with chemical fertilizers.

GOING GREEN IN THE AFTERLIFE

A 2004 poll conducted by the American Association of Retired Persons (AARP) revealed that 70% of respondents would prefer a "green" funeral. Good news: It's getting easier every year to do. Here are the three most popular green methods..

• **Cremation.** It may seem green, but conventional cremation does have some drawbacks. If it's preceded by a public viewing, then embalming, "beautification," and coffin expenses may still be incurred. The alternative is *direct cremation*, where the body is removed from the place of death and cremated immediately afterward. This typically runs about $1,800, although if you transport the body yourself and use a simple container, the cost may be lower.

The hazardous part of cremation is that all of the toxins that were trapped inside you (as well as in the materials of the coffin) will now be released into the atmosphere. These include nitrogen oxide, carbon monoxide, sulfur dioxide, particulate matter, mercury (from dental fillings), hydrogen fluoride, and hydrogen chloride. Although crematoriums are required to use smokestack scrubbers to control emissions, the process uses a large amount of fossil fuels to burn the body and the coffin. In the U.S., temperatures of 1,600 to 1,800°F are maintained for about two hours to reduce the body to ash and bone fragments. That amount of energy could power an average house for a month.

Cremation does, however, save land that would otherwise be used for a gravesite. Cremains (the cremated remains) may be distributed on private land, interred, or kept in the home. Some are scattered in waterways, depending on the local regulations. There is a growing market for creative ways to disperse the cremains, including shooting them into space, using them in bullets (for hunters), in fireworks, compressing them into "diamonds" to make jewelry, and mixing them with concrete to form artificial reefs.

• **Home Funerals.** Before embalming became the norm, the dead were laid out in the front parlor and passersby knew a death had occurred by the black wreath hung on the front door. Today there is a growing movement to bring death back to the home. Most states allow home funerals, but a few have regulations that make it difficult to do. The Funeral Consumers Alliance (www.funerals.org) has information on the legal requirements of each state.

Home funerals, it should be known, take a lot of work and are not for the squeamish—Americans, for the most part, have grown accustomed to letting someone else deal with the dead. Plenty of good online resources can guide you though the process of washing and clothing the body, as well as using dry ice to preserve it.

Once the proper paperwork is obtained, the body can be placed in a container—generally a simple wooden coffin, although a cardboard box may be used—and transported to its final resting place. And the emerging "green funeral" industry is now offering coffins made from recycled newspapers. You can even be buried in a moss-lined woven willow nest, a bamboo coffin, or even a hemp sack. The cost of a home funeral is typically under $1,000, not including the cost of the burial site.

• **Natural Burial.** The intent here is to allow the body to decompose as naturally as possible. To that end, the body is not embalmed, there is no vault at the burial site, and the body is buried in a biodegradable coffin or shroud.

Because no vault is used, most conventional cemeteries don't allow natural burials, though a select few do. The eco-friendliest burials take place in lands that have long-term covenants or deed restrictions that guarantee the area will remain a natural preserve.

Graves are marked by stones, shrubs, or trees native to the area. Costs of natural burials average $2,000, not including transportation costs and the cost of the burial container. While there are few natural burial preserves in the U.S. today, more are appearing as the market for them develops.

GOING DOWN

So if your wish is to be turned into a garden that your friends and family may enjoy for years, you may be able to swing it. But it's important to remember that if you don't make all of the arrangements ahead of time, there could be surprises that those left behind will have to deal with.

That's what happened to Claire Wallerstein of England when her father died in 2004. Her experience with a green funeral went so "horribly wrong" that she wrote about it in London's *Daily Mail*. Among the highlights: She had to call the gravedigger while her father was still alive, but barely, since the grave had to be dug in time for them to get his unembalmed body into the ground quickly. Also, her family didn't visit the site beforehand—it was two counties away—and they didn't find out until the funeral that the graveyard doubled as a *pet* cemetery. Then, when they went back a month later to plant a tree on the grave, no one could find the exact spot—not even the people who worked there.

Wallerstein's greatest surprise was the lack of professionalism from the funeral company. "Though we can now laugh at most of the 'lapses' we experienced," she says, "for other bereaved people these could have been utterly devastating."

So if "green" is for you, do your homework, ask around, find a place that you can trust, and visit beforehand. One of the latest trends: a GPS marker for your natural burial site so your descendants will always be able to visit you and thank you for helping give them a clean planet. That's a great way to rest in peace.

*   *   *

A LAME ENVIRONMENTAL JOKE

Q: Bob the environmentalist rides his bicycle to work every morning. How does he get home at night?

A: He recycles.

AND THEN?

We leave you with some words about what may come next. See you around.

"Civilization has risen from the Stone Age; it can rise again from the Wastepaper Age."
—**Jacques Barzun**

"We must ask ourselves whether we really wish some future universal historian on another planet to say about us, 'With all their genius and with all their skill, they ran out of foresight and air and food and water and ideas.'"
—**U Thant**

"The future is called 'perhaps,' which is the only possible thing to call the future. And the only important thing is not to allow that to scare you."
—**Tennessee Williams**

"The past can't see you, but the future is listening."
—**Destin Figuier**

"The best investment on Earth is Earth."
—**Louis J. Glickman**

"Nature provides a free lunch, but only if we control our appetites."
—**William Ruckelshaus**

"Our children may save us if they are taught to care properly for the planet; but if not, it may be back to the Ice Age or the caves. Then we'll have to view the universe above from a cold, dark place. No more jet skis, nuclear weapons, plastic crap, broken pay phones, drugs, cars, waffle irons, or television. Come to think of it, that might not be a bad idea."
—**Jimmy Buffet**

"The human brain now holds the key to our future. We have to recall the image of the planet from outer space: a single entity in which air, water, and continents are interconnected. That is our home."
—**David Suzuki**

"The ultimate test of man's conscience is his willingness to sacrifice something today for future generations whose thanks will not be heard."
—**Gaylord Nelson**

"I never think of the future. It comes soon enough."
—**Albert Einstein**

Eureka! Your brain produces enough electricity to power a light bulb.

UNCLE JOHN'S BATHROOM READER CLASSIC SERIES

Find these and other great titles from the *Uncle John's Bathroom Reader* Classic Series online at **www.bathroomreader.com**. Or contact us at:

Bathroom Readers' Institute
P.O. Box 1117
Ashland, OR 97520
(888) 488-4642

Also available
from Uncle John's
Bathroom Reader!

THE LAST PAGE

F ELLOW BATHROOM READERS:
The fight for good bathroom reading should never be taken
loosely—we must do our duty and sit firmly for what we
believe in, even while the rest of the world is taking potshots at us.

We'll be brief. Now that we've proven we're not simply a flush-
in-the-pan, we invite you to take the plunge: Sit Down and Be
Counted! Become a member of the Bathroom Readers' Institute.
Log on to *www.bathroomreader.com*, or send a self-addressed,
stamped, business-sized envelope to: BRI, PO Box 1117, Ashland,
Oregon 97520. You'll receive your free membership card, get discounts when ordering directly through the BRI, and earn a permanent spot on the BRI honor roll!

If you like reading our books...
VISIT THE BRI'S WEB SITE!
www.bathroomreader.com

- Visit "The Throne Room"—a great place to read!
- Receive our irregular newsletters via e-mail
- Order additional *Bathroom Readers*
- Become a BRI member

Go with the Flow...

Well, we're out of space, and when you've gotta go, you've gotta
go. Tanks for all your support. Hope to hear from you soon.
Meanwhile, remember...

Keep on flushin'!